ALL CALL
IONA HOME

*The genealogy of the founders of Iona
and their descendants ❧ 1800-1950*

S.R. MacNeil

*"S ged a leannainn air as ur,
Cha chuir mi chliu na's airde;
Ma theid sibh leam gu seall mi dhuibh
Gach cul is raon mar tha iad."*

Formac Publishing Company Limited
Halifax, Nova Scotia

Formac Publishing Company Limited acknowledges the support of the Cultural Affairs Section, Nova Scotia Department of Tourism and Culture. We acknowledge the financial support of the Government of Canada through the Book Publishing Industry Development Program (BPIDP) for our publishing activities.

We acknowledge the support of the Canada Council for the Arts for our publishing program.

National Library of Canada Cataloguing in Publication

MacNeil, S. R., 1897-
All call Iona home, 1800-1950 : the genealogy of the founders of Iona and their descendants / by S.R. MacNeil. — 2nd ed.

Reprint. First published: Antigonish, N.S. : Formac, 1979.
ISBN 0-88780-629-5

1. Iona Region, N.S.—Genealogy. I. Title.

FC2349.I55Z48 2004   929'.2'0971693
C2004-900551-0

Formac Publishing Company Limited
5502 Atlantic Street
Halifax, Nova Scotia, B3H 1G4
www.formac.ca

Printed and bound in Canada

Mr. and Mrs. S.R. MacNeil

Preface to the revised edition

Although the author took every precaution to ensure the accuracy of the information in *All Call Iona Home*, the book is solely based on oral collecting. As a result there are a number of errors and omissions. The Roots Cape Breton program of the Highland Village Museum/An Clachan Gàidhealach, welcomes additions and corrections, especially ones with corroborating evidence such as dates and places. As well, if you have concerns or require assistance with your family information please contact Roots Cape Breton by mail at 4119 Highway 223, Iona, NS, B2C 1A3 or e-mail at rootscapebreton@gov.ns.ca.

Rodney Chaisson, Director
Highland Village Museum/
An Clachan Gàidhealach

Deputy
Prime Minister

President of the
Privy Council

Vice-
Premier Ministre

Président du
Conseil privé

It is a pleasure for me to commend this
book by S.R. MacNeil to those interested in Iona and
the Scottish heritage of Nova Scotia. Mr. MacNeil's
research on the genealogy of the founders of Iona and
their descendants is a fitting extension of his valuable
contribution to the Iona Museum and to his community.

Allan J. MacEachen
Deputy Prime Minister

Ottawa
K1A 0A3

discover

CAPE BRETON ISLAND

NOVA SCOTIA

Place	Number on Map		
Barra Glen	3	MacKay's Point	13
Birch Point	19	MacKinnon's Harbour	9
Gillis Point	11	MacNeil's Vale	22
Gillis Point East	12	Murphy's Point	18
Grass Cove	2	Ottawa Brook	10
Highland Hill	21	Red Point	7
Iona	1	Red Point East	8
Iona Rear	4	St. Columba	20
Jamesville East	5	Upper Washabuck	16
Jamesville West	6	Washabuck Bridge	17
Lower Washabuck	14	Washabuck Center	15

My dear Readers:

From the lowly acorn the majestic oak tree grows. While I was Curator in the restored Highland Village in Iona, visitors constantly approached me for information on their people who once belonged to this area. Willingly I gave them what information I could, and they always went away seemingly grateful. Their many attempts to show me their gratitude made me the more painfully aware that I should perfect my own knowledge of the people of this area, and be able to present it in a more organized way. One thing led to another, and before long I felt a pressing need to preserve for future generations what I had succeeded in piecing together. This little book is an attempt to do just that. Experts caution that in a work of this kind a "cut-off" date is a "must," and I have decided that 1950 be mine.

My great-great-grandfather was Donald "Og" MacNeil. A soldier in the British Army, he took part in both the Siege of Louisburg in the year 1758 and in the Taking of Quebec in the year 1759. After the defeat of General Montcalm's army on the Plains of Abraham, Donald "Og" was ordered to raise the British flag, so as to mark Britain's taking possession of Canada. In the attempt to do so, he was killed by a French sniper and buried in Quebec. For several years before that, while scouting in and about Cape Breton Island, he was deeply impressed by the beauty of the Bras d'Or Lake and its surroundings. On his several trips to his home in Barra while serving in the British Army in America, he repeatedly impressed upon his relatives — and indeed on Barra men in general — that, if ever they migrated to Canada, they should settle in that part of the Lake's northern bank which we know today as the parish of Iona. Hence, were it for only the fact that MacNeils now form the majority of settlers in this parish, I make no apology for giving them first place in these pages. And, were it for only the fact that Donald "Og" was personally so eager to see his fellow Barra men the first settlers of Iona, I make no apology for giving him and his descendants first place among those MacNeils.

There are omissions in this book, and quite likely inaccuracies as well. I can assure my readers, however, that these blemishes are there not because of any half-hearted effort on my part to eliminate them. It is an exercise in patience and fortitude to try to obtain from people today information on their forebears. Many young people today know little or nothing about their relatives beyond those in their immediate families. Indeed, there are families today whose members would be hard put to give the correct Christian names of brothers and sisters whom they grew accustomed to call only Junior, Buddy, Sister, Bunny, T.D., and the like. There are families in this parish today — and in every parish — who show little enthusiasm for making the effort to get to know who their "relations" are. This may seem, at first, rather heartless of them, but there is an explanation for this apparent apathy, and that is the almost complete loss of the Gaelic language among our young.

Where the majority of people come from the same pioneers, and where families feel obliged to name their children after the same persons, a wide variety of "labels" is ever a necessity. It could be expected, therefore, that Christian names in our parish be interwoven with labels like "big," "small," "red," "white," "black," "farmer," "fisherman," "blacksmith," "tailor," and the like. Wherever Gaelic is the common language, the language itself presents a difficulty that is peculiarly its own. This difficulty stems from what is called the Gaelic "aspirated form," the form most frequently used in Gaelic to denote possession. We who speak English denote possession, merely by adding an 's to the end of a person's name. Thus we get "Neil's" from "Neil." Both are really forms of the one word, but obviously the name "Neil" is clearly audible and visible in both. Those who speak Gaelic denote possession, by putting a person's name in its aspirated form, and the aspirated form requires that a change be made within the name itself — something very different from merely adding 's to the end of a name. While the Gaelic name and its aspirated form are really two forms of the same word, those who do not speak Gaelic consider them as two different words. And to make matters worse, whenever a Gaelic name with a label is put in its aspirated form, both the name and the label suffer changes within themselves. This has to appear hopelessly entangling to those who do not speak Gaelic, but nothing could be simpler to those who do.

Wherever there are omissions and inaccuracies in this work, those who find them would do a great service to themselves and to the cause, if they would make note of these blemishes. They might send the corrected forms to the Museum in the Highland Village in Iona, where they could be kept on record. In this way, a future enthusiast who undertakes to bring this present work up to date could have the benefit of their interest and knowledge. In trying to preserve truth, one cannot be held back merely because, despite's one's best efforts, there happens to be associated with it a minor omission or some detail, which only those could know who are in possession of all the facts. For, were one to content oneself with only perfection, nothing would ever be accomplished in this imperfect world of ours.

It is now my sacred duty to thank my good wife, Annie Jane, for all her patience, encouragement and assistance. My heart is filled with gratitude also towards all who kindly put at my disposal what records they did have, and all who did what they could to help me to put their families on record. This will be their reward: If ever this little book brings any glory to God, any honour to our dead, and any enjoyment to our living, they can always feel that they had a hand in bringing this about.

I have provided that the infinite merits of our Lord and Redeemer be re-offered in a special Mass of Remembrance, so that those whom I mention in these pages and those whom I may fail to mention will all be remembered "at the Altar of the Lord." And now, after many years in this "labour of love," I end the work on this my eightieth birthday — and with this prayer: "God and Father of all gifts, we praise You, Source of all we have and are. Teach us to acknowledge always the many good things Your infinite love has given us, and help us to love You with all our heart and strength."

Barra Glen
Iona R.R. 2
August 8, 1978   **S.R. MacNeil**

Anderson, John **274** Barra Glen

Arsenault, Walter **275** Barra Glen

Bonaparte, Seward and Joseph   MacKinnon's Harbour

Bonaparte, Seward **276**

Roddie J./Seward **277**

Joseph **278**

Boyd, John C. **279** Washabuck

Brown, John **280** Washabuck

Campbell, Malcolm (John, Hector) **281** Iona

Hugh/Malcolm **282**

Malcolm/Hugh/Malcolm **283**

Archibald/Malcolm **284**

Alex/Archibald/Malcolm **285**

Campbell, Malcolm (pioneer) 286 Iona

Angus/Malcolm 287

Malcolm/Angus/Malcolm 288

Campbell, Hugh 289 Gillis Point East

Allan/Hugh 290

Hector/Allan/Hugh 291

John A./Hector/Allan/Hugh 292

George/Hugh 293

Peter/George/Hugh 294

Joseph S./Peter/George/Hugh 295

Angus/Hugh 296

Dan/Angus/Hugh 297

Campbell, Donald (Hector) 298 Jamesville West

Darby/Donald 299

Hugh/Darby/Donald 300.

John/Hugh/Darby/Donald 301

Dan/Hugh/Darby/Donald 302

James/Darby/Donald 303

Colin/James/Darby/Donald 304

Hector "Ban"/Donald **305**

Colin/Hector "Ban"/Donald **306**

Campbell, Neil (Donald) **308** Jamesville West

Rory/Neil **309**

John R./Rory/Neil **310**

Roddie/John R./Rory/Neil **311**

Frank/John R./Rory/Neil **312**

James/Neil **313**

Neil J.R./James/Neil **314**

Campbell, James "Beag" **315** Jamesville West

Campbell, Archie **316** Iona

John F./Archie **317**

Campbell, Arthur **318** Iona

Campbell, Donald   MacNeil's Vale

Hector "Ban"/Donald 319
John/Hector "Ban"/Donald 320

Carmichael, Donald 321 Washabuck

Devoe, Peter 322 MacKinnon's Harbour
Simon/Peter 323
Dan/Peter 324

Deveau, Bill 324a Grass Cove

Gillis, Ann (MacIntyre) 325 Jamesville West and
   MacKinnon's Harbour
Rory/Hugh 326
Donald/Rory/Hugh 327
James/Donald/Rory/Hugh 328
Neillie/James/Donald/Rory/Hugh 329
John Y./Donald/Rory/Hugh 330
Dan R./Donald/Rory/Hugh 331

Hugh N./Donald/Rory/Hugh 332

Michael A.J./ Donald/Rory/Hugh 333

John "Ban"/Hugh 334

Neil/John "Ban"/Hugh 335

Rory F./Neil/John "Ban"/Hugh 336 .

Neil J./Rory F./Neil/John "Ban"/Hugh 337

Jankowski, Victor 338 Iona

MacAulay, Donald   Washabuck

Allan/Donald 339

Alexander 339a

MacCormack, William L. 340 Iona

MacDonald, Donald (Malcolm) 341 Ottawa Brook

Philip/Donald 342

John/Philip/Donald 343

Donald/Philip/Donald 344

Angus/Donald/Philip/Donald 345

Dan A./Donald/Philip/Donald 346

Jonathan/Philip/Donald 347

James/Jonathan/Philip/Donald 348 .

John D./James/Jonathan/Philip/Donald 349

MacDonald, John "Lewis" 350   Ottawa Brook

Michael/John 351

Peter/Michael/John 352

James/Peter/Michael/John 353

John/Michael/John 354

Dan/Michael/John 355

MacDonald, Alasdair   St. Columba

Michael "Mor"/Alasdair 356

Alexander/Michael "Mor"/Alasdair 357

Stephen A./Alexander/Michael "Mor"/Alasdair 358

James/Michael "Mor"/Alasdair 359

Dan A./James/Michael "Mor"/Alasdair 360

Allan/Michael "Mor"/Alasdair 361

Michael A.J./Allan/Michael "Mor"/Alasdair 362

John A./Allan/Michael "Mor"/Alasdair 363

John/Michael "Mor"/Alasdair 364

James/Alasdair 365

Stephen/James/Alasdair 366

Donald/Alasdair 367

Alexander/Donald/Alasdair 368

Michael/Alexander/Donald/Alasdair 369

Hector/Alexander/Donald/Alasdair 370

Rory/Alasdair 371

Alexander/Rory/Alasdair 372

MacDonald, Ronald "Mor" 373 Washabuck

Rory R./Ronald "Mor" 374

Francis B./Rory R./Ronald "Mor" 375

Angus/Ronald "Mor" 376

Ranald/Angus/Ronald "Mor" 377

Angus/Angus/Ronald "Mor" 378

Dan F./Angus/Ronald "Mor" 379

MacDonald, Alasdair "Glas" 380 Washabuck

Murdock/Alasdair "Glas" 381

Rory C./Murdock/Alasdair "Glas" **382**

Malcolm/Rory C./Murdock/Alasdair **383**

MacDonald, Angus "Tuathach" **384** Washabuck

MacDonald, Donald "Soldier" **384a** Ottawa Brook

Hector/Donald "Soldier" **385**

MacDonald, Hector (Ronald) **386** Gillis Point

Ronald/Hector/Ronald **387**

MacDonald, James (Donald "Ban") **388** Gillis Point

MacDonald, James "Section-man" **390** Ottawa Brook

MacDonald, Rory "Mor" **391** MacKinnon's Harbour

Angus "Red"/Rory "Mor" **392**

MacDougall, Alexander (John "Miller") **393** Red Point

James/Alexander **394**

MacDougall, James "Miller" **395** Washabuck

Michael/James **396**

Jim A./Michael/James **397**

Walter/Jim A./Michael/James **398**

Dan/Michael/James **399**

Hugh A./Michael/James **400**

Michael R./Hugh A./Michael/James **401**

MacDougall, "Calum William" **402** Washabuck

Michael/"Calum William" **403**

MacDougall, Rory (Donald, Hector) **404** Upper
Washabuck

MacEachern, Hector **34** MacKinnon's Harbour

MacInnis, Rory **405** Iona

Michael/Rory **406**

Malcolm/Michael/Rory **407**

John/Michael/Rory **408**

Michael F./John/Michael/Rory **409**

John F./John/Michael/Rory **410**

MacInnis, Michael **411** Red Point

MacInnis, "Mac Iain Mhinistir" **412** MacKinnon's Harbour

MacInnis, John **413** Washabuck Bridge

MacInnis, Malcolm **414** Washabuck

MacIntosh **415** Lower Washabuck

MacIntyre, Roderick "Ur" **416** St. Columba

MacIsaac, Rod **417** Washabuck

MacIsaac **418** Red Point

MacIver, Colin **419** Washabuck

Henry/Colin **420**

"Dolly"/Henry/Colin **421**

Joe/"Dolly"/Henry/Colin **422**

John/John/Colin **423**

John C. **423a**

MacKay, George **424** Washabuck

MacKenzie, Archibald (Eachain) **425** Washabuck

Donald/Archibald **426**

Archibald/Donald/Archibald **427**

Daniel J./Archibald/Donald/Archibald **428**

John/Archibald **429**

Rory/Archibald **430**

Archie/Rory/Archibald **431**

Neil/Rory/Archibald **432**

Hector/Rory/Archibald **433**

MacKenzie, Alexander "Framer" **434** Washabuck

Charles/Alexander **435**

John S./Charles/Alexander **436**

MacKenzie, Murdock (Hector) **437** Washabuck

James/Murdock **438**

William/James/Murdock **439**

Tom/William/James/Murdock **440**

James/William/James/Murdock **441**

MacKenzie, Jonathan (Hector) **442** Washabuck

Hector/Jonathan **443**

Donald/Jonathan **444**

Peter/Donald/Jonathan **445**

MacKenzie, John D. (Alex) **446** Gillis Point

MacKinnon, John "Big" **447** Highland Hill

Neil/John "Big" **448**

Norman/Neil/John "Big" **449**

Michael/Neil/John "Big" **450**

Hector/John "Big" **451**

Rory/John "Big" **452**

John B./Rory/John "Big" **453**

Rory/John B./Rory/John "Big" **454**

MacKinnon, Johnnie **455** Iona Rear

Thomas/Johnnie **456**

Eoin/Thomas/Johnnie **457**

Paul/Thomas/Johnnie **458**

John P./Paul/Thomas/Johnnie **459**

Neil/Johnnie **460**

Jonathan/Neil/Johnnie **461**

Malcolm/Johnnie 462

John A./Malcolm/Johnnie 463

Neil A./Malcolm/Johnnie 464

MacKinnon, Donald "Ban" (Malcolm)   MacKinnon's
    Harbour

Allan/Donald "Ban" 465

John G./Allan/Donald "Ban" 466

Ambrose/John G./Allan/Donald "Ban" 467

Neil S./John G./Allan/Donald "Ban" 468

Donald/Allan/Donald "Ban" 469

Allan D./Donald/Allan/Donald "Ban" 470

Rory/Donald "Ban" 471

John/Rory/Donald "Ban" 472

Rory S./John/Rory/Donald "Ban" 473

Charles/Donald "Ban" 474

John/Charles/Donald "Ban" 475

John J./John/Charles/Donald "Ban" 476

Stephen J./John/Charles/Donald "Ban" 477

John M./Stephen J./John/Charles/Donald "Ban" 478

MacKinnon, Donald (Philip) **479** Washabuck

Murdock/Donald **480**

Rory/Murdock/Donald **481**

Dan A./Rory/Murdock/Donald **482**

Dan/Murdock/Donald **483**

Jimmie/Dan/Murdock/Donald **484**

MacKinnon, Michael "Dubh" **485** Washabuck

MacKinnon, Donald "Mor" **486** MacKinnon's Harbour

MacLean, Lachlan **487** Washabuck

Neil/Lachlan **488**

Michael/Neil/Lachlan **489**

John/Michael/Neil/Lachan **490**

Hector/Michael/Neil/Lachlan **491**

Andrew/Hector/Michael/Neil/Lachlan **492**

Allan/Michael/Neil/Lachlan **493**

Donald/Neil/Lachlan **494**

Neil S./Donald/Neil/Lachlan **495**

Peter/Neil/Lachlan 496

Neil P./Peter/Neil/Lachlan 497

Neil S./Neil P./Peter/Neil/Lachlan 498

Hector/Neil/Lachlan 499

Paul/Neil/Lachlan 500

Alexander/Lachan 501

Paul/Alexander/Lachlan 502

Malcolm/Lachlan 503

Peter F./Malcolm/Lachlan 504

Vincent / Peter F./Malcolm/Lachlan 505

Peter F./Vincent/Peter F./Malcolm/Lachlan 506

Michael A./Vincent/Peter F./Malcolm/Lachlan 507

Jonathan/Malcolm/Lachlan 508

Stephen/Malcolm/Lachlan 509

Roderick J./Stephen/Malcolm/Lachlan 510

Malcolm B./Stephen/Malcolm/Lachlan 511

Michael/Malcolm/Lachlan 512

Roderick/Lachlan 513

Donald/Roderick/Lachlan 514

"Red" Rory/Donald/Roderick/Lachlan 515

Joseph A./"Red" Rory/Donald/Roderick/Lachlan 516

Peter S./Roderick/Lachlan 517

Neil P.S./Peter S./Roderick/Lachlan 518

James A./Neil P.S./Peter S./Roderick/Lachlan 519
Lachlan/Roderick/Lachlan 520

MacLean, Neil, "Dubh" 521 Washabuck
Allan 522

MacLean, Allan "Leathaineach" 523 Washabuck

MacLean, Charles "Gobha" 525 Washabuck

MacLean, Archibald   Ottawa Brook
Rory/Archibald 526
Peter/Rory/Archibald 527
Rory/Peter/Rory/Archibald 528
Hugh/Peter/Rory/Archibald 529
Norman/Peter/Rory/Archibald 530
John/Rory/Archibald 531
Dan/Archibald 532
Rory/Neil/Archibald 533

MacLean, Neil (Eachain) 534

Hector/Neil 535

Eoin/Neil 536

John J./Eoin/Neil 537

Alex/John J./Eoin/Neil 538

Donald/Neil 539

John A./Donald/Neil 540

Leonard/John A./Donald/Neil 541

Angus/Eoin/Neil 542

MacLellan, Angus 543 Ottawa Brook

Peter A./Angus 544

MacLeod, Colin 545 MacKinnon's Harbour

MacNeil, Donald "Og"   Barra Glen

Rory/Donald "Og" 1

Malcolm/Rory/Donald "Og" 2

Eoin/Rory/Donald "Og" 3

Donald/Eoin/Rory/Donald "Og" 4

Rory/Eoin/Rory/Donald "Og" 5

Neil R./Rory/Eoin/Rory/Donald "Og" 6

Murdock/Eoin/Rory/Donald "Og" 7

Francis/Murdock/Eoin/Rory/Donald "Og" 8

Rory/Rory/Donald "Og" 9

Rory/Rory/Rory/Donald "Og" 10

Stephen/Rory/Donald "Og" 11

Michael/Stephen/Rory/Donald "Og" 12

Stephen R./Michael/Stephen/Rory/Donald "Og" 13

John R./Michael/Stephen/Rory/Donald "Og" 14

Rory/Stephen/Rory/Donald "Og" 15

Stephen M./Rory/Stephen/Rory/Donald "Og" 16

Neil/Stephen/Rory/Donald "Og" 17

John P./Neil/Stephen/Rory/Donald "Og" 18

Johnnie/Neil/Stephen/Rory/Donald "Og" 19

John/Rory/Donald "Og" 20

John/John/Rory/Donald "Og" 21

Johnnie/John/John/Rory/Donald "Og" 22

Michael/John/Rory/Donald "Og" 23

Murdock/Donald "Og" 24

Paul/Murdock/Donald "Og" 24a

Neil/Murdock/Donald "Og" 25

John/Murdock/Donald "Og" 26

Michael/Murdock/Donald "Og" 27

Stephen B./Michael/Murdock/Donald "Og" 28

Barra/Donald "Og" 29

MacNeil, Edward A. 30

Alasdair/Barra/Donald "Og" 31

John/Alasdair/Barra/Donald "Og" 32

Neil/Barra/Donald "Og" 33

Ben/Neil/Barra/Donald "Og" 35

MacNeil, Donald (Ruairi)   Iona

John/Donald 35a

Rory "Mor"/Donald 36

John/Rory "Mor"/Donald 37

Rory/John/Rory "Mor"/Donald 38

John/John/Rory "Mor"/Donald 39

Francis/John/Rory "Mor"/Donald 40

Donald "Mor"/Rory "Mor"/Donald 41

Rory D./Donald "Mor"/Rory "Mor"/Donald 41a

John/Donald "Mor"/Rory "Mor"/Donald 42

Malcolm/Donald "Mor"/Rory "Mor"/Donald 43

Michael D./Donald "Mor"/Rory "Mor"/Donald 44

Dan R./Michael D./Donald "Mor"/Rory "Mor"/Donald 45

John M./Michael D./Donald "Mor"/Rory "Mor"/Donald 46

John R./Michael D./Donald "Mor"/Rory "Mor"/Donald 47

Hector/Rory "Mor"/Donald 48

Francis H./Hector/Rory "Mor"/Donald 49

Donald "Beag"/Rory "Mor"/Donald 50

Michael D./Donald "Beag"/Rory "Mor"/Donald 51

Roddie/Michael D./Donald "Beag"/Rory "Mor"/Donald 52

Francis/Michael D./Donald "Beag"/Rory "Mor"/Donald 53

Murdock/Michael D./Donald "Beag"/Rory "Mor"/Donald 54

Dannie/Michael D./Donald "Beag"/Rory "Mor"/Donald 55

Daniel/Donald "Beag"/Rory "Mor"/Donald 56

MacNeil, Eoin (Donald, John)   Iona and Jamesville

Iain/Eoin 57

Eoin "Mor"/Iain/Eoin 58

James/Eoin "Mor"/Iain/Eoin 59

Murdock/Eoin "Mor"/Iain/Eoin 60

Michael D./Murdock/Eoin "Mor"/Iain/Eoin 61

Michael/Eoin "Mor"/Iain/Eoin 62

John J./Eoin "Mor"/Iain/Eoin 63

Stephen J./Eoin "Mor"/Iain/Eoin 64

Stephen/Iain Eoin 65

Donald/Stephen/Iain/Eoin 66

Stephen S./Stephen/Iain/Eoin 67

Stephen J./Stephen S./Stephen/Iain/Eoin 68

John/Iain/Eoin 69

Donald/John/Iain/Eoin 70

Neil/Eoin 72

John/Neil/Eoin 73

Rory J./John/Neil/Eoin 74

Malcolm/Neil/Eoin 75

Stephen/Malcolm/Neil/Eoin 76

James/Eoin 77

Jonathan/James/Eoin 78

Rory/James/Eoin 79

Donald/James/Eoin 80

Kenneth/James/Eoin 81

Michael K./Kenneth/James/Eoin 82

John/James/Eoin 83

Malcolm/James/Eoin 84

Rory A./Malcolm/James/Eoin 85

MacNeil, Hector and Donald (Neil)   Gillis Point

Hector/Neil 86

Neil/Hector/Neil   87

Murdock/Neil/Hector/Neil   88

Peter/Neil/Hector/Neil   89

Hector/Neil/Hector/Neil   90

Joseph A./Hector/Neil/Hector/Neil   91

James/Hector/Neil   92

Charles S./James/Hector/Neil   93

John A./Charles S./James/Hector/Neil   94

Donald/Neil   95

Philip/Donald/Neil   96

Dan F./Philip/Donald/Neil   97

Neil/Philip/Donald/Neil   98

John/Donald/Neil   99

Michael/John/Donald/Neil   100

Frank/Michael/John/Donald/Neil   101

Donald/John/Donald/Neil   102

Hector/John/Donald/Neil   103

Neil/Donald/Neil   104

Dan A./Neil/Donald/Neil   105

Donald/Neil/Donald/Neil   106

Roderick/Neil/Donald/Neil   107

Allan A./Roderick/Neil/Donald/Neil   108

John M./Roderick/Neil/Donald/Neil   109

Hector P./Neil/Donald/Neil 110

Alex P./Neil/Donald/Neil 111

Allan A./Alex P./Neil/Donald/Neil 112

Peter S./Neil/Donald/Neil 113

Philip B./Neil/Donald/Neil 114

MacNeil, Neil and Donald and Malcolm (Eoin)   Gillis
  Point

Neil/Eoin 115

Eoin/Neil/Eoin 116

Donald/Eoin 117

Donald/Donald/Eoin 118

Michael/Donald/Donald/Eoin 119

Donald D./Donald/Donald/Eoin 120

Murdock/Donald/Eoin 121

Dan S./Murdock/Donald/Eoin 122

John H./Dan S./Murdock/Donald/Eoin 123

Anthony/Dan S./Murdock/Donald/Eoin 124

Francis X./Dan S./Murdock/Donald/Eoin 125

Hector/Donald/Eoin 126

John/Hector/Donald/Eoin 127

Malcolm/Eoin 128

MacNeil, Alasdair "Mor" 129 Gillis Point

John/Alasdair "Mor" 130

James C./John/Alasdair "Mor" 131

Neil J./James C./John/Alasdair "Mor" 132

Neil/Alasdair "Mor" 133

James/Neil/Alasdair "Mor" 134

Allan/Alasdair "Mor" 135

James A./Allan/Alasdair "Mor" 136

Roderick/James A./Allan/Alasdair "Mor" 137

Alexander Jr./Alasdair "Mor" 138

Alex "Mor"/Alexander Jr./Alasdair "Mor" 139

James S./Alexander Jr./Alasdair "Mor" 140

Michael/Alasdair "Mor" 141

MacNeil, Rory (Rory) 141a Hector's Point

Hector "Mor"/Rory 142

Rory H./Hector "Mor"/Rory 143

Paul/Rory H./Hector "Mor"/Rory 144

Hugh/Hector "Mor"/Rory 145

Stephen U./Hugh/Hector "Mor"/Rory 146

John/Hector "Mor"/Rory 147

Joseph H./John/Hector "Mor"/Rory 148

John J./Joseph H./John/Hector "Mor"/Rory 149

Hector/Joseph H./John/Hector "Mor"/Rory 150

Hugh/Joseph H./John/Hector "Mor"/Rory 151

Eoin/Rory 152

Hector/Eoin/Rory 153

Malcolm/Eoin/Rory 154

Rory/Malcolm/Eoin/Rory 155

John/Eoin/Rory 156

Francis X.S./John/Eoin/Rory 157

Ronald/Francis X.S./John/Eoin/Rory 158

Edmund/Ronald/Francis X.S./John/Eoin/Rory 159

Roddie/Francis X.S./John/Eoin/Rory 160

John P./Francis X.S./John/Eoin/Rory 161

Roderick/John/Eoin/Rory 162

John P./John/Eoin Rory 163

MacNeil, Donald "Ban" 164 Iona

Dan/Donald/Donald "Ban" 165

John/Donald "Ban" 166

Stephen/John/Donald "Ban" 167

George/Stephen/John/Donald "Ban" 168

James/John/Donald "Ban" 169

MacNeil, Donald (Rory) **170** Iona, Barra Glen, and
Jamesville

Neil/Donald **171**

Donald "Mor"/Neil/Donald **172**

Michael/Neil/Donald **173**

Donald "Beag"/Neil/Donald **174**

Neil D./Donald "Beag"/Neil/Donald **175**

Dan A./Neil D./Donald "Beag"/Neil/Donald **176**

Rory D./Donald "Beag"/Neil/Donald **177**

James"Mor"/Donald **178**

Colin/James "Mor"/Donald **179**

Malcolm/James "Mor"/Donald **180**

James M./Malcolm/James "Mor"/Donald **181**

John H./Malcolm/James "Mor"/Donald **182**

MacNeil, Angus and John (Eoin)   Highland Hill

Angus/Eoin **183**

John/Angus/Eoin **184**

Dan A./John/Angus/Eoin **185**

Donald/Angus/Eoin **186**

Eoin/Angus/Eoin **187**

John/Eoin **188**

Murdock B./John/Eoin **189**

Thomas/Murdock B./John/Eoin **190**

Angus/John/Eoin **191**

Thomas/John/Eoin **192**

Thomas "Ban"/Thomas/John/Eoin **193**

MacNeil, Rory "Red" **194**, Iona Rear

Donald/Rory "Red" **195**

Hugh/Donald/Rory "Red" **196**

Rory/Hugh/Donald/Rory "Red" **197**

Hugh/Rory/Hugh/Donald/Rory "Red" **198**

John/Rory "Red" **199**

Donald/John/Rory "Red" **200**

Alex/John/Rory "Red" **201**

Rory/Alex/John/Rory "Red" **202**

Neil/Rory "Red" **203**

Rory/Neil/Rory "Red" **204**

Hugh/Neil/Rory "Red" **205**

Malcolm/Rory "Red" **206**

Michael/Malcolm/Rory "Red" **207**

John M./Michael/Malcolm/Rory "Red" **208**

Michael R./John M./Michael/Malcolm/Rory "Red" **209**

Neil M./Michael/Malcolm/Rory "Red" **210**

Angus/Malcolm/Rory "Red" **211**

Alex/Rory "Red" **212**

Michael/Alex/Rory "Red" **213**

Rory/Alex/Rory "Red" **214**

Roddie J./Rory/Alex/Rory "Red" **215**

Paul/Rory "Red" **216**

Rory/Paul/Rory "Red" **217**

MacNeil, Angus "Beag" and Eoin "Beag" (Donald)
   Ottawa Brook

Angus "Beag"/Donald **218**

Neil A./Angus "Beag"/Donald **219**

Dan H./Angus "Beag"/Donald **220**

Dan/Angus "Beag"/Donald **221**

John/Eoin "Beag"/Donald

Dan N./John/Eoin "Beag"/Donald **223**

MacNeil, James and Donald "Doctor"   Ottawa Brook
   and Red Point

James "Doctor" **224**

Donald "Doctor" **225**

Michael/Donald "Doctor" 226

Jim A./Michael/Donald "Doctor" 227

Dan J.J./Michael/Donald "Doctor" 228

Joseph/Donald "Doctor" 229

James L./Joseph/Donald "Doctor" 230

MacNeil, John and Neil "Roger"   Ottawa Brook and
   Highland Hill

John "Roger" 231

Neil "Roger" 232

Stephen/Neil "Roger" 233

Peter B./Stephen/Neil "Roger" 234

MacNeil, Malcolm (Iain "Ban") 235 Barra Glen

John/Malcolm 236

Hugh/Malcolm 237

Neil H./Hugh/Malcolm 238

MacNeil, John D. (James, Donald "Og") 239 Barra Glen

Roddie/John D. 240

MacNeil, James "Pearson" **241** Iona

Neil/James "Pearson" **242**

James N.P./Neil/James "Pearson" **243**

MacNeil, Stephen J. **244**

James Jr./James "Pearson" **245**

Alex P./James Jr./James "Pearson" **246**

MacNeil, Neil "Mor" **247** Ottawa Brook

Dan Y./Neil "Mor" **248**

Andrew/Dan Y./Neil "Mor" **249**

William/Dan Y./Neil "Mor" **250**

MacNeil, Michael "Saor" **251** Red Point

MacNeil, Alasdair **252** Ottawa Brook

Alexander "Seonaid"/Alasdair **253**

John A./Alexander "Seonaid"/Alasdair **254**

MacNeil, Donald (John, Donald John) **255** MacKinnon's Harbour

MacNeil, Stephen (Alasdair) **256** Grass Cove

James S./Stephen **257**

MacNeil, James "Lieutenant" **258** Grass Cove

MacNeil, John D. (Donald, Norman) **259** Grass Cove

James/John D. **260**

MacNeil, Francis F. **261** Barra Glen

MacNeil, Eoin **262** Washabuck Center

Michael/Eoin **263**

Johnnie A./Michael/Eoin **264**

MacNeil, Neil "Geal" **265** Washabuck

Rory/Neil **266**

MacNeil, "Red" Dan **267** Jamesville

MacNeil, Murdock "Beag" (Donald "Piper") **268** Washa-buck Bridge

John/Murdock **269**

Michael/Murdock **270**

MacNeil, Calum (I' "Ruadh") **271** Washabuck

MacNeil, Malcolm "Ruadh" **272** Washabuck

MacNeil, Jonathan (Seamus) **273** Iona

MacNeil, Malcolm Dan (Norman D.) **273a** Grass Cove

MacPhee **546** Lower Washabuck

MacRitchie, Kenneth **547** Washabuck

Norman/Kenneth **548**

John D./Norman/Kenneth **549**

Matheson, William **550** Washabuck

Morrison, John **551** Gillis Point

Donald "Beag"/John **552**

Rory/John **553**

Donald/Rory/John **554**

Munroe, Allan **555** Washabuck

Murphy, Donald "Og" **556** MacKinnon's Harbour

Joseph/Donald **557**

Hugh/Donald **558**

Joseph F./Hugh/Donald **559**

Peter/Joseph F./Hugh/Donald **560**

Murphy, Peter 561 Washabuck

Murphy, Peter 562 Washabuck

Alex/Peter 563

Dan P./Alex/Peter 564

Nash, Donald 565 St. Columba

Michael J./Donald 566

Dan N./Michael J./Donald 567

Northen, Charles 568 Ottawa Brook

Cosmos/Charles 569

O'Donnell, Philip 570 Jamesville West

Redquest, John 571 Red Point

Ross, William **572** Washabuck

Small, George **573** Red Point

Sutherland **574** Washabuck

Walker, Donald **575** Ottawa Brook

John H./Donald **576**

Dan/Donald **577**

MACNEIL

Donald "Og" MacNeil was a native of Barra in Scotland. He served in the British Army and took part in the Siege of Louisburg in 1758. That same year, he was aboard a British man-of-war on its way from Louisburg to Spanish River, now Sydney Harbour. A French vessel was sighted but, as it carried only ragged sails — purposely so as not to attract attention — the British vessel paid little attention to it. The cook aboard the British vessel was overheard, however, to make this remark in Gaelic: "Oh, French frigate, your sails may be ragged and dirty, but it is your cargo that is valuable." This remark was not lost on Donald "Og," who reported it immediately to the Captain. The British vessel was forthwith turned around and sent in hot pursuit of the French vessel. The chase continued all across the Atlantic, for it was not until both vessels were rounding the English coast that they came in close range of each other. Fortunately for the French vessel, it was too near the French coast to be attacked.

It was already too late in the Fall for the British man-of-war to return to Canada, so it tied up at an English port, while Donald "Og" and other members of the crew went to their homes. Back in Barra — as he did many times before — Donald "Og" lauded the beauty of the Bras d'Or Lake and re-affirmed his hope that, if any of them ever migrated to Canada, they would settle on the northern bank of that lake in what is now the parish of Iona. Rightly or wrongly, it was in these words that he painted for them the advantages of their doing so: "Besides fuel in the forests, water in the ground, and fish in the sea, you will find there more shelter from the North wind, better and earlier ripening harvests, and good fishing grounds."

Donald "Og" took part in the Taking of Quebec in 1759. It was his Captain, Donald "Gorm" MacDonald, who fooled the French sentry on that eventful night of September 12. Along with comrades, Donald "Og" helped to land six four-ton guns on the Quebec shore in the dead of night. Those guns are still preserved on the Plains of Abraham and are maintained by the Canadian Government. So also is the house in which General Montcalm died, as well as the house in which General Wolfe died, both of them dying from battle wounds. The battle itself is said to have lasted only about twenty minutes. When victory was assured, Captain MacDonald ordered Donald "Og" to hoist the British flag over Britain's new domain. He did so and was dismounting, when he was shot down by a French sniper in the nearby bushes. In his turn, this sniper was immediately shot down by one of Captain MacDonald's men.

Donald "Og" had three sons in Barra when he met his untimely death in Quebec. It was not until 1813 — that is, 54 years after their father's death — that the first two of his sons came to the New World. These sons of Donald "Og" were not the first MacNeils to come to Iona. That event in history must be credited to four who, along with others, left Barra and landed in Pictou in 1799. They were not immediate relatives of Donald "Og," but they were determined to carry out the instructions that Donald "Og" had detailed for them some forty years earlier.

The first four MacNeils to come to Iona were: Donald (Rory) and Eoin (Donald, John) who were not relatives; Donald's son Rory; and Eoin's son John. As was already said, the four had landed in Pictou the previous September. They made their way to Arisaig, where relatives and friends put at their disposal the humble huts that they themselves had abandoned for more comfortable quarters. In the Spring of 1800, the four set out for Iona in one small boat. They rowed to where the St. Peter's Canal was later cut, portaged their boat to the Bras d'Or Lake, and it is on record that they were greatly amazed at the size of the lake. They rowed along the southern shore, down to what is now East Bay, but they were not finding what they had long been hoping to find. Disappointed and fully aware of the difficulties that it involved, they decided to row back to what is now Orangedale, and it was not until they came in sight of the Barra Strait, that they saw themselves face-to-face with what Donald "Og" had so vividly described for them.

According to the legal requirements in vogue at the time for the "granting" of land, the MacNeils would have to set down a stake from which the Crown Surveyor could in time officially mark out their claims. The four MacNeils placed their stake at what was then the southernmost tip of land, where the Barra Strait was the narrowest. When the Intercolonial Railway was being built, however, that tip of land ceased to be southernmost, for what now lies between where the MacNeils placed their stake and the Iona entrance to the Grand Narrows Bridge was then filled in, so as to lessen the degree of curve for trains. Residents of the area recall the lighthouse that was long in service, adjacent to the C.N.R. Station in Iona. It would be more correct to say that the MacNeils placed their stake near where that lighthouse later stood. From that stake, as the legal marking point, a line was eventually drawn to Iona Rear, to about what was later the property of Rory G. MacNeil (Ruairi, Alasdair Iain). Donald and his son Rory took land to the West of that line; Eoin and his son John took land to its East.

The four MacNeils began immediately the formidable task of clearing the land — a formidable task indeed for Barra men, who, not having trees in their native land, never developed the art of "wielding the axe." They had already made a clearing and were burning the brush, when the smoke alerted the Indians. At that time, Redmen alone inhabited the interior of Cape Breton Island, as the French preferred to settle only along the Island's shores. Losing no time, the Indians came by canoe to investigate. Arriving on the scene, the Chief wanted to know by what right the Scots were clearing land. Donald (Rory) was hurriedly chosen to be spokesman for the four, and presumably because he was able to converse in French. To the Chief's question, Donald replied that they had permission from King George III. Donald produced a document to substantiate this, but the Chief refused to appear impressed. He made it clear to the four that he considered himself King in those regions and that he had no intention of recognizing another. A show-down was evidently imminent, and from weapons which the Indians carried in their canoes it was evident also that Highland blood was soon to be shed.

Realizing their plight, Eoin sought divine aid. He fell to his knees on the ground and signed himself with the Sign of the Cross. In those days, signing oneself with the Sign of the Cross and kneeling down were two actions that automatically went together. Divine aid was not long in coming, for all of a sudden the warlike Chief appeared friendly. He was friendly but cautious. Cautious lest this gesture could be a trickery-tactic on Eoin's part, the Chief very dubiously asked whether the four Scots might be Catholics. The Scots made every effort to establish their Catholicity to the satisfaction of the Chief, but the Chief still continued to appear skeptical. It was not until Donald went to his "ceiste," (his chest), and returned, holding a crucifix in the palm of his hand and presented it to the Chief, that the Chief, seeing the image of the Crucified Christ, made upon himself a huge Sign of the Cross and exclaimed aloud: "We are all brothers." The Scots were Catholics indeed, but they did not know that the Indians, too, were Catholics. The Jesuit missionary, now St. Anthony Daniel, had worked among the Indians in Northern Cape Breton, and it could well have been he who converted those same Indians to the Catholic Faith.

If they were all brothers, what better way could they show their brotherhood than by partaking together in a meal of friendship? The Chief ordered his men to procure eels from the canoes. As could be expected, the Scots did not take to the eels enthusiastically! Eels were never a part of the Barra men's diet, for their native shores were too sandy to afford at any time a haunt for eels. Yet so pleased were they with the sudden turn of events that day, that they could suppress their aversion even to eels! Accustomed to seasoning their fish with salt, the Scots offered some salt to the Indians. It was now their turn to become suspicious, for they were not accustomed to using what we call common salt. It was not that the Indians never seasoned their fish with salt, but that they always depended on the sea-water in which they boiled their fish to do this seasoning for them. As it turned out, the Chief was highly pleased with how common salt improved the taste of the fish, and he asked that he be allowed to take some of it back home with him. For the moment the Scots were nonplussed, for they had no container. Resourcefully, the Chief ordered one of his men to weave for him a suitable container from the bark of a birch tree. From that day on, there have always been peace and harmony between the Micmac Braves and the Gaels. As for the Gaels, however, they saw far more in this episode than the sparing of their lives.

When there was being planned in Christmas Island parish the hundredth anniversary of St. Barra's Church, once also the Mother Church of those living on the Iona side of the Barra Strait, a committee of representatives from both parishes was set up to make preparations for the jubilee. My double-first-cousin and I, then in our teens, were often taken along by the committee because of the ease with which we could read records written in Gaelic. We were thus able to witness first-hand the valiant efforts of Hector (Rory "Mor") MacNeil of Iona — a grandson of Donald who brought his crucifix to the Indian Chief on that memorable day in 1800—to have it put on record at the Christmas Island celebration that the four MacNeils, on that occasion, were favoured by Providence with a miracle. Father Roderick MacKenzie, then parish priest of Iona — himself a native of Christmas Island — was reluctant publicly to appear as if anticipating a decision of the Church, whose province alone it is to pass judgment on matters of this kind. Hector (Rory "Mor") pressed his case with vigour until it was apparent that his pastor was not going to go along with his desire. If only Hector (Rory "Mor") had been allowed to have his own way, this is what he wanted to see officially put on record in the Christmas Island celebration, and in his own most carefully phrased seven separate parts:

i) The four MacNeils had known many times before what it meant to sacrifice for the Faith. ii) They had witnessed many times before how timely Providence can come with Its heavenly aid. iii) They had seen with their own eyes how it was the Sign of the Cross that completely changed the heart of the Chief. iv) They were convinced that it was the Crucified Christ Himself who had summoned both Micmac and Gael as brothers of His own. v) They recognized in the speared eels the symbol of sacrifice. vi) The salt recalled to their minds the Salt of Wisdom used in the rite of Baptism for the preservation of the Faith. vii) And how could anyone say that they were being deceived in their inner-most thoughts when — without their even knowing it — the very ground on which they were then standing was later to be consecrated to the offering of Christ's Sacrifice of the Cross? For there, where all this happened in 1800, there stands today the parish church of Iona, dedicated to the patronage of St. Columba of Iona in Scotland."

Donald "Og" MacNeil was married twice in Barra. From his first wife he had two sons, Rory and Murdock, and from his second wife a son, Barra. At the time of his death on the Plains of Abraham, his sons were in the Old Country and likely still quite young.

Rory (Donald "Og") and Ben came to the New World in 1813 and settled with their families in Barra Falls, now Rear Big Beach in the parish of Christmas Island. Murdock was in ill health when his brothers left for the New World, and it was not until

1821 (or 1822) that he attempted to cross the Atlantic with his wife and family. Unfortunately Murdock died on the voyage across, but not before he entrusted his wife and children to Alasdair "Mor" MacNeil, a cherished friend of his and a fellow-immigrant aboard the Ship "Harmony." Alasdair "Mor" MacNeil settled eventually in Gillis Point, and he undertook immediately to stake out land adjoining his own and to build on it a log-cabin home for the deceased Murdock's wife and family.

Rory (Donald "Og") married Margaret MacKinnon in Barra and their family: Donald, Malcolm, Eoin, Rory, Stephen, John, Mary, Annie, Sarah, and Catherine. After settling for a time in Barra Falls — in about 1817 — the family, with the exception of Donald, moved to Barra Glen in the Parish of Iona. **1**

Annie (Rory, Donald "Og") married Darby (Donald, Hector) Campbell, Irish Vale, lived in Barra Glen, and later moved to Jamesville (see **299**). Sarah married John ("Big" Rory) MacNeil, Iona (see **37**), lived in Iona, and had a family. Mary married Malcolm (John "Ban") MacNeil from Barra, lived in Barra Glen (see **235**), and had a family. Catherine married Malcolm (Tormad) MacNeil, Piper's Cove, lived in Piper's Cove, and had a family.

Malcolm (Rory, Donald "Og") married first Christy, daughter of Neil "Geal" MacNeil, Washabuck (see **265**). They lived in Barra Glen and had a son Michael "Brook," at whose birth the mother died. This Michael was brought up by his aunt, Jane (Neil "Geal") MacNeil, Washabuck Center. In a second marriage Malcolm married Sarah (Malcolm) Campbell, Iona (see **286**). They lived in Barra Glen and their family: Rory, Malcolm, Donald, Christy, and Mary. The family later moved to Glace Bay. **2**

Rory (Malcolm) married a Miss MacPhee, Louisburg, lived in Glace Bay, and had a family. Malcolm married in Glace Bay and had a family. Donald married first Pennie Mac-Innis, Mabou, lived in Bridgeport, had a family; and in a second marriage he married a Miss MacNeil, Scotch Hill, Margaree. Christy married Michael (Neil, Donald) Mac-Neil, Iona Rear (see **173**), lived in Iona, had a large family, and later two of her sons — Neil and Angus — together with their parents returned to Iona. Mary did not marry and lived with her brother in Glace Bay.

Eoin (Rory, Donald "Og") married Catherine (Neil, Eoin) Mac-Neil, Gillis Point (see **115**). They lived in Barra Glen and their family: Donald, Rory, Murdock, Stephen, Neil, Mary, Margaret, and Annie. **3**

Mary (Eoin) married Donald "Tailor" MacNeil, Highland Hill (see **186**), lived in Highland Hill, and had a family. Margaret married John (James) MacNeil, Iona (see **83**), lived in Iona, and had a family. Annie married Malcolm (Seamus "Mor") MacNeil, Jamesville (see **180**), lived in Jamesville, and had a family. Stephen married in Boston, had a family, and later moved to British Columbia.

Donald (Eoin) married Flora (Angus, Eoin) MacNeil, Highland Hill (see **183**). They lived in Barra Glen and their family: Rory, Thomas, Catherine, and Margaret Monica. **4**

Rory (Donald) married Flora (Iain "Ban") MacKinnon, Highland Hill (see **453**), lived in Sydney, and had no family. Thomas married in the United States and had no family. Catherine married Stephen J. (John, Charles) MacKinnon, MacKinnon's Harbour (see **477**) and had a family. Margaret Monica married Rory S. (Iain, Ruairi) MacKinnon, MacKinnon's Harbour (see **473**) and had a family.

Rory (Eoin) married first Mary (Neil, Eoin) MacNeil, Iona (see **72**). They lived in Barra Glen and had a son, Neil R. In a second marriage Rory married Sarah (Philip, Donald) MacNeil, Gillis Point (see **96**) and their family: two girls, one of whom died young and the other married in Boston. **5**

Neil R. (Rory) married Mary Ann (Michael, Calum "Mor") MacNeil, Rear Iona (see **207**). They lived in Barra Glen and their family: Michael Rory, Joseph, and two girls who died young. **6**

Murdock (Eoin), a competent shoemaker, married Mary

MACNEIL

(Neil) Campbell, Jamesville West (see **308**). They lived in Barra Glen and their family: Francis, Rory Joseph, Mary Jane, Katie Ann, and five other girls who went to the United States. **7**

> Rory Joseph (Murdock) and Katie Ann died unmarried. Mary Jane married Angus MacNeil, Bridge-tender, Grand Narrows, lived in Grand Narrows, and had no family.

> Francis (Murdock) married Margaret (Norman D.) MacNeil, Benacadie. They lived in Barra Glen and their family: Margaret Ann, Mary Francis, Murdock Dan, Norman, Angus, Neil Murdock, and Duncan Joseph. **8**

> Norman (Francis) married Elizabeth(Rory D.) MacNeil, Barra Glen (see **177**). They lived in Sydney and had a family.

Neil (Eoin), a school teacher in his younger days, a Victoria County Councillor, and later a C.N.R. freight officer in Sydney, married Elizabeth (Angus, Eoin) MacNeil, Highland Hill (see **183**). They had a daughter Katie Ann.

> Katie Ann (Neil) was adopted by her aunt Mary, the wife of Donald "Tailor" MacNeil, Highland Hill. Later she married Frank MacInnis, Castle Bay and lived in Winnipeg. After the death of her husband, she moved back to Highland Hill.

Rory (Rory, Donald "Og"), commonly known as "Rory Glen Mor," married Catherine (Iain, Eoin) MacNeil, Jamesville (see **57**). They lived in Jamesville and their family: Rory, Sarah, Margaret, Catherine, Mary, Annie, and Mary Ann. "Rory Glen Mor" met with a singularly tragic ending. He and his daughter Catherine along with two MacNeil brothers who were neighbours of theirs but not relatives — Thomas and Angus MacNeil of Highland Hill — were coming from Baddeck on May 22, 1863. As they passed through the Grand Narrows Strait about dusk, the wind suddenly shifted from North to Northwest. It rose to such gale proportions, that landing at Jamesville was out of the question. Instead, they were forcefully driven out into the center of the Big Lake, and so furious a storm raged all night that the four of them perished. Indians sighted their boat the next morning off Indian Island (Johnstown). They left immediately for the scene and, together with others who had been scouting the lake, they came upon the gruesome spectacle of the four corpses securely fastened to the boat's interior. For the genealogy of the two MacNeil brothers from Highland Hill, see **191-193**. **9**

Catherine ("Rory Glen Mor") perished with her father. Sarah married Hugh (Malcolm) Campbell, Barra Glen (see **282**), lived in Barra Glen until the death of her husband, when she moved to St. Columba. Margaret married Patrick Kiely, Big Baddeck, lived in Big Baddeck, and had a family. Mary married Hector (Larry) MacDougall, Christmas Island, lived in Christmas Island, and had a family. Annie was the second wife of Neil (Philip) MacNeil, Barra Glen (see **98**), lived in Barra Glen, and had no family. Mary Ann died unmarried.

Rory ("Rory Glen Mor") was only fourteen when his father perished. He later married Mary (James, Michael) MacDonald, St. Columba (see **359**). They lived in Barra Glen and their family: Annie, Annie Catherine, Katie Eliza, and a son who died in infancy. Arthur Campbell was adopted in their home. **10**

Annie (Rory) married Frank (Michael, Iain "Ban") MacDonald, Irish Cove, lived in Glace Bay, and had no family. Annie Catherine married John D. (Seamus, Donald "Og") MacNeil, Castle Bay (see **239**), lived in Barra Glen and had a family. Katie Eliza died unmarried in the United States. For Arthur Campbell, see **318**.

Stephen (Rory, Donald "Og") married Mary (Neil, Eoin) MacNeil, Gillis Point, a sister of Eoin's wife (see **115**). They lived in Barra Glen and their family: Michael, Rory, Neil, Mary, Catherine, Margaret, and Paul. **11**

Mary (Stephen) married Stephen (Domhnull, Ruairi) MacNeil, Benacadie, lived in Benacadie, and had a family. Catherine married Paul (Thomas, Johnnie) MacKinnon, Iona Rear, lived in Iona Rear, and had a family (see **458**).

MACNEIL

Margaret and Paul were unmarried.

Michael (Stephen) married Catherine (Hugh, Malcolm) Campbell, Barra Glen (see **282**). They lived in Barra Glen and their family: Mary, Mary Lucy, Christena, Mary Catherine, Stephen, Hughie, Sarah, Hugh Francis, Mary Ann I, Mary Ann II, Stephen R., and John R. **12**

We digress here for an insert on Michael (Stephen) by his grandson, Reverend J.H. Gillis, Ph.D., Saint Francis Xavier University in Antigonish.

"Iona was a mission of Christmas Island parish until it became a parish in its own right in 1873. It was St. Barra's pastor's zeal to keep a catechist in Iona who would, as they say in Gaelic, 'put the catechism to the children.' It so happened that the catechist in Iona was getting up in years and desirous of being relieved of his post. 'What can we do to replace you?' asked the parish priest. 'Well, I'll just tell, you,' said the catechist, 'I have a boy in my class in Iona who knows the catechism exceptionally well. Therefore all you have to do, Father, is to find out who it is who teaches him, and put him or her in my place.' The pastor thought this a fortunate solution, so he sent word to Stephen (Rory) in Barra Glen that he should come to see him in Christmas Island and bring along with him his son Michael. There was great consternation in the MacNeil home in Barra Glen that night, for evidently the priest had something against the boy that as yet the parents did not know. Young Michael protested his innocence vigorously, but nothing could deter the father from coming to this decision: 'First thing early in the morning, you and I are going to the priest in Christmas Island.'

"It simply had to be. Together they walked through the woods to Iona, ferried themselves across the Strait, and then continued to walk on to Christmas Island. Arriving there, the father knocked at the glebe's backdoor, stated his mission, and was ushered into the pastor's study. As he went there, he left his son in the kitchen. Expecting nothing but the worst, the father was completely cowed by the priest's words: 'I sent for you to find out who it is who teaches your son the catechism, for I hear that he knows it exceptionally well.' Breathing now more easily, the father replied: 'Oh, nobody teaches him, for where we live in Barra Glen nobody can read or write. But the boy is in the kitchen, Father, and you can ask him to speak for himself.' It was now Michael's turn to face the bar of justice! He, too, was taken off guard when he heard the priest say: 'Tell me how it is that you know your catechism so well, as they tell me that you do.' Very coyly Michael said in his own defence: 'I just listen to the rest, Father.' For evidently Michael's secret strategy had been to listen intently to his classmates, as the same catechism question was put to each of them in turn. By the time that the question was put to Michael, he had already snatched its answer from the air.

"Clearly pleased with Michael's reply, the priest very paternally patted him on the head and said: 'Many a person you will teach in the years to come.' Then he handed Michael a book. It was a real book, and a real book that he was to have as his very own. It was a Gaelic catechism and, opening it at its first page, the priest read from it in Gaelic: 'Who created you? God created me. Who is God? God is the Creator of heaven and earth and of all things.' Michael himself had long before this snatched that much from out of the air waves. But the priest meant business. As if mysteriously catapulting himself into the age of the 'Look-and-Say' technique in reading, the priest said to Michael: 'Whenever you see a word that looks like this one here, it will be **God**. Whenever you see one that looks like this one here, it will be **Creator**. Whenever you see one that looks like this one here, it will be **heaven**.' Michael's only kindergarten-lesson was evidently to be in how to hold the book right-end-up!

"On the way home that evening, Michael would run ahead of his father, sit down by the roadside, and pore over the leaves of the book, until his father caught up with him. He would then take off again for a few more moments at trying to unearth its treasures. So great was his determination — even then — to conquer that book! And whenever anyone asked during the months that followed: 'Where is Michael?' his mother was always heard to reply: 'You will find him somewhere with his head buried in that book that the priest gave him.' How he managed to do it, we can never know, but Michael so mastered that book that he could read it from cover to cover with ease. Yet he knew nothing of an alphabet, and still less of how to recite one!

"All this happened in 1858 when Michael was twelve years old. From the first, even as he himself was conquering the book, he gathered unto himself disciples, willing to come under his tutelage. His first 'graduates' in reading by sight were his own brother-in-law, Paul (Thomas, Johnnie) MacKinnon, Iona Rear (see **458**) and his friend, Rory (Alasdair, John Rory 'Red') MacNeil, Iona Rear (see **202**), and they, too, took a hand in holding catechism classes of their own. Our author himself 'graduated' from his father's First Communion Catechism Class in 1909, a fact that establishes that his father had taught catechism classes on a regular basis for over a half century. Who will not say that St. Barra's pastor was speaking under inspiration when — in 1858 — he said to Michael: 'Many a person you will teach in the years to come'?

"Not content with conquering the catechism, Michael purchased a Gaelic Bible, and from it he regularly gave readings in public. Who were his hearers? They were his male peers from far and near, who regularly came in numbers by night, who sat around the kitchen walls, and who were often so absorbed in what the Lord Jesus did and said, that many a session ended only because the morning sun had already risen in the sky. In Michael's latter days, the local postmaster subscribed for the **Mac Talla**, a Gaelic newspaper. Its arrival was always the signal for the 'old faithful' to gather once again in the 'kitchen academy,' but this time to hear read aloud gems from the English classics that had been translated into Gaelic. Because she had been reared in that 'kitchen academy,' our mother could regale us at home with legends of King Arthur and the Knights of the Round Table.

"A word on that Gaelic Bible. When after Michael married and left his father's house for a home of his own close by, he left the Bible in the old homestead, where it was always venerated as a priceless heirloom. When the Reverend Duncan J. Rankin became pastor of Iona in 1926, he had occasion to scout around for a Gaelic Bible, as it had always been his custom to read the Gospel at Sunday Mass in both English and Gaelic. Michael's Bible found itself in Father Rankin's hands, and from it, periodically re-dressed and reinforced by the good Sisters, Father Rankin read the Gospel in Gaelic every Sunday for the quarter century that he was pastor of Iona. The least we can say is that here was a book that many times over bore fruit in abundance!

"I myself was born three years before my grandfather died. As he had done, a year before, to a sister of mine who, like myself, had been born prematurely, he put the water of Baptism on me. At the time, Iona's pastor was on a sick-call in another end of the parish, and mine was clearly a case of necessity. So it was my grandfather who baptized me. The pastor came to our home, put his hat on the kitchen table, and said to my grandfather: 'Baptize that hat, as you baptized the child.' My grandfather, who had so often drilled his classes on how to act in such an emergency complied, and the pastor's reaction was: 'The child is truly baptized — for I could do no better myself.'

"After I graduated from college, I was fortunate enough to be sent to Rome to prepare for the Holy Priesthood, and to be housed there in the National College of the Scots. Returning home in 1935, I visited Scotland and — with neither plan nor design — I came upon the rectory of Craigston church in Barra. It was a Saturday evening, and the pastor did not hesitate to suggest that I take the parish Mass in the morning and preach. He was as unaware as I was that, on the morrow, I would be in the very church where — 136 years before — my great, great, grandmother prayed for a whole day, trying to persuade the Lord to make 'a pact' with her. She was the wife of Donald (Rory) MacNeil who — as it is told elsewhere in this book — accosted the Indian Chief on the Iona beach on that memorable day in 1800. Donald (Rory) had made up his mind to migrate to the New World, but his wife Margaret was fearful, lest he and she and their children die without the Last Rites in that primitive land. This was therefore the burden of her day-long vigil in the Craigston church in 1799. It was completely lost on me that, besides being the first priest to be ordained from the parish of Iona, I was her great-great-grandson. Yet, although the whole thing was sadly lost on me, there were luckily others who could see the hand of God tieing together the two events. No sooner did the news of my offering Holy Mass in Craigston church reach the home of Francis (Hector "Mor," Donald Rory) MacNeil in New Waterford, than his son John Dan took his facile pen to record the event for history. Dramatically he sketched the 'pact with the Lord' and how she and her husband and all their children managed to receive the Last Rites in this land — some of them, to say the least, in circumstances that were unusual. Margaret MacNeil was John Dan's great-great-grandmother through her son Rory, and mine through her son John. My chance-presence, as a priest, in Craigston church — even before, as a priest, I met my own people in the New World — was seen by him as the crowning proof that God does indeed hear the prayers of His people and abandons them not.

"John Dan MacNeil's historical manuscript was published in the Sydney **Post Record** in 1946 and, to say the least, 'it made the rounds.' In making those rounds, it was officially offered by

MACNEIL

Michael A. MacKinnon, formerly of East Bay and then of Dorchester, Mass., to both Professor Charles Dunn of Harvard University and Sister Margaret Beaton of the then Saint-Francis-Xavier-University-in-Sydney, for preservation in their collection of Scottish immigrant history." **J.H.G.**

Stephen (Michael), Mary Ann I, and Hughie died in infancy. Mary married Joseph F. Murphy, MacKinnon's Harbour (see **559**), lived in MacKinnon's Harbour, and had a family. Mary Lucy married Hugh N. (Donald) Gillis, MacKinnon's Harbour (see **332**), lived in MacKinnon's Harbour, and had a family. Christena married Michael Black, Mira, lived in Sydney, and had a family. Sarah became a Sister of Sion. Mary Ann II became a Sister of Notre Dame. Hughie Francis and Mary Catherine died young.

Stephen R. (Michael) married Annie Jane Bishop, Boisdale. They lived in Barra Glen and their family: Theresa, Josephine, Sarah, Michael, Martena, Joseph who died in infancy, and Camillus whom they adopted. **13**

John R. (Michael) married Elizabeth ("Red" Rory) MacLean, Washabuck (see **515**). They lived in Barra Glen and their family: Lex, Elaine, Monty, and Dolores. **14**

Rory (Stephen) married Sarah (Hugh, Malcolm) Campbell, Barra Glen, sister of Michael's wife (see **282**). They lived in Barra Glen and their family: Mary, Mary Ann, May Ann, Mary Lizzie, Mary Catherine, and Stephen Michael. **15**

Mary Lizzie (Rory) and Mary Catherine died young. Mary married Roddie (Frank) MacNeil, Iona (see **160**), lived in Iona, and had a family. Mary Ann married Rod S. (Michael, Alasdair) MacDonald, Jamesville West (see **369**), lived in Sydney, and had a family. May Ann married Hugh F. (Archie) MacKenzie, Christmas Island, lived in Grand Narrows, and had a family.

MACNEIL

Stephen Michael (Rory) married Annie (MacNeil) Lahey, Big Pond. They lived in Barra Glen and had no family. **16**

Neil (Stephen) married Annie (Malcolm, Johnnie) MacKinnon, Rear Iona (see **462**). They lived in Gillis Point and their family: Stephen, John P., Thomas, Johnnie, Margaret, Mary Catherine, Mary Lizzie, Effie, and Lucy. **17**

Thomas (Neil), Margaret, and Effie are unmarried. Stephen married and has a family in Ontario. Mary Catherine married Rannie J. (Ruairi, Eachain) MacNeil, Beaver Cove, lived in Sydney, and had a family. Mary Lizzie married James A. (Aillean, Alasdair) MacNeil, Gillis Point (see **136**), lived in Gillis Point, and had a family. Lucy married James (John D.) MacNeil, Grass Cove (see **260**), lived in Grass Cove, and had a family.

John P. (Neil) married Jessie Campbell, Sydney. They live in Gillis Point and their family: Margaret, Mary Effie, and Pauline. **18**

Johnnie (Neil) married Mary E. (Dan D.) MacNeil, Grass Cove (see **120**). They live in Grass Cove and their family: Dannie, Neil, Ann Marie, and Kenzie. **19**

John (Rory, Donald "Og") married a daughter of John (Mac'in Tailleir) MacPhee, Shenacadie. They lived in Barra Glen and their family: John, Michael, Jane, and Catherine. **20**

Jane (John) married Michael (Malcolm "Big") MacNeil, Rear Iona (see **207**), lived in Rear Iona, and had a family. Catherine married Hector (Domhnull, Ruairi) MacNeil, Rear Christmas Island, lived in Christmas Island, and had no family.

John (John) married Annie (Donald "Mor") MacKinnon, MacKinnon's Harbour (see **486**). They lived in Barra Glen and their family: Dan, Johnnie, Mary Jane, Margaret, Flora, and Peggy Ann. **21**

MACNEIL

Dan (John) and Peggy Ann died unmarried. Margaret died young. Flora married John J. (Eoin "Mor") MacNeil, Jamesville (see **63**), lived in Jamesville, and had a family. Mary Jane married Angus D. MacDonald, Whitney Pier, lived in Whitney Pier, and had no family.

Johnnie (John), known as "Johnnie Ban," married Mary (James, Domhnull a Chull) MacNeil, Benacadie. They lived in Barra Glen and their family: James, Angus, Mary, Katie, Michael, Annie Flo, Murdock, Jackie, Roddie, and others who died in infancy. **22**

James ("Johnnie Ban") died unmarried. Mary married in the United States. Annie Flo married and lived in Toronto. Roddie, unmarried, was killed in World War II. Katie married Dan Joe MacNeil, "Ferryman," Grand Narrows, lived in Grand Narrows, and had a family. Michael married a Miss MacKenzie, Christmas Island, lives in Sydney, and has a family. Murdock, married Catherine (Dan Angus) MacNeil, Highland Hill (see **185**), lives in Grand Narrows, and has a family. Angus married Mary Jane (Michael D.) MacNeil, Iona (see **51**), lives in Grand Narrows, and had a family. Jackie married Faye ("Red" Rory) MacLean, Washabuck (see **515**), lives in Toronto, and has a family.

Michael (John) married Catherine (Alasdair, Rory "Red") MacNeil, Rear Iona (see **212**). They lived in Barra Glen and had a family of three who died young. **23**

Murdock (Donald "Og") died during the passage from Barra to Cape Breton. It was in 1821 (or 1822) and aboard the immigrant Ship "Harmony." His widow and children, after leaving Sydney, went with their companions up through the Bras d'Or Lake and finally settled in Gillis Point. The widow's name was evidently MacInnis, and she was probably from South Uist. She and her children had been entrusted to the care of Alasdair "Mor" MacNeil, as was already mentioned. Murdock's family was:

Paul, Neil, John, Michael, Christy, and Margaret. **24**

Paul (Murdock, Donald "Og") married Margaret (Domhnull, Eoin) MacNeil, Gillis Piont (see **117**), lived in Gillis Point for a time, but moved with his family to the United States. Christy married Neil (Hector) MacNeil, Gillis Point (see **87**), lived in Gillis Point East, and had a family. Margaret married Donald (Hector) MacNeil, Piper's Cove, lived in Piper's Cove, and had a family. **24a**

Neil (Murdock, Donald "Og") married Margaret (Calum "Ruadh") MacNeil, Gillis Point (see **128**). They had two sons: Neil who died young, and Rory who married in Springhill and had a family. **25**

John (Murdock, Donald "Og") married Jane (Neil "Geal") MacNeil, Lower Washabuck (see **265**). They lived in Washabuck Center and their family: Peter, John, Neil, and Kate — all of whom died unmarried. **26**

Michael (Murdock, Donald "Og") married Margaret (Alasdair "Mor") MacNeil, Gillis Point (see **129**). They lived in Gillis Point and their family: Stephen B., Peter, Alex, Murdock, Catherine I, Elizabeth, Sarah, and Catherine II. **27**

Alex (Michael) and Murdock died unmarried. Peter lived in New Brunswick. Catherine I married John (Michael "Lewis") MacDonald, Ottawa Brook (see **354**), lived in Ottawa Brook, and had a family. Elizabeth married James (Eoin "Mor") MacNeil, Jamesville (see **59**), lived in Jamesville, and had a family. Sarah married a Mr. Young, Little Bras d'Or and had no family. Catherine II married Peter B. MacDonald, Ottawa Brook (see **352**), lived in Ottawa Brook, and had a family.

Stephen B. (Michael), known as "Piper" and a watchmaker by trade, married a Miss MacPhee, daughter of Angus (Ruairi, Aonghas), Boularderie. They lived in Gillis Point, but later moved to Port Hawkesbury. **28**

MACNEIL

Ben or Barra (Donald "Og") married in Barra, Scotland Sarah (Donald) MacNeil. They settled in Barra Falls (that is, Rear Big Beach) and their family: Donald, John, James, Alexander, Neil, Mary I, Peggy, Mary II, and Catherine. **29**

Donald (Barra, Donald "Og") and John have many descendants in Christmas Island, and James has descendants in Boisdale and Sydney Mines.

Edward MacNeil, a great-grandson of John (Barra), was for many years a merchant, postmaster, and collector of customs in Iona. He married Margaret Josephine (James N.) Campbell, Jamesville West (see **313**] and their family: John A.J., James R.J., and Catherine Flora May. **30**

Alasdair or Alexander (Barra, Donald "Og") married Catherine (Angus, Eoin) MacNeil, Christmas Island. They lived in Christmas Island, but later moved to Ottawa Brook. Their family: Annie, Katie I, Katie II, Sarah, Mary I, Mary II, Annie, John I, Michael, John II, and Angus. **31**

Katie I (Alasdair) married Peter MacInnis, Castle Bay, lived in Castle Bay, and had a family. Mary I married John (Mac Sheumais) MacNeil, Big Beach, and had a family. Mary I and Michael died young. Katie II and Angus died unmarried. Annie married James MacDougall, Red Point (see **394**), lived in Red Point, and had no family, but they adopted Michael MacInnis (see **411**). Sarah married Donald (Iain, Ruairi "Ruadh") MacNeil, Iona Rear (see **200**), lived in Iona Rear, and had a family that died young. Mary II married Neil (Iain "Ban") Gillis, Jamesville West (see **335**), lived in Jamesville West, and had a family.

John I (Alasdair) married Margaret (Hector, Domhnull Eoin) MacNeil, Gillis Point (see **126**). They lived in Ottawa Brook and their family: Alex and Hector. In a second marriage John I married Betsy Nash (see **565**) and had no family. **32**

Alex (John I) married Sarah (Francis, Eachain Ruairi "Mor") MacNeil, Iona (see **49**), lived in New Waterford, and his family: Margaret, Francis, Mary Monica, Agnes, Rita, Bernie, Michael, Irene, Raymond, Jerrand, and Sylvester. Hector (John I)

MACNEIL

married Katie Jane (Rory, Domhnull "Mor") MacNeil, Red Point (see **41a**), lived in New Waterford, and his family: James, Madeline, Margaret, John, Regina, Roy, and Matthew.

Neil (Barra, Donald "Og"), a tailor, moved his family from the parish of Christmas Island to Red Point. He married Catherine (Rory "Saor") MacInnis, Iona (see **405**) and their family: Murdock, Rory, Donald, Michael, Patrick, Ben, John, Ann, Peggy, Mary I, Christy, Mary II, and Teresa. **33**

Peggy (Neil) and Mary II died unmarried. Ann married Michael "Saor" MacNeil, Red Point (see **251**), lived in Red Point, and had a family. Christy married Eoin (Neil, Hector) MacLean, Ottawa Brook (see **536**), lived in Ottawa Brook, and had a family. Mary I married John (Michael "Mor") MacDonald, St. Columba (see **364**), lived in St. Columba, and had a family. Theresa married a Mr. MacEachern, Arichat and had a son Hector.

Hector MacEachern, son of Theresa (Neil, Barra) MacNeil, was a blacksmith in MacKinnon's Harbour for some years. He married Mary, commonly known as "Maiseag," and they had a son Simon who married, lived in Glace Bay, and had a family. **34**

John (Neil), the Reverend John MacNeil, as a young man, lived with Presbyterian relatives near Little Narrows, where he attended school for some years. He became interested in the Protestant faith, studied for the ministry, and was ordained. He married a woman from Ontario where he had his first pastoral charge. Later he was minister to the Presbyterian congregation in Baddeck Forks. He had a family, and one of his sons, Grant MacNeil, was Member of Parliament for Vancouver North, having been elected on the C.C.F. ticket in 1935.

Ben (Neil) married first Katie MacNeil, Shenacadie. They lived in Big Beach and had a large family. Later they moved with their son "Boston Dan" and their daughter Catherine to Red Point. In a second marriage Ben married Sarah (Donald "Doctor") MacNeil, Ottawa Brook (see **225**) and their family: Dan Neil, Donald John, and John. **35**

MACNEIL

Dan Neil (Ben), Donald John, and John were unmarried. Catherine married first Malcolm (Donald "Mor") MacNeil, Red Point (see **43**), lived in Red Point, had no family; and in a second marriage she married George Small, Glace Bay (see **573**), lived in Red Point, and had a family.

● ● ●

Donald (Ruairi) MacNeil and his son Rory "Mor" were two of the first four MacNeils to come to Iona. It was in 1800. Donald had married Margaret MacNeil in Barra and their family: Rory "Mor," Donald, Michael, John, Hector, Margaret, Sarah, Christy, and Mary.

Donald (Donald, Ruairi) married Catherine, daughter of John "Brown" MacNeil, settled for a time in Arisaig, and later moved to Big Beach. Michael apparently lived in Pictou and quite likely moved later to Guysborough. Hector died young. Margaret apparently lived in Pictou. Sarah married Rory "Miller" MacDougall, Big Beach and had a family. Christy married Allan (Donald "Ban") MacKinnon (see **465**), lived in MacKinnon's Harbour, and had a family. We have no information on Mary.

John (Donald, Ruairi) married Catherine (Darby) Campbell, Big Pond. They settled in Ottawa Brook, near where later Dan Y. MacNeil lived. John's family apparently consisted of five daughters. **35a**

Flora (John, Donald Ruairi) was the second wife of Donald (Rory) Gillis, MacKinnon's Harbour (see **327**) and had a family. Another daughter was the first wife of Hector (Neil, Hector) MacLean, Ottawa Brook (see **535**), lived in Ottawa Brook, and died shortly after her marriage. A third daughter was the wife of Neil "Mor" MacNeil, Ottawa Brook (see **247**), lived in Ottawa Brook, and had a family. We have no definite information on the other two daughters. Evidence, still incomplete, would lead one to believe that one of John's other daughters was the wife of Donald "Soldier" MacDonald, Ottawa Brook (see **384a**) and that her name was Christy. If this be true, John's fourth daughter would be the mother-in-law of Angus "Beag" (Donald, Rory) MacNeil, Ottawa Brook (see **218**). There is also strong evidence that the fifth of John's daughters was the wife of Alexander (John "Miller") MacDougall, Red Point (see **393**); and, if this be true, she was the mother of Flora, the third wife of Archibald Campbell, Red Point (see **284**).

Rory "Mor" (Donald, Ruairi) married first Mary, daughter of Malcolm Campbell, Iona (see **286**). They lived in Iona and their family: John, Donald "Mor," Annie I, Flora, Sarah, Annie II, and Elizabeth. In a second marriage he married Mary Campbell, widow of Eoin (Seamus) MacNeil, Iona (see **273**) and sister of Malcolm (John, Hector) Campbell, Barra Glen (see **281**). They lived in Iona and their family: Hector, Donald "Beag," Catherine, and a son on whom we have no information. **36**

Annie I (Rory "Mor," Donald Ruairi) married Hector MacLean, Pictou, lived in Pictou, and had a family. Flora married Michael Campbell, Antigonish and Margaree, lived in Iona, and had a son Archie (see **316**). Sarah married Malcolm "Mor" (Rory "Red") MacNeil, Iona Rear (see **206**), lived in Iona Rear, and had a family. Annie II married Stephen "Beag" MacNeil, Beaver Cove, and had a family. Elizabeth and Catherine were unmarried.

John (Rory "Mor," Donald Ruairi) married Sarah (Rory, Donald "Og") MacNeil (see **1**). They lived in Iona and their family: Rory, John, Malcolm, Francis, Mary, Margaret, and Peggy Ann. **37**

Mary (John) married Angus (Neil, Eachain) MacLean, Washabuck (see **542**), lived in Washabuck Bridge, and had a large family. Margaret married Rory MacMillan, Red Islands, lived in East Bay, and had a family. Peggy Ann married Dan MacNeil, "Ferryman," Grand Narrows, lived in Grand Narrows, and had a family. Malcolm married in the United States and had a family.

MACNEIL

Rory (John) married first Annie (Murdock, Alasdair) MacDonald, Upper Washabuck (see **381**). They lived in Upper Washabuck and their family: Elizabeth and others who died young. In a second marriage he married Katie (Peter, Neil) MacLean, Washabuck Center (see **496**) and their family: Mary, Frances Ann, Josephine, Annie May, and Peter Malcolm. **38**

Elizabeth (Rory) married Angus (Ronald) MacDonald, Upper Washabuck (see **376**), lived in Upper Washabuck, and had a family. Mary became a Sister of St. Martha. Frances Ann was the second wife of Neil H. (James) Gillis, MacKinnon's Harbour, (see **329**), lived in MacKinnon's Harbour, and had a family. Josephine married a Mr. Reeves and lived in Boston. Annie May married James (Dan) MacKinnon, Cain's Mountain (see **484**), lived in MacKinnon's Harbour, and had a family. Peter Malcolm married Bridgit MacDonald, Glace Bay, lived in Upper Washabuck, and had no family.

John (John) married in the United States and had a family. After the death of his wife, he returned to Washabuck, married a Mrs. Morrison, and had no family. **39**

Francis (John) married Mary MacIntosh, East Bay. They lived in Iona and their family: Sadie, Stephen L., Jessie, John Malcolm, Roderick, Mary Frances, and Mary Catherine who died young. **40**

Sadie (Francis) married Allan Austin (Rory N.) MacNeil, Gillis Point (see **108**), lived in Gillis Point, and had a family. Stephen L. married Helen (Vincent) MacLean, Lower Washabuck (see **505**), lived in Sydney, and had a family. Jessie married Alex MacLean, Grand Narrows, lived in Grand Narrows, and had a family. John Malcolm died unmarried. Roderick married a Miss Morrison, East Bay, lived in Sydney, and had no family. Mary Frances married John Hector (Dan S.) MacNeil, Gillis Point (see **123**), lived in Dartmouth, and had a family.

Donald "Mor" (Rory "Mor," Donald Ruairi) married Sarah (Hector, Neil) MacNeil, Gillis Point (see **86**). They lived in Red

MACNEIL

Point and their family: Hector, Rory I, John, Rory II, Michael D., Malcolm, Mary I, Sarah, Mary II, Margaret, and Annie. **41**

Hector (Donald "Mor") died unmarried. Rory II was killed in the Springhill Explosion in 1891. Mary I married Martin Maloney, Joggins Mines. Annie married Dan MacNeil, Joggins Mines. Sarah married Rory (John "Roger") MacNeil, Ottawa Brook (see **231**), lived in Iona, and had no family. Mary II married Malcolm (Michael) MacInnis, Iona (see **407**), lived in Iona, and had a family. Margaret married James "Banker" MacNeil, Iona (see **169**), lived in Iona, and had a family.

Rory I (Donald "Mor") married first Sarah (Angus "Lord") MacDonald, Washabuck Bridge (see **384**). They lived in Red Point and their family: Sarah, Christy, and Katie Jane. In a second marriage he married Bella Beaton, Mabou and their family: Sarah Ann, a son who died in infancy, and Mildred MacKenzie whom they adopted. **41a**

Sarah (Rory I) married Michael MacInnis, Red Point (see **394**), lived in Red Point, and had no family. Christy married Alex (Archibald) Campbell, Red Point (see **285**), lived in Red Point, and had a family. Katie Jane, brought up by Donald (Isabella) MacNeil, Jamesville (see **70**), married Hector (Iain, Alasdair Barra) MacNeil, Ottawa Brook (see **32**), lived in New Waterford, and had a large family. Sarah Ann married Dan J.J. (Michael "Doctor") MacNeil, Ottawa Brook (see **228**), lived in Ottawa Brook, and had a family.

John (Donald "Mor") married Lizzie (Mor, Iain "Roger") MacNeil, Ottawa Brook (see **231**). They lived in Ottawa Brook and had no family. **42**

Malcolm (Donald "Mor") married Catherine (Barra, Neil Barra) MacNeil, Red Point (see **35**). They lived in Red Point and had no family. **43**

Michael D. (Donald "Mor") married Elizabeth White, Mabou. They lived in Red Point and their family: Cassie, Peggy, Sadie, Kaye, Martha, Sarah Margaret, Chrissie, Dan R., John Malcolm, John T., and John Robert. **44**

MACNEIL

John T. (Michael D.) died unmarried. Cassie married Joe Mancini, North Sydney, lived in St. Peter's, and had a family. Peggy married John Doucet and had no family. Sadie married Arthur Cox and had a family. Kaye married Sam Medjuck and had a family. Martha married John Young and had a family. Sarah Margaret married Jerome Gillis and had no family. Chrissie married William Dixon and had a family.

Dan R. (Michael D.) married Ellen (Murdock) Gillis, Cain's Mountain. They lived in Red Point and their family: Gladys, Hugh, Melvin, Jean, Michael, Bruno, Murdock J., Carleton, Francis, Sheila, and Verna. **45**

John Malcolm (Michael D.) married Cecilia (Joseph) Bonaparte, MacKinnon's Harbour (see **278**). They lived in Red Point and their family: John Felix, Mary Bell, and Roy J. **46**

John Robert (Michael D.) married Margaret Fickey, Sydney. They lived in Little Narrows and their family: Michael, Theresa, John and Catherine. **47**

Hector (Rory "Mor," Donald Ruairi) married Margaret MacNeil, Grand Narrows. They lived in Iona and their family: John, Rory, Hector, Dan, Francis H., Mary Jane, and a daughter who married Hugh Campbell, Springhill. **48**

John (Hector) lived in the United States. Hector lived in Alaska. Dan was killed in Iona in the constructing of the Intercolonial Railroad. Mary Jane married first Malcolm MacIsaac, Sydney, had a family; and in a second marriage she married Joseph MacKinnon, Beaver Cove, and had a family. Rory married Mary (John, Aonghas Eoin) MacNeil, Highland Hill (see **184**), lived in the United States, and had a large family.

Francis H. (Hector) married Mary II (Murdock, Domhnull Eoin) MacNeil, Gillis Point (see **121**). They lived in Iona, but later moved to New Waterford with their family: Dannie, Michael, Murdock, John Dan, John Malcolm, Hector, Hector Joseph, Margaret, Sarah, Annie, Mary

Jane, and Monica. **49**

Donald "Beag" (Rory "Mor," Donald Ruairi) married Mary (James, Donald "Ban") MacDonald, Gillis Point (see **388**). They lived in Iona and their family: Michael D., Daniel, James C., Roderick, Mary Ann, Katie, and Mary. **50**

Roderick (Donald "Beag") and Mary died unmarried. Mary Ann married Hector MacSween, Boisdale, and had a family. Katie married Danny MacSween, brother of Mary Ann's husband, Boisdale, and had a family. James C. married Maggie (Eachain, Eoin) MacNeil, Iona (see **153**), lived in Sydney, and had a family.

Michael D. (Donald "Beag") married first Mary Jane Cash, Irish Cove. They lived in Iona and their family: Joe, Margaret, Catherine, and Roddie. In a second marriage he married Katie (Murdock B.) MacNeil, Highland Hill (see **189**) and their family: Murdock, Francis, Dannie A., and Mary Jane. **51**

Joe (Michael D.) married first a Miss MacKinnon, Beaver Cove, lived in Sydney, had a family; and in a second marriage he had a family in Western Canada. Margaret married Neil Joseph (Peter S.) MacNeil, Gillis Point (see **113**), lived in New Waterford, and had a family. Catherine married first Daniel (Francis H., Hector) MacNeil, Iona (see **49**), lived in New Waterford, had a family; and in a second marriage she married Neil MacDonald, lived in Waterford, and had a family. Mary Jane married Angus (John A.J.) MacNeil, Barra Glen (see **22**), lived in Grand Narrows, and had a family.

Roddie (Michael D.) married Margaret (Joseph "Doctor") MacNeil, widow of James P. (Peter B.) MacDonald, Ottawa Brook (see **353**). They lived in Ottawa Brook and had no family. **52**

Francis (Michael D.) married Agnes (Rod F.) Gillis, Jamesville West (see **336**). They lived in Iona and their family: Hector, Jimmy, Michael, Carleton, Bernadette, Colleen, and Judy (Dan Neil) Nash (see

MACNEIL

567) whom they adopted. **53**

Murdock (Michael D.) married Margaret (Rory, Peter) MacLean, Ottawa Brook (see **528**). They lived in Iona and their family: Jerry, Michael D., Catherine, Anita, Joanne, and Larry. **54**

Dannie A. (Michael D.) married Kaye (John Y.) MacLean, Orangedale. They lived in Iona and their family: Jackie, Connie, Roddie, Bernice, Tipton, and Dan E. **55**

Daniel (Donald "Beag") married Mary Beaton, Mabou. They lived in Iona and their family: Elizabeth, Maggie, Mary Jane, Mary, John Angus, Dan Rory, and Alex R. The family moved to New Waterford, but one of the daughters, Elizabeth, returned to Iona, married John Francis (Archie) Campbell (see **317**) and had a family. **56**

● ● ●

Eoin (Donald, John) MacNeil and his son John were the two other MacNeils who — with Donald (Ruairi) MacNeil and his son Rory "Mor" — made up the first four MacNeils to come to Iona. Eoin (Donald, John) had married in Barra Margaret Campbell, sister to Malcolm Campbell, the first Campbell to come to Iona (see **288**) and their family: Iain or John, Neil, James, and Margaret. **56a**

Margaret (Eoin, Donald John) married Donald (Ruairi) MacNeil, lived for a time in Iona, and moved with her sons — Neil and James "Mor" — to Jamesville (see **170**).

Iain (Eoin, Donald John), whose wife's name we do not know, lived for a time in Iona, but later moved to Jamesville with his family: Eoin "Mor," Stephen, John, Elizabeth, Catherine, Annie, and Mary. **57**

Elizabeth (Iain, Eoin) married John "Banker" MacNeil, Iona (see 166), lived in Iona and had a family. Catherine married Rory (Rory "Glen Mor") MacNeil, Barra Glen (see 9), lived in Barra Glen, and had a family. Annie married John (Donald, Neil) MacNeil, Gillis Point (see 99), lived in Gillis Point, and had a family. Mary married Donald "Og" Murphy, MacKinnon's Harbour (see 556), lived in MacKinnon's Harbour, and had a family.

Eoin "Mor" (Iain, Eoin) married Catherine (James "Pearson") MacNeil, Iona (see 241). They lived in Jamesville and their family: James, Murdock, Michael, Catherine, Alex, Stephen J., Flora, John J., and Mary Ann. **58**

Alex (Eoin "Mor") died unmarried. Catherine married Colin (Hector "Ban") Campbell, lived in Jamesville, and had a family (see 306). Flora married Michael D. MacNeil, Piper's Cove, lived in Piper's Cove, and had a family. Mary Ann married Alex MacDonald, Soldier's Cove, lived in Soldier's Cove, and had a family, one of whom, Catherine, married Joseph A. (Hector, Neil) MacNeil, Iona (see 91), and had a family in Iona.

James (Eoin "Mor") married Elizabeth (Michael, Murdock) MacNeil, Gillis Point (see 27). They lived in Jamesville and their family: Mary Ann, Mary Lizzie, and John T. **59**

Mary Ann (James) married Archie (Archibald, Donald) MacKenzie, Rear Christmas Island, lived in Christmas Island, and had a family. Mary Lizzie and John T. were unmarried.

Murdock (Eoin "Mor") married Mary (Domhnull, Tormad) MacNeil, Piper's Cove. They lived in Jamesville and their family: John K., Colin, Michael Dan, Jimmie, Hugh D., Dan Rory, Lizzie, Mary C., and Christy. **60**

Colin (Murdock) and Lizzie died young. John K. and Dan Rory were unmarried. Christy married in the United States. Hugh D. married Agnes Morrison, lived in Sydney, and had no family. Jimmy married Ann MacPherson, Big Beach, lived in Big Beach, and had a family. Mary C. married John H. (Malcolm, Seamus "Mor") MacNeil, Jamesville (see 182), lived in Jamesville, and had a family.

Michael Dan (Murdock) married Helen MacNeil, Point Tupper. They lived in Jamesville and their family: Murdock, Colin, Donnie, Diana, Mary Catherine, and Margaret. **61**

Mary Catherine (Michael Dan) married Roddie (Joseph) Murphy, MacKinnon's Harbour (see **559**) and has a family.

Michael (Eoin "Mor") married Catherine (Eachain, Eoin) MacNeil, Iona (see **153**). They lived in Jamesville and their family: Mamie, Florence, Bessie, and Hector B. **62**

> Hector B. died unmarried. Bessie married Dan L. MacNeil, Sydney, lived in Sydney, and had a family. Mamie married a Mr. Parago, lived in Sydney, and had a family. Florence married John Alex MacNeil, Big Beach and had no family.

John J. (Eoin "Mor") married Flora (John, John) MacNeil, Barra Glen (see **21**). They lived in Jamesville and their family: John James, John Angus, and Maggie Catherine. **63**

> John James (John J.) married in the United States and had no family. John Angus married and had a family. Maggie Catherine went to the United States.

Stephen J. (Eoin "Mor") married Mary (Donald "Tailor") MacNeil, Highland Hill (see **186**). They lived in Jamesville and their family: Mary Catherine, Mary Ann, Colin, James R., Sarah, Lizzie, Regis, and a boy who died young. **64**

> Colin (Stephen J.), James R., and Regis were unmarried. Mary Ann married Alex Chisholm, lived in the United States, and had no family. Sarah married J.J. MacKinnon, lived in Sydney, and had no family. Lizzie married in Winnipeg and had a family. Mary Catherine married Neil H. (James) Gillis, MacKinnon's Harbour (see **329**), lived in MacKinnon's Harbour, and had no family.

MACNEIL

Stephen (Iain, Eoin) married Ann Dunn, Benacadie. They lived in Jamesville and their family: Patrick, John, Donald, Mary Ann, Katie, and Stephen S. **65**

Patrick (Stephen) and Mary Ann died unmarried. Katie married Thomas MacNeil, Benacadie and had a family. John married Bessie (James, Donald "Ban") MacDonald, Gillis Point (see **388**), lived in New Waterford, had a large family, and married a second time.,

Donald (Stephen) married Sarah (Malcolm "Big") MacNeil, Rear Iona (see **206**). They lived in Barra Glen and their family: Stephen, Mary Catherine, and Sarah Ann. They also adopted Jim Francis MacNeil and Patrick Ratchford. **66**

Stephen (Donald) was unmarried. Mary Catherine was the second wife of Charles S. MacNeil, Red Point (see **93**), lived in Red Point, and had a son Daniel who married a daughter of Rory H. MacNeil, Benacadie and has a family in Toronto. Sarah Ann married Dan Devoe (see **324**) and had a daughter Magdalen who married Vincent MacDonald and has a family in Sydney.

Stephen S. (Stephen) married Katie (Sandy) MacNeil, Benacadie. They lived in Barra Glen and their family: Patrick, Stephen John, Mary Ann, Mary Catherine, Katie, Alex Rory, Katie Ann, Mary Sarah, and Dolly Ratchford whom they adopted — a sister of Patrick Ratchford, both being grandchildren of John (Stephen) above. **67**

Patrick (Stephen S.) died young. Alex Rory is unmarried. Mary Ann married Michael Campbell, Boisdale and had a family. Mary Catherine married John P. MacKinnon, Shenacadie and had a large family. Katie married John James MacKinnon, Big Beach and had a family. Katie Ann married Neil MacDonald, Sydney. Mary Sarah married Eddie MacNeil, Big Beach and had no family. Dolly Ratchford married Hugh (Joseph H.) MacNeil, Iona (see **151**), lived in Iona, and had a family.

Stephen John (Stephen S.) married first Margaret

MACNEIL

Burke, adopted daughter of Francis F. MacNeil, Barra Glen (see **261**). They lived in Iona and their family: Catherine, Stephen or Buddy, and Marie. In a second marriage Stephen John married Rita MacLean, Big Beach, lived in Sydney, and had a family. **68**

John (Iain, Eoin) married Isabel (Hector, Neil) MacNeil, Gillis Point (see **86**). They lived in Jamesville and their family: Donald, Peter, and James. **69**

James (John) died young. Peter married Catherine Campbell and had no family.

Donald (John) married first Mary (Donald, Rory) Gillis, MacKinnon's Harbour (see **327**). They lived in Jamesville and had twin daughters who died in infancy. In a second marriage he married a woman from Sydney Mines. **70**

Neil (Eoin, Donald John) married Mary (Rory "Red") MacNeil, Iona Rear (see **194**). They lived in Iona and their family: John, Malcolm, Stephen, Michael, Ann, Elizabeth, Catherine, Rory, and Mary. **72**

Elizabeth (Neil, Eoin) married Angus Campbell, Grand Narrows, and had a family. Catherine married Jonathan (Neil, Eoin) MacNeil, Gillis Point (see **116**), lived in Gillis Point, and had a family. Mary married Rory "Plant" MacNeil, Barra Glen (see **5**) and had a family. We have no information on Stephen, Ann, and Rory. For Michael see **513**.

John (Neil, Eoin) married Mary (Roderick, Lachlan) MacLean (see **513**). They lived in Iona and their family: Ann, Neil, Mary Ann, Mary I, Elizabeth, Katie, Rory John, and Katie II. **73**

Ann (John) and Neil were unmarried. Mary Ann married Stephen (Paul) MacLean, Baddeck (see **500**). Mary I married Dan D. (Donald, Eoin) MacNeil, Gillis Point (see **120**), lived in Gillis Point, and had a family. Elizabeth married Marshall Lewis. Katie died young. Mary II married John (Paul) MacLean, Washabuck (see **500**), lived in Baddeck, and had a family.

MACNEIL

Rory John (John) married Mary Sarah (Iain, Seumus) MacNeil, Iona (see **83**). They lived in Iona and their family: Catherine, Rose, John Joseph, Jackie, Clara, Marguerite, and Theresa. **74**

Catherine (Rory John) married Victor Jankowski (see **338**), lived in Iona, and had a family. Rose and John Joseph were unmarried. Clara died in a drowning accident. Jackie married Susan Bourassa, lives in Toronto, and has a family. Marguerite married and has a family in California. Theresa married Fraser Gillis, East Bay and has a family.

Malcolm (Neil, Eoin) married Ann (Neil, Iain) MacNeil, Cooper's Pond. They lived in Iona and their family: Neil F., Michael, Stephen, Catherine, Mary, and Elizabeth. **75**

Neil F. (Malcolm), a town clerk in Glace Bay, married Alice Gouthro, lived in Glace Bay, and had a family. Michael married Elizabeth MacLean and had a family of four boys who died young. We have no information on Catherine, Mary, and Elizabeth.

Stephen (Malcolm) married Ann MacGillivray. They lived in Iona and their family: Neil, Angus, and Alex Rory. **76**

Alex Rory (Stephen), a C.N.R. Station Agent, married Mary Chisholm, Antigonish, lived in West Bay Road, and their family: Stephen, Annie, and Louise. We have no information on Neil (Stephen) and Angus.

James (Eoin, Donald John) married Sarah MacLeod, "Mor Coinneach," in Scotland. They lived in Iona and their family: Jonathan, Rory, Donald, Kenneth, John, Michael, Christy Ann, Ann, and Malcolm. **77**

Michael (James, Eoin) married a Miss Donovan and lived in the mining districts of Cape Breton. Ann married James (James "Pearson") MacNeil, Iona (see **245**), lived in Iona, and had a family. Christy Ann married Hector MacKenzie, Christmas

Island, lived in Christmas Island, and had a family.

Jonathan (James, Eoin), often known as John "Mason" MacNeil, married Margaret (Hector, Ban Sine) Campbell, Gillis Point (see **319**). They lived in Gillis Point and their family: Annie, Flora, Betsy, Mary, Sarah, Dan J., Rod, Jim, John J., and another who died young. **78**

> Annie (Jonathan) married John (Michael, Rory) MacInnis, Iona (see **408**), lived in Iona, and had a family. Flora married John MacKenzie, Washabuck, lived in Washabuck, and had no family. Betsy married Neil P.S. MacLean, Washabuck (see **518**), lived in Washabuck, and had a family. Mary married Angus "Red" MacNeil, Glace Bay and had a family. Dan J. married Mary MacLean, Washabuck, lived in Sydney, and had a family. Sarah married a Mr. Gracie, Glace Bay, and had a family. Rod and John J. died unmarried. Jim married Flora MacGillivray, Antigonish, lived in Sydney, and had a family.

Rory (James, Eoin) married Catherine MacNeil, Middle Cape. They lived in Iona but left for the mining area of Cape Breton. They had a son Neil who married Margaret (Alasdair "Mor") MacNeil, Iona (see **212**) and had no family. **79**

Donald (James, Eoin) married Sarah MacMillan, Hay Cove. They lived in Iona and their family: Neil D., Hector D., Margaret, Mary Ann, Sally, James, Annie, and Sarah Belle. **80**

> Neil D. (Donald) married first Catherine Campbell, Grand Narrows, had no family; and in a second marriage he married Lucy (Neil, Johnnie) MacKinnon, Iona Rear (see **460**) and lived in Sydney. Hector D. married and had a family in Reserve Mines. Mary Ann married Allan (Michael, Neil) MacLean, Washabuck (see **493**) and lived in Washabuck Center. Sally married Dan J. (Hugh, Darby) Campbell, Jamesville (see **302**), lived in Jamesville, but later moved the family to Halifax. Sarah Belle married Neil A. (Malcolm, Johnnie) MacKinnon, Iona Rear (see **464**), lived in Iona, and had a family. Margaret married Rory G. MacNeil, Iona Rear (see **202**) and had a family. James and Annie died unmarried.

Kenneth (James, Eoin) married Mary (Alasdair "Mor") MacNeil

Iona Rear (see **212**). They lived in Iona and their family: James, Michael K., Mary Ann, and Elizabeth. **81**

James (Kenneth) died young. Mary Ann married Alex S. (Alasdair) MacNeil, Gillis Point (see **139**), lived in Iona, and had no family. Elizabeth married Dan H. "Painter" MacNeil, Ottawa Brook (see **220**), lived in Ottawa Brook, and had no family.

Michael K. (Kenneth) married Flora (Paul, Thomas) MacKinnon, Iona Rear (see **458**). They lived in Iona and their family: Mary Ann, James, and Kenneth. **82**

Mary Ann (Michael K.) became a Sister of St. Martha. James did not marry. Kenneth married and has a family in Lower River Inhabitants.

John (James, Eoin) married Margaret (Eoin "Plant") MacNeil, Barra Glen (see **3**). They lived in Iona and their family: Katie Ann, Sarah, Ann, Flora, Mary Sarah, James, John Rory, and Malcolm J. **83**

Ann (John) was the first wife of Stephen U. (Hugh, Hector) MacNeil, Hector's Point (see **146**) and died in childbirth along with her child about a year after her marriage. Katie Ann married Joseph H. (John, Hector) MacNeil, Iona (see **148**), lived in Iona, and had a large family. Sarah, James, John Rory, and Malcolm J. died unmarried. Flora married John T. Leonard and had no family. Mary Sarah married Rory John (John, Neil) MacNeil, Iona (see **74**), lived in Iona, and had a family.

Malcolm (James, Eoin) married Maggie (Neil, Iain) MacNeil, Cooper's Pond. They lived in Iona but later moved to North Sydney with their family: James, Neil, Rory Allan, Colin Stephen, Agnes, Sarah, and Mary Ann. **84**

James (Malcolm), Neil, and Colin Stephen lived away from the parish. Agnes married Michael MacIvor and had a family. Mary Ann married a Mr. Francis and had a family. Sarah died unmarried. Rory Allan, unmarried, lived in Iona on the property of Hector (Eoin, Ruairi) MacNeil. **85**

● ● ●

MACNEIL

Hector and Donald, sons of Neil MacNeil, Barra came to the New World, Hector in 1813 and Donald in 1817. Like so many other Barra men, they belonged to sea-faring people who had little experience with tilling the soil. It was likely Hector's admiration for the fine harbour in Gillis Point that attracted him to settle in that more rugged part of the parish. Donald landed in Shenacadie and immediately he prepared "to grant land" there. As it was then too late in the season to work the land, he went to pass the winter with his brother Hector in Gillis Point East. Record has it that Hector had "to ration the potatoes" that winter. During that winter, Donald was having second thoughts about settling in Shenacadie, and his final decision was "to grant land" near his brother's property in Gillis Point and to surrender his rights over the property in Shenacadie to his cousin, Charles MacNeil. An incident relative to Donald's ineptitude at handling the plough has come down to us. One day, in utter disgust, he complained to his wife: "I give up! That implement manages to go everywhere but where it should." Wishing to be helpful and remembering his reputation as an oarsman, his good wife said to him: "I am sure that you would have much better success if only you imagined that it was a boat you were steering and not a plough." Donald took her advice seriously and — explain it as you will — from that day on, although he was then sixty, Donald successfully mastered the art of ploughing. And fortunately so, for there lay before him many more years at "following the plough."

Hector (Neil) married in Scotland Margaret MacNeil and they had a son Neil. In a second marriage he married Mary (Seamas MacEachain) MacNeil, Grand Narrows and their family: Sarah, Isabella, and James. **86**

· Sarah (Hector, Neil) married Donald "Mor" (Ruairi "Mor") MacNeil, Iona (see **41**), lived in Iona, and moved to Red Point, Isabella married John (John, Eoin) MacNeil, Jamesville (see **69**), lived in Jamesville, and had a family.

Neil (Hector, Neil) married Christy (Murdock, Donald "Og") MacNeil, Gillis Point (see **24a**). They lived in Gillis Point and their family: Murdock, John, Donald, Peter, Hector, Margaret, Sarah I, Catherine, Mary, Elizabeth, Sarah II, and another who died young. **87**

John (Neil, when still a young man, was drowned in the constructing of the St. Peter's Canal. Donald married Annie (Donald) Murphy, MacKinnon's Harbour (see **556**), lived in the United States, and had a family, one of whom, Christena, became a Sister of Notre Dame. Catherine and Sarah I died unmarried. Margaret married John (Malcolm, Eoin) MacNeil, MacNeil's Vale (see **128**), lived in MacNeil's Vale, and had a family. Mary married Michael "Dubh" MacKinnon, Lower Washabuck, but died soon after her marriage (see **485**). Elizabeth married John (Michael, Neil) MacLean, Washabuck Center (see **490**), lived in Washabuck Centre, and had a family. Sarah II married George Kent, Boston.

Murdock (Neil) married Mary (Michael, Neil) MacLean, Washabuck Center (see **489**). They lived in Gillis Point East — to the North of the Harbour — and their family: John, Annie and Betsy. **88**

John (Murdock) married Mary MacDougall and had no family. Annie married Charles King, Little Bras d'Or and had an adopted family. Betsy married Albert King and had a daughter Mary.

Peter (Neil) married Mary (Rory "Geal") MacNeil, Washabuck (see **266**). They lived in Gillis Point East and their family: Donald, Michael Joseph, John, Roddie Neil, Katie, Christy, and Mary Ann. After the father's death, the family moved to the United States. **89**

Donald (Peter) married in the United States and had no family. Michael Joseph married and had two sons. John graduates from Saint Francis Xavier University and was an architect by profession. Roddie Neil also attended Saint Francis Xavier University, but died before graduation. Katie and Christy became Sisters of Notre Dame. Mary Ann died in the United States.

Hector (Neil) married Mary (Allan, Michael) MacDonald, St. Columba (see **361**). They lived in Gillis Point East and their family: John Neil, Joseph A., Christena, and Sadie Maria. They also adopted Mary Sarah or "Chippy" Gillis

MACNEIL

(see **333**). **90**

John Neil (Hector) died unmarried. Christena became a Sister of Notre Dame. Sadie Maria married George (Stephen "Banker") MacNeil, Iona (see **168**), lived in Ottawa Brook, and had a family.

Joseph A. (Hector) married Catherine (Alex) Mac-Donald, Soldier's Cove (see **58**). They lived in Iona and their family: John Augustine and Marguerite, both of whom married away from the parish. **91**

James (Hector, Neil) married Ann (Charles, Domhnull "Ban") MacKinnon, MacKinnon's Harbour (see **474**). They lived in Gillis Point East and their family: Charles S., Ann, Mary I, Mary II, Betsy, Sarah, Christy, and Katie. The family later moved to Red Point. **92**

Ann (James) married a Mr. MacDonald, River Deny's, lived in Ottawa Brook, and had a son, commonly known as "James Section-man" (see **389**). Mary I married a Mr. Freelhan. Mary II married Michael (Alasdair "Mor") MacNeil, Iona Rear (see **213**), lived in Barra Glen, and had a family. Betsy and Sarah were unmarried. Christy married John Redquest, Red Point (see **571**), lived in Red Point, and had a family. Katie married Rory MacNeil, Long Island.

Charles S. (James) married first Mary Sarah (Colin, Hector "Ban") Campbell, Jamesville (see **306**). They lived in Red Point and their family: Jim Colin, Jim Charles, John Alex, Bennie and Francis (twins), Mary Elizabeth, Katie Ann, Sarah Elizabeth, and Annie Bell. In a second marriage he married Mary Catherine (Donald S.) MacNeil, Jamesville (see **66**), and had a son Daniel. Charles also adopted James "Section-Man" MacDonald and Michael MacDon-nell. **93**

Jim Colin (Charles S.), Bennie and Francis, Sarah Elizabeth, and Annie Bell live in Toronto. Jim Charles died unmarried. Mary Elizabeth married a Mr. Hall, Sydney Mines. Daniel married and has a family in Toronto. Katie Ann is unmarried.

MACNEIL

John Alex (Charles S.) married Murdena Moody, Orangedale. They lived in Red Point and their family: Shirley, Betty, Ivadell, Anson, James and Zelda. **94**

Donald (Neil) married Catherine (Philip) MacKinnon in Barra and their family: Philip, John, Annie, Christy, Mary, Sarah, Katie, and Neil. **95**

Annie (Donald, Neil) married John (Iain, Ruairi) MacNeil, Iona West (see **141a**), lived in Iona and had a family. Christy married Alexander (Alasdair "Mor") MacNeil, Iona Rear (see **212**), lived in Iona Rear, and had a family. Mary, Sarah, and Katie died unmarried.

Philip (Donald, Neil) married Ann (Neil ic Lachlain) MacLean, Washabuck (see **488**). They lived in Gillis Point and their family: Mary, Sarah, Ann "Mhor," Katie, Ann "Beag," John F., Neil, Dan F., Hector, and Elizabeth whom they adopted. **96**

Mary (Philip) married Hector (Donald) Campbell, MacNeil's Vale (see **305**), lived in MacNeil's Vale, and had a family. Sarah married Rory P. (Jonathan, Rory) MacNeil, Barra Glen (see **5**), lived in Barra Glen, and had a family. Ann "Mhor" married first Hector "Soldier" MacDonald, Ottawa Brook (see **385**), lived in Ottawa Brook, and had a family; and in a second marriage she married Ben Warren from Newfoundland. Katie married Neil (Johnnie) MacKinnon, Iona Rear (see **460**), lived in Iona Rear, and had no family. Ann "Beag" and John F. died unmarried. Hector married Ann (John G.) MacKinnon, MacKinnon's Harbour (see **466**), lived in Boston, and had a family.

Dan F. (Philip) married Margaret (Murdock) MacNeil, MacNeil's Vale (see **121**). They lived in Gillis Point and had no family. **97**

Neil (Philip) married first Mary (Iain, Charles) MacKinnon, MacKinnon's Harbour (see **475**). They lived in Barra Glen and their family: Peter Charles and Lizzie Ann. In a second marriage he married Ann (Rory "Glen Mor") MacNeil, Barra Glen (see **9**) and had no family. And in a third marriage he married a Mrs. MacNeil, Big Beach and had no family. **98**

Peter Charles (Neil) married and had a family in Little Bras d'Or. Lizzie Ann married Dr. Alex MacNeil, Mabou, lived in Mabou, and had a family.

John (Donald, Neil) married Ann (Iain, Eoin) MacNeil, Jamesville (see **57**). They lived in Gillis Point and their family: Michael, Donald, Hector, Ann "Mhor," Ann "Beag," Catherine, Elizabeth, Margaret, and Sarah. **99**

Ann "Mhor" (John) married Archie (Flora) Campbell, Iona (see **316**), lived in Iona, and had a family. Ann "Beag" married James G. (Neil, Alasdair) MacNeil, MacNeil's Vale (see **134**), lived in MacNeil's Vale, and had a family. Catherine married John (Philip) MacDonald, Ottawa Brook (see **343**), lived in Ottawa Brook, and had a family. Elizabeth died unmarried. Margaret married Dan (Michael "Lewis") MacDonald, Ottawa Brook (see **355**), lived in Ottawa Brook, and had a family. Sarah married Captain Angus (Malcolm "Mor") MacNeil, Iona Rear (see **211**), lived in Iona Rear, and had a large family.

Michael (John) married Bessie (Domhnull, Domhnull Eoin) MacNeil, Gillis Point (see **118**). They lived in Gillis Point and their family: John Alex, John Allan, Joe, Lizzie Ann, Katie Maria, and Frank. **100**

John Alex (Michael), John Allan, Joe, and Katie Maria were unmarried. Lizzie Ann married Murdock MacLean and had no family.

Frank (Michael married Katie Ann (Roderick, Neil) MacNeil, Gillis Point (see **107**). They lived in Gillis Point and their family: Joe, Roderick, Michael, Carleton, and Sylvia. **101**

Donald (John) married Mary Ann (Hugh, Malcolm) Campbell, Barra Glen (see **282**). They lived in Gillis Point and had a son John Hugh, who was killed in a mining accident in Glace Bay at the age of twenty. **102**

Hector (John) married Bessie (Paul) MacNeil, Iona Rear (see **216**). They lived in Iona Rear and their family: John, Mary, Bessie Ann, and Annie. **103**

MACNEIL

John (Hector), Bessie Ann, and Annie died unmarried. Mary married Dan G. (James, Neil Alasdair) MacNeil, MacNeil's Vale (see **134**), lived in Gillis Point, and had no family.

Neil (Donald, Neil) married first Sarah (Rory "Red") MacNeil, Iona Rear (see **194**). They lived in Gillis Point and their family: Donald, Roderick, Michael, and Mary. In a second marriage he married Sarah (Domhnull, Eachain) MacKenzie, Christmas Island and their family: Hector P., Alex P., Peter S., Dan A., Philip B., and Paul. **104**

Michael (Neil) died young. Paul married Elizabeth Fluke from P.E.I., lived in the United States, and had no family. We have no information on Mary.

Dan A. (Neil) married Ann (Iain, Alasdair) MacNeil, Gillis Point (see **130**). They lived in Gillis Point and had no family. **105**

Donald (Neil) married Christy (Michael "Saor") MacInnis, Iona (see **406**). They lived in Iona, West of John (Michael) MacInnis, and their family: Mary, Sarah I, Mary Ann, Lizzie, Annie, Sarah II, Mick John, and Neil. **106**

Mary (Donald) married John A. MacDougall, Glace Bay and had a child who died young. Sarah I, Annie, Sarah II, Mick John, and Neil were unmarried. Mary Ann married Rod MacIsaac and had a family in Glace Bay. Lizzie married Jack MacInnis and had a family in Sydney.

Roderick (Neil) married first Elizabeth (Alasdair, Michael) MacDonald, St. Columba (see **357**). They lived in St. Columba and their family: Sally, Katie, Mary, Katie Ann I. In a second marriage he married Mary (Murdock, Donald Eoin) MacNeil, MacNeil's Vale (see **121**). They lived in Gillis Point and their family: Sarah Ann, Neil Archie, Allan Austin, John Murdock, Katie Ann II, and Bessie. **107**

Sally (Roderick) married Cornelius Auburn, Boston[*] and had a family. Katie disappeared while working in Boston. Mary was unmarried in the United States. Katie Ann I died young. Sarah Ann married W.M.

Moley in the United States and had a family. Neil Archie died unmarried. Katie Ann II married Frank (Michael, John Donald) MacNeil, Gillis Point (see **101**), lived in Gillis Point, and had a family. Bessie married Angus (Norman D.) MacNeil, Benacadie and had a family.

Allan Austin (Roderick) married Sadie (Francis, Iain Ruairi) MacNeil, Iona (see **40**). They lived in Gillis Point and their family: Frances, Cecilia, Lucille, Mary Crescentia, Elizabeth Madeline, Murdock Allan, Joseph Augustine, and John Stanislaus. **108**

Frances (Allan Austin) married Malcolm MacLennan, Benacadie, lives in Sydney, and has a family. Cecilia, Mary Crescentia, Elizabeth Madeline, Murdock Allan, and Joseph Augustine married in the United States. Lucille married John MacKenzie, Benacadie, lives in Gillis Point (see **446**), and has a family. John Stanislaus married Catherine (Anthony, Dan S.) MacNeil, (see **124**) and has a family in Western Canada.

John Murdock (Roderick) married Tena (Simon) Devoe (see **323**). They live in Gillis Point and their family: Mary Columba, Cecil, Rhodena, Evelyn, Lexena, Agnes, Marie, and Simon who died in infancy. **109**

Hector P. (Neil) married Ann (Domhnull, Eoin) MacNeil, MacNeil's Vale (see **118**). They live in Gillis Point and their family: John Michael, Neil, Dan Allan, and John D. The family later moved to Baddeck. **110**

John Michael (Hector P.), a photographer for Dr. Alexander Bell in Beinn Breagh, Baddeck died unmarried. Neil, manager-clerk for John E. Campbell, Baddeck and later manager of Iona Co-operative, was unmarried. Dan Allan married Mary MacKinnon, Barrachois, lived in the United States, and had a family. John D., a customs officer in Baddeck, married Freda Casey, Glace Bay and had a son Neil.

MACNEIL

Alex P. (Neil) married Catherine (Murdock) MacNeil, MacNeil's Vale (see **121**). They lived in Gillis Point and their family: Sarah, Neil Ambrose, Michael Roderick, Murdock, Katie Ann, Mary T., Ambrose, Allan Alex, and John Alex. **111**

Neil Ambrose (Alex P.), Michael Roderick, and Katie Ann died young. Mary T. died unmarried in the United States. Murdock, a veteran of both World Wars, died unmarried. Sarah married Stephen U. (Hugh, Hector) MacNeil, Iona (see **146**) and had a large family in Sydney. John Alex died in World War II. Ambrose married Ann MacDougall, Creignish, lives in Troy, and has a family.

Allan Alex (Alex P.) married Tena (Devoe) MacNeil (see **323**). They lived in Gillis Point and had a son Dennis who was drowned. **112**

Peter S. (Neil) married Bessie (Rory, Eachain) MacNeil, Gillis Point (see **143**). They lived in Gillis Point and their family: Neil Joseph, Rory Hector, John Michael, Mary Ann, Margaret, Allan, Lawrence and Catherine. **113**

John Michael (Peter S.) and Allan, both war veterans, died unmarried. Lawrence lives in the United States. Neil Joseph married Margaret (Michael D.) MacNeil, Iona (see **51**), lived in New Waterford, and had a family. Rory Hector married and had a family in Western Canada. Mary Ann married a Mr. Peterson and had a family in the United States. Margaret married David MacNeil from P.E.I. and lived in Regina. Catherine married and had a family in the United States.

Philip B. (Neil) married Elizabeth (Murdock, Donald) MacNeil, MacNeil's Vale (see **121**). They lived in Baddeck and their family: Louise, Cecilia, Ambrose, Joe, Neil Ambrose, Murdock, Michael Allan, and Ann. **114**

Louise (Philip B.) was unmarried. Neil Ambrose, Murdock, and Michael Allan died young. Ann was a nurse in the United States. Ambrose was killed in the World War. Cecilia married a Mr. Flag and had a

MACNEIL

family. Joe married Mary (Hector) MacDonald, Jamesville West (see **370**) who was brought up by Donald (Isabella) MacNeil, Jamesville (see **70**).

●　　　●　　　●

Neil, Murdock, Donald, Malcolm, James, and Rory MacNeil — six brothers — came to the New World together. Their parents remained in Barra, Scotland. Their father was Eoin MacNeil, and their mother was Christy, a sister of Hugh Gillis, whose widow (Ann MacIntyre Gillis) settled with her family in Jamesville West (see **325**). Neil settled in Gillis Point. Murdock settled in P.E.I. Donald and Malcolm settled in MacNeil's Vale. James and Rory settled in Big Pond. Our interest concerns, therefore, Neil, Donald, and Malcolm.

Neil (Eoin) married Mary MacLean in Scotland. They lived in Gillis Point and their family: Eoin, John, Catherine, Mary, Christy, Ann, and Maggie. **115**

John (Neil, Eoin), Christy, and Maggie were unmarried. Catherine married Jonathan (Rory, Donald "Og") MacNeil, Barra Glen (see **3**), lived in Barra Glen, and had a family. Mary married Stephen (Rory, Donald "Og") MacNeil, Barra Glen (see **11**), lived in Barra Glen, and had a family. Ann married Paul (Rory "Red") MacNeil, Iona Rear (see **216**), lived in Iona Rear, and had a family.

Eoin (Neil, Eoin) married Catherine (Neil, Eoin) MacNeil, Iona (see **72**). They lived in Gillis Point and their family: Neil J., Katie, Catherine, Annie, Mary and Sarah. **116**

Neil J. (Eoin) and Katie died unmarried. Sarah married Rod "Beag" (Neil) Campbell, Jamesville West (see **308**), lived in Highland Hill, and had a daughter who died young. Catherine, Annie and Mary were employed for several years in the United States, and in their latter years they built a home in Iona which eventually became St. Columba Convent.

MACNEIL

Donald (Eoin) married Annie Campbell in Scotland. She was the daughter of Iain MacEachain, whose brother Calum settled in Barra Glen. Donald and Annie lived in MacNeil's Vale and their family: Donald, Murdock, Hector, Margaret, Catherine, and Eliza. **117**

Margaret (Donald, Eoin) Married Paul (Murdock, Donald "Og") MacNeil (see **24a**), lived in Gillis Point, and later moved the family to the United States. We have no information on Catherine and Eliza.

Donald (Donald, Eoin) married Elizabeth (Alasdair "Mor") MacNeil, Gillis Point (see **129**). They lived in MacNeil's Vale and their family: John, Donald D., Margaret, Betsy, Michael, Annie and Katie. **118**

> John (Donald) died young. Margared died unmarried. Betsy married Michael (Iain, Domhnull) MacNeil, Gillis Point (see **100**), lived in Gillis Point, and had a family. Annie married Hector P. (Neil) MacNeil, Gillis Point (see **110**) and had a family. We have no information on Katie.

> Michael (Donald) married Flora (Rory, Hector) MacNeil, Gillis Point East (see **143**). They went to the United States and had a family. **119**

> Donald D. (Donald) married Mary (Eoin, Neil) MacNeil, Iona (see **73**). They lived in Gillis Point and their family: Donald, John Michael, Mary, and a son who died young. **120**

>> Donald (Donald D.) is unmarried. John Michael became a priest in the Oblates of Mary Immaculate. Mary married John (Neil S.) MacNeil, Gillis Point (see **19**), lived in Gillis Point and had a family.

Murdock (Donald, Eoin) married Sarah (Alasdair "Mor") MacNeil, Gillis Point (see **129**). They lived in MacNeil's Vale and their family: Mary I, Katie, Peggy, Dan S., Eliza, Mary II, and Alex. **121**

> Mary I (Murdock) married first Jonathan (Eoin, Thomas)

MACNEIL

MacKinnon, Iona Rear (see **457**), had no family; and in a second marriage she married Rory (Neil, Donald) MacNeil, Gillis Point (see **107**), lived in Gillis Point, and had a family. Katie married Alex P. (Neil, Donald) MacNeil, Gillis Point (see **111**). Peggy married Donald (Philip) MacNeil, Gillis Point (see **97**) and had no family. Eliza married Philip MacNeil, Baddeck. Mary II married Francis (Hector) MacNeil, Iona (see **49**), lived in Iona, had a family, and later moved to New Waterford. Alex, a C.N.R. Conductor, married Lexie MacDonald, lived in Sydney, and their family: Dan, Viola, and Nina.

Dan S. (Murdock) married Katie (Allan, Michael "Mor") MacDonald, St. Columba (see **361**). They lived in Gillis Point and their family: Sadie, Allan, John Hector, Leo, Francis X., Eliza, Margaret, Mary and Anthony. **122**

> Allan (Dan S.) died unmarried. Leo was killed in World War I. Sadie married Jerry Tracey, lived in Iona, and later moved the family to Saint John. Eliza married in the United States. Margaret married Francis B. (Rory R.) MacDonald, Washabuck (see **375**), lived in Gillis Point, and had a family. Mary married Stephen, adopted son of Jim "Fisherman" MacNeil, Iona (see **244**), lived in Iona and had a family.

> John Hector (Dan S.) married Mary Frances (Francis, Iain Ruairi) MacNeil, Iona (see **40**). They lived in Dartmouth and their family: Sadie and Shirley. **123**

> Anthony (Dan S.) married Mary Agnes, adopted daughter of Allan D. MacKinnon, MacKinnon's Harbour (see **470**). They lived in Iona and their family: Leo, Arnold, Isabel, Catherine, Agnes, Allan, Jeanette, Francesca, Lawrence, and Eleanor. **124**

> Francis X. (Dan S.) married Catherine, adopted daughter of Francis X.S. MacNeil, Iona (see **157**). They lived in Iona and their family: Francis X. Jr., Sharon, Louise, Marguerite, and Paul and Pius (twins). **125**

Hector (Donald, Eoin) married Catherine (Allan, Domhnull "Ban") MacKinnon, MacKinnon's Harbour (see **465**). They lived in MacNeil's Vale and their family: Peggy "Mor," John, Ann, Margaret, Mary, Christy, Michael, and Rod.   **126**

> Christy (Hector) was unmarried. Michael and Rod died in the United States. Peggy "Mor" married Michael "Dubh" (Donald) MacKinnon, Washabuck (see **485**). Ann married John (Angus, Eoin) MacNeil, Highland Hill (see **187**), lived in Highland Hill, and had a family. Margaret married John (Barra) MacNeil, Ottawa Brook (see **32**), lived in Ottawa Brook, and had a family. Mary married Rory "Gosgie" MacNeil, Iona Rear (see **204**), lived in Iona Rear, and had a family.

John (Hector) married Maggie "Tailor" MacNeil, Highland Hill (see **186**). They lived in MacNeil's Vale and their family: Lizzie Ann, Hector, Dan Joe, Mary, Margaret, Michael Stephen, Annie May, and Sadie.   **127**

> Michael Stephen (John) and Annie May are unmarried. Dan Joe, Mary, Margaret, and Sadie are married in the United States. Hector is married in Antigonish. Lizzie Ann married a Mr. MacEachern, Boularderie, lived in New Waterford, and had a family.

Malcolm (Eoin) lived in MacNeil's Vale, East of where his brother Donald lived. His family was: John, Margaret, Joanna, and Mary.   **128**

John (Malcolm, Eoin) married Margaret (Neil, Hector) MacNeil, Gillis Point East (see **87**) and had a family. Joanna married George MacEachern, Glace Bay, and both are buried in Iona. Mary was unmarried. Margaret married John (Murdock, Donald "Og"), lived in Gillis Point, and had a family (see **25**).

● ● ●

Alasdair "Mor" MacNeil made the voyage from Barra on the Ship "Harmony", along with the ailing Murdock (Donald "Og")

MacNeil in 1821 or 1822. It was to him that Murdock entrusted the care of his wife and family, a trust that Alasdair "Mor" honoured most nobly. Alasdair "Mor" married Catherine MacNeil, whose relatives are in Boisdale. They lived in Gillis Point and their family: John, Neil, Allan, Alexander Jr., Michael, Elizabeth, Sarah, Margaret, and Rachel. **129**

Rachel (Alasdair "Mor") married Roderick Johnstone, Beaver Cove, lived in Beaver Cove, and had a family. Margaret married Michael (Murdock, Donald "Og") MacNeil and had a family (see 27). Sarah married Murdock (Donald, Eoin) MacNeil, Gillis Point and had a family (see 121). Elizabeth married Donald (Donald, Eoin) MacNeil, Gillis Point and had a family (see 118).

John (Alasdair "Mor") married Mary (Ruairi ic Lachlain) MacLean, Washabuck (see 513). They lived in Gillis Point and their family: Katie, James C., Angus J., Alex, Rory, Mary, Ann, and a son who died in infancy. **130**

Angus J. (John, Alasdair "Mor") died unmarried. Katie married James (Neil) Campbell, Jamesville West (see 313), lived in Jamesville West, and had a family. Alex married Catherine MacKinnon, Framboise, lived in Sydney, and his family: Mary Florence and an adopted daughter Catherine. Ann married Donald (Neil) MacNeil, Gillis Point (see 105), lived in Gillis Point, and had no family. Mary married Hector (Allan, Hugh) Campbell, Gillis Point East (see 291), lived in Gillis Point East, and had a family.

James C. (John, Alasdair "Mor") married Jane (James, Darby) Campbell, Jamesville (see 303). They lived in Gillis Point and their family: John Angus and Neil James. **131**

John Angus (James C.) married Annette Borden, Donkin and had a family in Johnstown.

Neil James (James C.) married first Katie MacNeil, Benacadie. They lived in Gillis Point and their family:

MACNEIL

Francis, Mary, Michael, and Georgina. In a second marriage he married Margaret Beaton, Scotch Lake and has no family. **132**

Neil (Alasdair "Mor") married Annie MacNeil, Gillis Point. They lived in MacNeil's Vale and their family: James, Sandy "Mor," Katie, Annie, and another daughter. **133**

Sandy "Mor" (Neil, Alasdair "Mor") and Annie died unmarried. Katie married Neil MacIsaac in the Cape Breton mining area. The other daughter married Joseph (Eoin "Mor") MacNeil, Christmas Island.

James (Neil, Alasdair "Mor") married Annie "Beag" (Iain, Domhnull) MacNeil, Gillis Point (see **99**). They lived in MacNeil's Vale and their family: John Neil, John Allan, Dan G., and Margaret Ann. **134**

John Neil (James), a war veteran, married Genevieve (Ronald, Francis) MacNeil, Iona (see **158**) and had no family. Margaret Ann died unmarried.

Allan (Alasdair "Mor") married Mary MacNeil, Gillis Point. They lived in Gillis Point and their family: Neil A., Michael, James A., Joe Ambrose, John Michael, and Sarah. **135**

Neil A. (Allan, Alasdair "Mor") and Michael died unmarried. John Michael is married in South Africa. Joe Ambrose married Molly Moran and their family: Mary, Allan and John Ambrose. Sarah married Donald (Angus) Campbell, Gillis Point East (see **297**), and had a large family, and moved to the United States.

James A. (Allan, Alasdair "Mor") married Mary Elizabeth (Neil, Stephen) MacNeil, Gillis Point (see **17**). They lived in Gillis Point and their family: Michael Allan, Mary Ann, Roderick, Annie, Donald, and Columba. **136**

Michael Allan (James A.) married Beatrice Sampson,

Louisdale, lives in Louisdale, and has a family. Mary Ann married Michael Dan ("Red" Rory) MacLean, Washabuck (see **515**), lived in Washabuck, had a family, and later moved to Baddeck. Annie married Angus (Angus, Ronald) MacDonald, Washabuck (see **378**), lived in Washabuck, and had a family.

Roderick (James A.) married Betsy (James) MacKenzie, Washabuck (see **441**). They live in Gillis Point and have a family. **137**

Alexander Jr. (Alasdair "Mor") married Sarah MacKenzie and their family: Alex "Mor," James S., Neil, Katie Ann, Anastasia, Mary Ann, and Catherine. **138**

Neil (Alexander Jr., Alasdair "Mor") died young. Catherine and Anastasia died unmarried. Mary Ann married Malcolm MacNeil, lived in Gillis Point, and later their family — Michael and Johnnie — was adopted by Alexander Jr. Katie Ann married Anthony MacNeil, Glace Bay and had a family.

Alex "Mor" (Alexander Jr., Alasdair "Mor") married Mary Ann (Kenneth, James) MacNeil, Gillis Point (see **81**). They lived in Gillis Point, had no family, and moved to Iona. **139**

James S. (Alexander Jr., Alasdair "Mor") married Mary Jane (Hugh "Gosgie") MacNeil, Gillis Point (see **205**). They lived in Gillis Point and their family: Katie May, Walter, Alexander, Michael, Elizabeth, Bridgit, and Hugh Francis who died young. The family moved to Sydney. **140**

MACNEIL

Michael (Alasdair "Mor") married Ann MacLean, Washabuck. They lived in Gillis Point and their family: Alexander, Neil, Michael, Stephen B., John Joseph, Peter Francis, Mary, and Katie. The family grew up away from the parish.   **141**

• • •

Rory (Rory) MacNeil came from Barra and settled in Hector's Point, Iona. He had married a sister of Donald "Ban" MacNeil (see **164**) and their family: Hector "Mor," Eoin, Neil, John, Ann, and another daughter.   **141a**

Ann (Rory, Rory) married Neil "Gosgie" MacNeil, Iona Rear (see **203**) and had a family. The other daughter married a Mr. MacDonald, Mabou Harbour. We have no information on Neil. John married Annie (Donald, Neil) MacNeil, lived in Iona West, and had a family (see **95**).

Hector "Mor" (Rory, Rory) married Ann (Rory "Red") MacNeil, Iona Rear (see **194**). They lived in Hector's Point and their family: Rory H., Hugh, John, and Catherine.   **142**

Catherine (Hector "Mor," Rory Rory) married Allan (Hugh "Red") Campbell, Gillis Point East (see **290**), lived in Gillis Point East, and had a family.

Rory H. (Hector "Mor," Rory Rory) married Sarah (Hugh "Red") Campbell, Gillis Point East (see **289**). They lived in Gillis Point East and their family: Paul, Dan, John, Hector, Flora, Betsy, Maggie Ann, Mary Catherine, and Annie.   **143**

MACNEIL

Hector (Rory H.) was unmarried in the United States. Mary Catherine died young. Dan married Elizabeth MacDonald and had no family. John married Agnes MacNeil in Boston and their family: Florence, Jean, Ethel, and Mary Margaret. Flora married Michael D. (Donald, Donald) MacNeil, Gillis Point (see **119**), lived in the United States, and had a family. Betsy married Peter S. (Neil, Donald) MacNeil, Gillis Point (see **113**), lived in Gillis Point, and later moved to the United States. Maggie Ann married Stephen "Tailor" MacNeil, Christmas Island. Annie married Michael P. MacKinnon, Antigonish, lived in Antigonish and had a family.

Paul (Rory H.) married Nora MacLean, Bay St. Lawrence. They lived in Gillis Point East and their family: Hughie, Mary, Sarah Ann, Catherine, Flora, and a son who died young. **144**

Hughie (Paul) was killed in an explosion in the United States, while still a young man. Mary married John Burke and had a family in the United States. Sarah Ann and Catherine were unmarried in the United States. Flora married Pepin Arsenault, lived in Baddeck, and had no family.

Hugh (Hector "Mor," Rory Rory) married Flora (John "Ban") Gillis, Jamesville West (see **334**). They lived in Iona and their family: Annie I, Annie II, John, and Stephen Urban. **145**

Annie I (Hugh) died young. Annie II married Angus (Domhnull "Beag") MacKenzie, Sydney and had a family. John married Mary MacGillivray and had no family.

Stephen Urban (Hugh) married first Annie (John, James) MacNeil, Iona (see **83**). She died in childbirth a year after her marriage, and in a second marriage he married Sarah (Alasdair, Neil) MacNeil, Gillis Point (see **111**) and their family: Annie Florence, Hughena, Catherine, Joanna, Pauline, Monica, Lexis, and Murdock Alexander. The family lived in Iona but later moved to Sydney. **146**

John (Hector "Mor," Rory Rory) married Mary MacLean, Bay St. Lawrence. They lived in Iona and their family (Joseph H., J.T.,

Hector, and others who died young. **147**

J.T. (John) married Margaret Verchers, Arichat, lived in Sydney, and their family: John Hector, and seven daughters, one of whom married John Rory (Michael) Nash, St. Columba (see **566**). We have no information on Hector (John).

Joseph H. (John) married Katie Anne (John, James) MacNeil, Iona (see **83**). They lived in Iona and their family: Maria, Annie May, Mary Elizabeth, Margaret, Florence, Mary Ann, Mary Catherine, Hector, Hugh, John Joseph, Neil, Michael, and Sarah. **148**

Maria (Joseph H.) married John MacKinnon, Beaver Cove and had a family. Florence, Sarah, Mary Ann, and Mary Catherine married in Sydney and have families. Annie May, Mary Elizabeth, and Margaret became Sisters of Notre Dame. Michael, unmarried, died in the Army. Neil was unmarried.

John Joseph (Joseph H.) married Mary Brown, Bay St. Lawrence. They lived in Iona and had no family. **149**

Hector (Joseph H.) married Annie (James M. "Red") MacNeil, Jamesville (see **181**). They lived in Iona and had a family. **150**

Hugh (Joseph H.) married Dolly Ratchford, adopted daughter of Stephen S. MacNeil, Jamesville (see **67**). They lived in Iona and had two daughters. **151**

Eoin (Rory, Rory) married Annie MacNeil. They lived in Iona and their family: Hector, Malcolm, Rory, John, Catherine, Peggy, Elizabeth, Sarah and Katie. **152**

Rory (Eoin, Rory Rory) married and had a family in Boston. Catherine, Peggy, and Elizabeth who was drowned, died unmarried. Sarah married Allan (Michael "Mor") MacDonald, St. Columba (see **361**), lived in St. Columba, and had a family.

MACNEIL

Katie married Donald "Beag" Morrison, Gillis Point (see **552**), lived in Gillis Point, and had a family. Mary married Alexander (Iain) MacNeil, Iona Rear (see **201**), lived in Iona Rear, and had a family.

Hector (Eoin, Rory Rory) married Flora (Niall, Iain) MacNeil. Cooper's Pond. They lived in Iona and their family: Katie, Mary Elizabeth, Maggie, Sarah, and Flora. **153**

> Katie (Hector) married Michael (Eoin "Mor") MacNeil, Jamesville (see **62**), lived in Jamesville, and had a family. Mary married D.C. (Murdock, Donald Barra) MacNeil, Christmas Island. Elizabeth married Dan Martin and had a son Hector. Sarah married Roderick MacDonald, Glace Bay and had no family. Maggie married James C. (Donald "Beag") MacNeil, Iona (see **50**), lived in Sydney, and had a family. Flora was unmarried.

Malcolm (Eoin, Rory Rory) married Bessie (Michael "Saor") MacInnis, Iona (see **406**). They lived in Iona and their family: Rory, Peter, John V., Michael, Michael John, Christy, Mary Ann, and Michael "Beag." **154**

> John F. (Malcolm) and Mary Ann died unmarried. Michael, Michael "Beag," and Michael John died young. Christy married Dan H. MacNeil, Grand Narrows and had a family in Glace Bay. Peter married Bessie MacNeil, Grand Narrows, and had a family in Sydney.

> Rory (Malcolm) married Margaret (Jim "Banker") MacNeil, Iona (see **169**). They lived in Iona and had a family. **155**

John (Eoin, Rory Rory), known as "Yankee," married a daughter of Neil (Iain) MacNeil, Cooper's Pond. They lived in Iona and their family: Francis X.S., Roderick, John P., Mary Ann, Katie, Maggie, and Jane. Two others, Francis and John, died in infancy. **156**

> Mary Ann, (John) and Katie died young. Maggie was unmarried. Jane married a Mr. Moriarty and had a family.

> Francis X.S. (John) married Christy MacDougall, Christmas Island. They lived in Iona and their family: Ronald, Roddie, John S., John Paul, Angus, Mary Louise, Mary,

Gertrude, and Catherine. They also adopted Edmund and Genevieve MacNeil (see **158**), Catherine MacNeil, and Gregory MacNeil. **157**

John S. (Francis X.S.) and Mary Louise died unmarried. Catherine died young. Angus married a woman from Mira and had no family. Mary married Jack Ryan, a C.N.R. Conductor, lived in Point Tupper, and had a family. Gertrude married Angus MacDonald, Ballantyne's Cove and died within a week of her marriage. Catherine, the adopted daughter, married Francis X. (Dan S.) MacNeil, Iona (see **125**), lived in Iona and had a family.

Ronald (Francis X.S.) married Jessie MacLean, Baddeck. They lived in Sydney and their family: Edmund and Genevieve. Both children were brought up by the father's father in Iona. **158**

Genevieve (Ronald) married first John Neil (James, Neil Alasdair) MacNeil, Gillis Point (see **134**); in a second marriage she married in Western Canada; she had no family from either marriage.

Edmund (Ronald) married Agnes (Hector) MacDonald, Gillis Point (see **386**). They lived in Iona and had a family. **159**

Roddie (Francis X.S.) married Mary (Rory, Stephen) MacNeil, Barra Glen (see **15**). They lived in Iona and their family: Margaret Teresa, and George MacIntosh. **160**

Margaret Teresa (Roddie) married Peter (Joseph F.) Murphy, MacKinnon's Harbour (see **560**), lived in Iona and had a family. George MacIntosh married and had a family in Saint John.

John Paul (Francis X.S.) married Georgina Beaton, Inverness. They lived in Iona and had a family. **161**

Roderick (John), a merchant in Iona, married Bella

MacDonald. They lived in Iona and had a family. **162**

John P. (John) married first Mary (Alasdair, Ruairi) MacDonald, Gillis Point (see **372**). They lived in Iona and their family: Gordon, Cassie I, and Mary Regis. In a second marriage he married Mary Catherine (John, Michael "Mor") MacDonald, St. Columba (see **364**). They lived in Iona and their family: John Alex, Mary Ann, Joseph, Cassie II, Irene, Albert, Margaret, Louise, and Mary. **163**

> Gordon (John P.) married Annie Laurie MacNeil, lived in Grand Narrows, and had a son Gordon. Cassie I married C.H. Cederburgh and had a family. Mary Regis married William Kelley and had a family. John Alex married Margaret Burns and had no family. Mary Ann married Charles Perry and had a family in New York. Joseph married in Ontario. Albert married in Scotland. Cassie II, an excellent teacher, and Mary died unmarried. Margaret and Louise became Sisters of Notre Dame. Irene married William L. MacCormack, a railway Station Agent, Lower River Inhabitants, lived in Iona, and had a family (see **340**).

● ● ●

Donald "Ban" MacNeil, his brother John, and three of his four sisters came from Barra to the New World. John settled in Pictou. One sister, whose name we do not know, married Rory (Rory) MacNeil (see **141a**); another, Flora, married Malcolm Campbell, the first Campbell to come to Iona (see **286**); and the third, Catherine, married John MacDougall, Christmas Island. Donald "Ban" was already married to Ann (Kenneth) MacLeod, a sister of Sarah, wife of James (Eoin) MacNeil (see **77**). They lived in Iona and their family: John, Donald, Patrick, Kenneth, James Jonathan, Mary I, Mary II, Marcella, Kate, and Ann. **164**

Marcella (Donald "Ban") died unmarried. Jonathan went away young. James, a sea-captain, was married and died on one of his voyages. Kenneth went to the United States. Mary I married Neil MacNeil, Grand Narrows and died within a year of her marriage. Ann married Angus Campbell, Boisdale. Kate married Joseph Garringhi, lived in the United States, and had no family. Patrick married a Miss MacLean, Boisdale, had a family, and moved to the United States. Mary II, known as "Mairi Dubh," married Murdock (Rory, Murdock) MacNeil, Iona and had a son Kenneth.

Donald (Donald "Ban") married a Miss MacLean, sister of Patrick's wife. They lived in Barrachois and their family: Dan, James, and two daughters who married.

James (Donald, Donald "Ban"), a ship-mate with Captain Rory (Hector, Rory) MacNeil, sailed West for a number of years, married the Captain's daughter, and had no family.

Dan (Donald, Donald "Ban") married Kate (Michael "Lewis") MacDonald, Ottawa Brook and had no family (see 351). **165**

John (Donald "Ban"), known as "Banker," married Elizabeth (Eoin "Mor") MacNeil, Jamesville (see 57). They lived in Iona and their family: Jonathan, Catherine I, Catherine II, Elizabeth, Ann, Mary, Dan, John, Stephen, James, and John MacGillivray whom they adopted. **166**

Jonathan (John, Donald "Ban") and Catherine I died young. Ann, Mary, Dan, and John who lived to be 104, died unmarried. Catherine II married John H. (Hector "Ban") Campbell, Iona (see 320) lived in Iona, had no family, but adopted Annie Morrison.

Stephen (John, Donald "Ban") married Mary (George, Hugh) Campbell, Gillis Point (see 293). They lived in Gillis Point and their family: George, John Francis, Elizabeth, Flora, and Mary. **167**

Elizabeth (Stephen), Flora, and Mary died young. John Francis died unmarried.

MACNEIL

George (Stephen) married Sadie Maria (Hector, Neil) MacNeil, Gillis Point East (see **90**). They lived in Ottawa Brook and their family: Bernard, Hector, and Angela. **168**

James (John, Donald "Ban") married Margaret (Domhnull "Mor") MacNeil, Red Point (see **41**). They lived in Iona and their family: Elizabeth, Marcella, Mary Jane, Mary, Mary Ann, Mary Margaret, Roderick, and others who died in infancy. **169**

> Elizabeth (James) married Joe MacDonald and had a family. Marcella and Mary Jane were unmarried. Mary married John Cameron, Antigonish and had a family. Mary Ann married Simon Morrison, Glace Bay and had a family. Mary Margaret married Rory (Calum, Eoin) MacNeil, Iona (see **155**) and had a family. Roderick married Flora MacNeil, Boisdale, lived in Iona, and had no family.

● ● ●

Donald (Rory) MacNeil came, in 1802, with several friends from Scotland. All of them eventually settled on both sides of the Barra Strait. Donald married Margaret (Eoin, Donald John) MacNeil (see **56a**), and lived in Iona, on the property once owned by "Francis Hector," then by "Dan A.," and today by "Stephen Dan A." Donald and Margaret had two sons, Neil and James "Mor." After the father's death, the widow and her sons left Iona and went to settle in Jamesville, and next to the property of her brother Eoin. Donald (Rory) was the first of the new settlers to die in Iona. He was also the first to be buried in the Christmas Island parish cemetery. It happened this way. Donald (Rory) had a sister who was married to Neil "Ban" MacNeil, Grand Narrows. This Neil "Ban" had laid claim to the property now owned by the descendants of Joseph "Gobha" MacNeil, as well as the eastern property later owned by Edward and Donald "Ban" MacNeil. On the day that Donald (Rory) died in Iona, his sister came to Iona. She inquired where her brother was to be buried and, hearing that no definite place had been decided upon, she offered that he be buried on her own property in Cooper's Pond. Donald (Rory) was therefore buried next to the spot, where later there was built the "windowless log-cabin church" in Christmas Island, to which Bishop Plessis made reference in his diary. **170**

Neil (Donald, Rory) married Margaret, sister of Hector "Ban" Campbell, Jamesville (see **305**). They lived in Jamesville and their family: Donald "Mor," Michael, Rory and Peggy (twins), Mary, Christy, and Donald "Beag." **171**

Donald "Mor" (Neil, Donald Rory), Rory, Peggy, and Mary died unmarried. Christy married Malcolm (Aonghas, Calum) Campbell), Iona (see **288**), lived in Iona, and had a family. **172**

Michael (Neil, Donald Rory) married Christy (Malcolm, Calum Ruairi) MacNeil, Barra Glen (see **2**). They lived in Iona Rear and their family: Angus, Neil, Johnnie, Peter, four daughters, and probably another son. **173**

> Angus (Michael), a war veteran, was killed in a railroad accident. Johnnie was killed in World War I. Neil lived in Jamesville unmarried. Peter, brought up by his aunts and uncles, married a Miss McMullin, Rear Boisdale, lived in Boisdale, and had a family. One daughter of Michael (Neil, Donald Rory) married a Mr. Didgue; another married a Mr. Pittman; and the other married in Glace Bay.

Donald "Beag" (Neil, Donald Rory) married Sarah (Paul, Rory) MacNeil, Iona Rear (see **216**). They lived in Barra Glen and their family: Lawrence, Paul, Neil D., Rory D., Annie, and Margaret Ann. **174**

> Annie (Donald "Beag") married Rory Joseph (Hector "Big") MacNeil, Piper's Cove and had a family. Margaret Ann married a Mr. MacEachern, Inverness and had a family in the United States. Lawrence died young. Paul married a daughter of Patrick (Iain, Tormad) MacNeil, Piper's Cove, lived in the Cape Breton mining area, and had a family.

> Neil D. (Donald "Beag") married Katie MacLean, Boisdale. They lived in the Cape Breton mining area but moved to Jamesville in 1933, settling on the grandfather's farm. Their family: Dan Alex, Michael, Josephine, Sarah, Vincent, Jessie, Neil, and a child who died in infancy. **175**

>> Dan Alex (Neil D.) married Mary Decoste, Big Pond. They lived in Iona and had a son Neil. **176**

MACNEIL

Rory D. (Donald "Beag") married Mary Josephine (Michael, Neil Calum) MacNeil, Benacadie West. They lived in Barra Glen and their family: Lawrence, Bernie, Roy, Sadie, Betty, and an adopted daughter Margaret. **177**

James "Mor" (Donald, Rory) married Kate, sister of Hector "Ban" (Donald) Campbell, Jamesville (see **298**). They lived in Jamesville and their family: Colin, Jonathan, Malcolm, and Margaret or "Bayac." **178**

Jonathan (James "Mor," Donald Rory) and Margaret or "Bayac" died unmarried.

Colin (James, "Mor," Donald Rory) married Annie (Michael "Saor") MacInnis, Iona (see **406**). They lived in Jamesville and their family: Katie, Mary and Margaret. **179**

Katie (Colin), a teacher, was unmarried. Mary married Rory MacNeil, a blacksmith in Grand Narrows. Margaret married Hector MacDonald and lived in Arichat (see **370**).

Malcolm (James "Mor," Donald Rory) married Annie (Eoin, Rory Donald "Og"), MacNeil, Barra Glen (see **3**). They lived in Jamesville and their family: James M. "Red," John H., Michael M., Mary, Donald, Katie, and John Marie. **180**

Donald (Malcolm), Katie, and John Marie died young. Michael M. and Mary died unmarried.

James M. "Red" (Malcolm) married Sadie (James, Neil) Campbell, Jamesville West (see **313**). They lived in Jamesville and their family: James C., Malcolm, Annie, and Catherine Josephine. **181**

Annie (James M. "Red") married Hector (Joseph H.) MacNeil, Iona (see **150**), lived in Iona, and had a family.

John H. (Malcolm) married Mary Catherine (Murdock, Eoin "Mor") MacNeil, Jamesville (see **60**). They lived in

Jamesville and their family: Micky, Annie May, Catherine Ann, Betty, Josephine, Jemina, and two boys who died in infancy. **182**

●   ●   ●

Angus (Eoin) MacNeil and his twelve-year-old son came from Barra and settled in Highland Hill. A half-brother of Angus (Eoin), whose name was also Angus, settled in Christmas Island, where he married three times and had a family from each wife. This half-brother Angus was accustomed to winter in the Gulf, even though he "granted" land in Christmas Island and did work the land. It seems also that Angus (Eoin) who settled in Highland Hill did his own share of wandering about. At any rate, it is clear that by 1846 Angus (Eoin) who had first settled in Highland Hill and John, another brother of his, were permanently settled in Highland Hill. Two sisters of theirs had also come to America.

Sarah (Eoin) was unmarried. Katie married Neil (Hector) MacLean, Ottawa Brook (see **534**), lived in Ottawa Brook, and had a family.

Angus (Eoin) married in Scotland Margaret Breton or Brittain, daughter of Donald (Malcolm). They lived in Highland Hill and their family: John, Donald, Malcolm, John A., Eoin, Effie, Flora, Maggie, Elizabeth, Mary and Katie. **183**

Malcolm (Angus, Eoin) married Bessie MacKenzie, Washabuck (see **426**), lived in Sydney, and had a family. John A. married a Miss English, Sydney Mines, lived in Sydney Mines, and their family: Gus, Mary, John, Ambrose, Alphonse, Joseph, Elizabeth, and Ethel. Mary married John J. (John, Charles) MacKinnon, MacKinnon's Harbour (see **476**) and had a family. Elizabeth married Neil "Plant" MacNeil, Barra Glen (see **8**), lived in Barra Glen, and had a family. Effie married Malcolm (Johnnie) MacKinnon, Iona Rear (see **462**), lived in Iona Rear, and had a family. Maggie married Rory "Mor" (Neil) Campbell,

MACNEIL

Jamesville West (see **309**), lived in Jamesville West, and had a family. Flora married Donald "Plant" MacNeil, Barra Glen (see **3**), lived in Barra Glen, and had a family. Katie died unmarried.

John (Angus, Eoin) married Catherine (Charles, Donald "Ban") MacKinnon, MacKinnon's Harbour (see **474**). They lived in Highland Hill and their family: John Charles, Mary, Catherine, Katie, Ann, and Dan Angus. **184**

> John Charles (John) died unmarried. Mary married Rory H. (Hector, "Big" Rory) MacNeil, Iona (see **48**), lived in the United States, and had a family. Catherine married Samuel Cornell and had a family in the United States. Katie married Angus MacEachern, Creignish and had a family. Ann married Neil A. (Angus "Beag") MacNeil, Ottawa Brook (see **219**), lived in Ottawa Brook, and had a family.

> Dan Angus (John) married Katie Ann MacCormack, Boisdale. They lived in Highland Hill and their family: Charles, Annie, Effie, Catherine, Maxie, and one who died young. **185**

>> Annie (Dan Angus) married Lloyd Turner and has a family in Toronto. Effie married Hudson Morrisey and had a family. Catherine married Murdock (Johnnie "Ban") MacNeil, Barra Glen (see **22**), lived in Grand Narrows, and had a family. Maxie married and has a family in Toronto.

Donald (Angus, Eoin), commonly called "Tailor," married Mary (Eoin) MacNeil, Barra Glen (see **3**). They lived in Highland Hill and their family: Stephen D., Angus D., Margaret, Mary, Catherine, and John Rory. **186**

> Stephen D. (Donald), Angus D., and Catherine were unmarried. John Rory died young. Margaret married John H. (Hector, Donald) MacNeil, MacNeil's Vale (see **127**), lived in MacNeil's Vale, and had a large family. Mary married Stephen J. (Eoin "Mor") MacNeil, Jamesville (see **64**), lived in Jamesville, and had a family.

Eoin (Angus, Eoin) married Annie (Hector) MacNeil, MacNeil's Vale (see **126**). They lived in Highland Hill and their family: Dan Hector, Margaret, Elizabeth, Bessie, Lucy, Mary Catherine,

John Rory, and Maggie **187**

Maggie (Eoin) died unmarried. Dan Hector died young. Elizabeth married Joe Murphy and lived in New Waterford. Bessie married Freeman MacDonald and had a family. John Rory married in the United States and had no family. Mary Catherine married Allan J. MacNeil, Christmas Island and had a family. Lucy married Rory J. (Rory, Alasdair) MacNeil, Iona Rear (see **215**), lived in Iona Rear, and had a family. Margaret married Hector (Iain "Ban"), MacKinnon and had a family.

John (Eoin) married Sarah MacKinnon. They lived in Highland Hill and their family: Murdock B., Malcolm, Annie, Thomas, and Angus. **188**

Malcolm (John, Eoin) and Annie died unmarried.

Murdock B. (John, Eoin) married Mary (James, Alasdair) MacDonald, Washabuck (see **365**). They lived in Highland Hill and their family: Angus, John F., Thomas, James C., Katie, Sarah, and Betsy Ann. **189**

James C. (Murdock B.), a postmaster, died unmarried. Angus J. married a Miss Petrie, lived in Sydney, and had a son Murdock Ralph. John F. married Mary Elizabeth (Captain Angus) MacNeil, Iona Rear (see **211**), lived in Winnipeg, and had no family. Katie married Michael D. (Donald "Beag") MacNeil, Iona (see **51**), and had a family. Sarah married R.J. (Stephen, Malcolm) MacLean, Washabuck (see **510**), lived in Washabuck, and had an adopted family. Betsy Ann married Rory (Iain "Ban") MacKinnon, Highland Hill (see **454**), lived in Highland Hill, and later moved to Sydney.

Thomas (Murdock B.) married first Jessie (Donald) Walker, Ottawa Brook (see **575**), lived in Highland Hill, and had no family. In a second marriage he married Peggy MacDonald, Ottawa Brook, lived in Highland Hill, and had no family. **190**

MACNEIL

Angus (John, Eoin) married A Miss MacLean from P.E.I. Unfortunately he perished in the Bras d'Or Lake, off Jamesville, on May 22, 1863. There perished with him his brother Thomas, his neighbour Rory "Glen Mor" MacNeil, and Rory's daughter Catherine. After the tragedy, Angus' widow and her two children (Lauchie and Sarah) left Highland Hill and went to P.E.I. (John, grandson of Lauchie, now lives and has a family in Beach Point, Murray Harbour, P.E.I.) **191**

Thomas (John, Eoin), who perished with his brother Angus, had married Isabella (Rory, Ian "Mor") MacKinnon, Highland Hill (see **452**). They lived in Highland Hill, where a son, Thomas "Ban," was born after his father's untimely death. **192**

Thomas "Ban" (Thomas) married Bessie (Neil "Pearson") MacNeil, Iona (see **242**). They lived in Iona and had their family: Tom, Mary, Sarah, Maggie Bell, and a son who died young. After the death of Thomas "Ban," his widow married William (James) MacKenzie, Washabuck (see **439**), lived in Washabuck, and had a family. **193**

● ● ●

Rory "Red" MacNeil married Mary MacKinnon in Scotland. They and their family came from Barra and settled in Iona Rear in about 1822. Their family: Donald, John, Neil, Malcolm, Alex, Paul, Katie, Sarah, Mary, and Ann. **194**

Katie (Rory "Red") married Rory "Big" MacPhee, Boisdale, lived in Boisdale, and had a family. Sarah married Neil (Donald) MacNeil, Gillis Point (see **104**), lived in Gillis Point, and had a family. Mary married Neil (Eoin) MacNeil, Iona (see **72**), lived in Iona, and had a family. Ann married Hector "Big" MacNeil, Iona (see **142**), lived in Hector's Point, and had a family.

Donald (Rory "Red") married Sarah (Hugh "Ban") Gillis, Christmas Island. They lived in Christmas Island and their family Elizabeth, Hugh, Rory I, John, Michael, Murdock, Ann,

Stephen, Hector, and Rory II. **195**

Elizabeth (Donald, Rory "Red") married Thomas (Johnnie) MacKinnon, Iona Rear (see **456**) and had a family.

Hugh (Donald, Rory "Red") married first Mary (John "Shoemaker") MacKinnon, Benacadie. They had a son, who on the death of his mother was adopted in Christmas Island. Hugh moved to Iona and "granted" land — a holding of one hundred and forty acres — between Barra Glen and St. Columba, adjacent to the property of Thomas MacKinnon, his brother-in-law. To this day, that section of land is often referred to as "cuil Eoghain Domhnull," that is, "Hugh Donald's back land." In a second marriage Hugh married Peggy (Calum John, Hector) Campbell, Barra Glen (see **281**) and their family: Michael, Paul, Rory, Angus, and John V. **196**

Michael (Hugh) married and lived in St. Peter's. Paul and John V. moved away early in life. Angus was unmarried.

Rory (Hugh) married Elizabeth, adopted daughter of Philip (Donald Neil) MacNeil, Gillis Point (see **96**). They lived in Gillis Point and their family: Hugh I, John Hugh, Hugh II, Mary, and Michael. **197**

John Hugh (Rory) died unmarried. Hugh II died young. Mary married Joe Parson from Newfoundland and had no family. Michael married Flora MacInnis, Shenacadie, lived in Sydney, and had a family.

Hugh I (Rory) married first Elizabeth (John, Michael Neil) MacLean, lived in Sydney, and had a family. In a second marriage, he married Margaret Boudreau, lived in Gillis Point, and their family: Theresa, Helen, Lorraine, Alex, and Joseph. Later the family moved to Halifax. **198**

John (Rory "Red") married Mary (Donald "Ban") MacKinnon, Cooper's Pond. He settled on a part of his father's farm in Rear Iona and his family: Rory, Alex, Neil, Donald, Catherine, Ann, and Mary. **199**

Rory (John, Rory "Red") was drowned in New Brunswick, while still a young man. Neil, a school teacher, died in a storm on his way home from Baddeck. Catherine, Ann, and Mary died unmarried.

Donald (John, Rory "Red") married Sarah (Alex, Ben) MacNeil, Ottawa Brook (see **31**). They lived in Ottawa Brook and had a family of four who all died in infancy. **200**

Alex (John, Rory "Red") married Mary (John, Rory) MacNeil, Iona (see **152**). They lived in Rear Iona and their family: John and Rory. **201**

John (Alex) died young.

Rory (Alex) married first Margaret Ann (Captain Michael) MacKinnon, Big Beach. He lived in Rear Iona and had a son Alex. In a second marriage he married Margaret (Donald, James) MacNeil, Iona (see **80**) and their family: John G., Margaret, Sadie, Dan Joe, John Dan, and Louise whom they adopted. **202**

Neil (Rory "Red"), commonly known as "Gosgie," married first Ann (Rory, Rory) MacNeil, Hector's Point (see **141a**). They lived in Iona Rear and their family: Rory I, Hugh, Malcolm, and Ann. In a second marriage he married Christy (Hector "Tailor") MacLean, Middle Cape. They lived in Iona Rear and the family: Mary I, Catherine, Mary II, and Rory II. **203** ·

Rory I (Neil, Rory "Red") and Malcolm went away early. Ann married Angus ("Red" Hector) MacDonald, Christmas Island and had a family. Mary I married Donald "Roger" MacNeil, Glace Bay and had a large family. Catherine married Michael Gouthro, Frenchvale and had no family. Mary II married John Campbell, Frenchvale and had a family.

Rory II (Neil, Rory "Red") married Mary (Hector, Donald) MacNeil, MacNeil's Vale (see **126**). They lived in Iona Rear and their family: Katie Ann, Annie, Christy, Mary Catherine, Betsy, and Sarah. They all married and had families in the Cape Breton mining area. **204**

Hugh (Neil, Rory "Red"), a sailor, married Elizabeth (John "Red") MacNeil, Christmas Island. They lived in Iona Rear and their family: John R., Katie Ann, Mary Lizzie, David, Mary Jane, and Bridgit. **205**

John R. (Hugh), a lawyer, married Mary Ann (Malcolm, Norman) MacNeil, Piper's Cove, lived in the United States, and had a family. Katie Ann married Rod MacDonald, Sydney and had a family. Mary Lizzie married John R. Martin, Sydney and had a family. David, a C.N.R. Conductor, married in Sydney and had a family. Mary Jane married James S. (Alasdair, Alasdair "Mor") MacNeil, Gillis Point (see **140**), lived in Gillis Point, and later moved the family to Sydney. Bridgit died young.

Malcolm (Rory "Red") married Sarah (Rory "Big") MacNeil, Iona (see **36**). He lived on part of his father's farm in Iona Rear and his family: Mary I, Christy, Rory, Michael, Mary II, Sarah, Margaret, and Angus. **206**

Mary I (Malcolm, Rory "Red") married Hugh (Malcolm, Iain) Campbell, Barra Glen (see **282**), lived in Barra Glen, and had a family. Christie married Archie (Malcolm, Iain) Campbell, Barra Glen (see **284**), lived in Barra Glen, and had a family. Rory died young. Mary II married Michael (Sandy) MacNeil, Grand Narrows, lived im Grand Narrows, and had a family. Sarah married Donald (Dunn) MacNeil, Jamesville (see **66**), lived in Jamesville, and had a family. Margaret married John Cameron, Big Beach.

Michael (Malcolm, Rory "Red") married Jane (John, Rory Donald "Og") MacNeil, Barra Glen (see **20**). They lived in Iona Rear and their family: John M., Rory M., Mary Lizzie, Neil M., and Mary Ann. **207**

Rory M. (Michael) married Theresa (Rory, Neil) Campbell, Jamesville (see **309**), lived in Iona Rear, and had a son Rory Michael who died unmarried. Mary Lizzie married first

MACNEIL

Dan MacGillivray, Sydney, had a large family; and in a second marriage she married a Mr. Agnew from Newfoundland, lived in Sydney, and had a family. Mary Ann married Neil R. (Rory, Eoin) MacNeil, Barra Glen (see **6**), lived in Barra Glen and had a family.

John M. (Michael) married Christy (Hector, Donald "Soldier") MacDonald, Ottawa Brook (see **385**). They lived in Barra Glen and their family: Michael Hector, Michael Rory, Janie, Annie, John Joseph, Lizzie and Sarah. Rory Angus and others died young. **208**

> Michael Hector (John M.) married in Toronto and has a family. Jane married in the United States and has a family. Annie married a Mr. Campbell and has a large family in Sydney. Lizzie married Bernie MacNeil and has a family in Sydney. Sarah married a Mr. Campbell and has a family in Sydney. John Joseph is unmarried.

> Michael Rory (John M.) married Euphemia Gillis, Lake Ainslie. They lived in Barra Glen and their family: John, Neil, Malcolm, Hector, Alex, Norman, Christena, Mary, Theresa, Jenny, Colin, and Elizabeth. **209**

Neil M. (Michael) married Christy (Rory, Calum "Gobha") MacLean, Rear Christmas Island. They lived in Iona Rear and their family: Michael Rory, Janie, Flora, Neil and Mary Lizzie (twins), Mary Catherine, and Roddie Francis. **210**

> Neil (Neil M.) died unmarried. Mary Catherine married Joe Gillis, Mira and has a family in Sydney. Roddie Francis married Helen Gillis, Mira, lived in Sydney, and had a son. Janie married a Mr. MacNeil, Big Pond, lives in Sydney, and had a family. Michael Rory married Annie (John J.) MacNeil, Jamesville (see **182**), lived in Iona, and has no family.

Angus (Malcolm, Rory "Red") married Sarah (John, Donald Neil) MacNeil, Gillis Point (see **99**). They lived in Iona Rear and their family: Christy, Malcolm, Sarah, Mary Ann, and Mary

Lizzie. **211**

> Christy (Angus), a nurse, married a Mr. Ouelette in Boston and had a family. Sarah married John MacNeil and lived in New Waterford. Mary Ann lived in the United States. Mary Lizzie married John F. (Murdock B.) MacNeil, Highland Hill (see **189**), lived in Winnipeg, and had no family. Malcolm married Mary Lizzie (Hector "Lighthouse") MacLean, Gillis Point (see **491**), lived in Gillis Point, and had an adopted son James.

Alex (Rory "Red") married Christy (Donald, Neil) MacNeil, Gillis Point (see **95**). He settled on part of his father's farm in Iona Rear and his family: Michael, Mary, Catherine, Rory, Elizabeth, Sarah, and Margaret. **212**

Mary (Alex, Rory "Red") married Kenneth (James) MacNeil, Iona (see **81**) and had a family. Catherine married Michael J. (John, Rory Donald "Og") MacNeil, Barra Glen (see **23**), lived in Barra Glen, and had a family of four who died young. Elizabeth died young. Sarah died unmarried. Margaret married Neil (Rory, James) MacNeil, Iona (see **79**), lived in Dominion, and had no family.

Michael (Alex, Rory "Red") married Mary (James, Hector) MacNeil, Gillis Point (see **92**). They lived in Barra Glen and their family: James, Alex, Mary Ann, Lizzie I, Lizzie II, Neil J., and Christy. **213**

> James (Michael), Alex, Lizzie I, Mary Ann, Neil J., and Christy died unmarried. Lizzie II married Rory MacNeil, Castle Bay and had a family in Sydney.

Rory (Alex, Rory "Red") married Margaret (Michael) MacLean, Washabuck Center (see **489**). They lived in Iona and their family: John Alex, Mary Lizzie, Michael J., and Roddie J. **214**

> John Alex (Rory) died young. Mary Lizzie married Dan Redquest (see **571**) and had a family in Sydney. Michael J. married Margaret MacArthur, Mira and had a family.

Roddie J. (Rory) married Lucy (Eoin Angus) MacNeil, Highland Hill (see **187**). They lived in Iona Rear and their family: John Joseph, Mary, Catherine, Bernie, and Rhodena. **215**

Paul (Rory "Red") married Ann (Neil, Eoin) MacNeil, Gillis Point (see **115**). He settled on part of his father's farm in Iona Rear and his family: Elizabeth, Mary, Sarah, and Rory. **216**

Elizabeth (Paul, Rory "Red") married Hector (John, Donald) MacNeil, Gillis Point (see **103**), lived in Gillis Point, and had a family. Sarah married Donald "Beag" MacNeil, Barra Glen (see **174**), lived in Barra Glen, and had a family. Mary died unmarried.

Rory (Paul, Rory "Red") married first Mary (James Jr., James "Pearson") MacNeil, Iona (see **245**). They lived in Iona Rear and their family: Paul and Mary who both died young. In a second marriage he married Margaret (Malcolm, Johnnie) MacKinnon, Iona Rear (see **462**) and their family: Paul, Mary E., Effie, Margaret Ann, Catherine and Malcolm. **217**

Paul (Rory) died unmarried. Effie married Allan MacNeil, Christmas Island, lived in Glace Bay, and had a large family. Mary E., Margaret, Catherine, and Malcolm were unmarried.

●　　●　　●

Donald (Rory) MacNeil came from Barra to Pictou in 1802 and settled in Christmas Island. He had already married a Mary MacNeil and he had three sons: Angus, Angus "Beag," and Eoin "Beag."

Angus (Donald, Rory) married Catherine "Big" MacNeil and settled in Christmas Island.

Angus "Beag" (Donald, Rory) married Flora (Donald "Soldier") MacDonald, Ottawa Brook (see **384a**). They lived in Ottawa Brook and their family: Neil A., Dan H., Dan, and Christy. **218**

Christy (Angus "Beag," Donald Rory) was adopted by Francis (John G.) MacKinnon, MacKinnon's Harbour (see **466**) and died unmarried.

Neil A. (Angus "Beag," Donald Rory) married Annie (John, Aonghas Eoin) MacNeil, Highland Hill (see **184**). They lived in Ottawa Brook, had a large family, and later moved to Sydney. **219**

Dan H. (Angus "Beag," Donald Rory), known as "Painter," married Elizabeth (Kenneth, James) MacNeil, Iona (see **81**). They lived in Ottawa Brook, had no family, but adopted Margaret MacNeil who married in Glace Bay. **220**

Dan (Angus "Beag," Donald Rory), known as "Bangor Dan," married a woman from Irish Cove, sister of the wife of Jim Alex (Michael "Doctor") MacNeil, Ottawa Brook. They lived in Ottawa Brook, had a large family, and later moved away. **221**

Eoin "Beag" (Donald, Rory) married Peggy (Neil, Malcolm) Campbell, Benacadie and settled in Benacadie West.

John (Eoin "Beag," Donald Rory) married Mary (James "Doctor") MacNeil, Ottawa Brook (see **224**). They lived in Ottawa Brook and their family: Dan N., Mary, Eliza, Peggy, and three who died young. **222**

Mary (John) a deaf and mute, was a dressmaker in Sydney where she married a Mr. Bartholem and had a family. Eliza married in the United States. Peggy married Donald Nash, St. Columba (see **565**), lived in St. Columba, and had a family. The three who died young died of diphtheria and, to prevent the disease from spreading, were buried near the site of their own home in Ottawa Brook.

Dan N. (John) married Mary Sarah (Michael "Doctor")

MACNEIL

MacNeil, Ottawa Brook (see **226**). They lived for a time in Ottawa Brook, and moved to Halifax with their family of four. **223**

● ● ●

James MacNeil and his brother Donald, both known by the label "Doctor," came to Ottawa Brook from Doctor's Brook in Antigonish County. We have it on reliable authority that they and relatives came to Doctor's Brook from a hamlet in Barra called "Spiris," which is the Gaelic word for "Roost." Our information is that on this Barra hill-top there lived a family of MacNeils, known there as the "Doctors" and that alongside of them lived another family of MacNeils, known there as the "Rogers." It is quite likely, therefore, that this explains the origin of the place-name "Doctor's Brook" in Antigonish County, and also the fact that "Doctors" and "Rogers" are found living side-by-side in Ottawa Brook. We do not know for certain the date of the arrival of the "Doctor" brothers in Iona parish, but we know that they came to visit Catherine, a sister of theirs, who at that time was married in Ottawa Brook, the wife of a Philip MacDonald. Evidently the brothers like what they saw in Ottawa Brook, for they did not return to Doctor's Brook.

James "Doctor," whose wife's name we do not know, had a daughter Mary who married John (Eoin "Beag") MacNeil, Ottawa Brook (see **222**) and had a family. **224**

Donald "Doctor" married Mary (Alexander "Miller") Mac-Dougall, Red Point (see **393**). They lived in Ottawa Brook and their family: Michael, Joseph, John and Sarah. **225**

John (Donald "Doctor") was killed in the lumbering woods in Maine. Sarah was the second wife of Ben MacNeil, Red Point (see **35**), lived in Red Point, and had a family.

Michael (Donald "Doctor") married Catherine (Michael, Domhnull a Chuil) MacNeil, Benacadie. They lived in Ottawa

MACNEIL

Brook and their family: Jim Alex, Michael, Malcolm, Donald John, Neil Joseph, Kate, Theresa, Mary Ann, Margaret, and Mary Sarah. **226**

Michael (Michael) married Margaret, widow of Thomas (Murdock B.) MacNeil, Highland Hill, lived in Ottawa Brook, and had no family. Malcolm married first a Miss Campbell, and in a second marriage he married Margaret Kennedy, Inverness. Neil Joseph married a Miss MacPhee, lived in the Cape Breton mining area, and had an adopted family. Kate married Rod MacKenzie, Christmas Island; and in a second marriage she married Hector MacKinnon and lived in Toronto. Theresa married a Mr. Boutilier, Florence, lived in Sydney, and had a large family. Mary Ann married Michael MacDonnell who was adopted by Charles S. MacNeil, Red Point (see **93**), and had a large family. Margaret married Jim "Section Man" MacDonald who was also adopted by Charles S. MacNeil, Red Point (see **390**), lived in Ottawa Brook, and had a large family. Mary Sarah married Dan N. (John, Eoin "Beag") MacNeil, Ottawa Brook (see **223**), lived for a time in Ottawa Brook and moved the family to Halifax.

Jim Alex (Michael) married Mary Agnes ("Bard Ruadh") MacNeil, Irish Cove. They lived in Ottawa Brook and their family: Michael, Kaye, Christy, Joe Pius, John Archie I, Sydney, Catherine, Theresa, Duncan, James Alex, and John Archie II who died in infancy. **227**

Donald John (Michael) married Sarah Ann (Rory I) MacNeil, Red Point (see **41a**). They lived in Ottawa Brook and their family: Michael, Rhodena, and Isabella. **228**

Joseph (Donald "Doctor") married Sarah (James, Domhnull a Chuil) MacNeil, Benacadie. They lived in Red Point and their family: Mary Ann, Sadie, Margaret, May, Gertrude, Bessie, Donald, James and Hugh. **229**

Hugh (Joseph) was killed in World War II. Donald married and lived in Toronto. Mary Ann was unmarried in the United States. Sadie and Bessie married in the United States. Gertrude married John Fitzgerald, lived in Glace Bay, and had a family. Margaret married first James (Peter B.) MacDonald, Ottawa Brook (see **353**), lived in Ottawa

MACNEIL

Brook, had a family; and in a second marriage she married Roddie (Michael D.) MacNeil, Iona (see **52**), lived in Ottawa Brook, and had no family. May married Rannie (Michael A.J.) Gillis, a C.N.R. Conductor (see **333**), lived in Sydney and had a family.

James (Joseph) married Laura (Dan Y.) MacNeil, Ottawa Brook (see **248**). They lived in Red Point and their family: Hugh, Joseph, Gerard and Bernadette. **230**

● ● ●

John MacNeil and his brother Neil, both known by the label "Roger," came to Ottawa Brook from Barra. It was already stated that in Barra MacNeils with the label "Doctor" lived side-by-side with MacNeils who had the label "Roger." They still do in Ottawa Brook.

John "Roger" married Catherine (Donald, John) MacNeil, Grand Narrows. They lived in Ottawa Brook and their family: Michael, Rory, Sarah, and Lizzie whom they adopted. **231**

Michael (John "Roger") and Sarah were unmarried. Lizzie married John (Donald "Mor") MacNeil, Red Point (see **42**), lived in Ottawa Brook, and had no family. Rory married Sarah (Donald "Mor") MacNeil, Red Point (see **41**), lived in Ottawa Brook, and had no family.

Neil "Roger" married Mary (Donald, John) MacNeil, Grand Narrows, sister of John's wife (see **231**). They lived in Highland Hill and had a son Stephen. **232**

Stephen "Neil "Roger") married Christy (Michael "Mor") MacDonald, St. Columba (see **356**). They lived in Highland Hill and their family: Peter B., John V., Sarah, Annie, Mary, and Catherine. **233**

MACNEIL

John V. (Stephen) died unmarried. Sarah married Angus MacKenzie, Benacadie, lived in Benacadie, and had no family. Mary married Michael MacNeil, Bangor and had a family. Annie married Charles "Framer" MacKenzie, Washabuck (see **435**) and had a family. Catherine married Norman (Neil) MacKinnon, Highland Hill (see **449**), lived in Highland Hill, and had a family.

Peter B. (Stephen) married Christy (John, Calum) MacNeil, Barra Glen (see **236**). They lived in Highland Hill and had no family. **234**

● ● ●

Malcolm (Iain "Ban") MacNeil came from Barra with Rory (Donald "Og") MacNeil, to whose daughter he was married. He settled in Barra Glen and his family: John, Hugh, Christy, Mary, Peggy, and Sarah. **235**

Christy (Malcolm, Iain "Ban") married a Mr. O'Handley, Bridgeport and had no family. Peggy died unmarried. Mary married Donald (Norman) MacNeil, Piper's Cove and had a family. Sarah married Alexander MacPhee, Shenacadie, lived in the Cape Breton mining area, and had a family. One of Sarah's daughters, Betsy, married John MacVarish, North Sydney and, after the death of her husband, she and her daughter, Etta, spent their last days in Barra Glen.

John (Malcolm, Iain "Ban") married Elizabeth (Calum "Mor") MacDonald, Big Beach. They lived in Barra Glen and their family: Hugh, Mary, Christy, Mary Lizzie, and Katie. **236**

Hugh (John) went to the United States. Mary married Alexander (John) MacNeil, Rear Big Pond and had a family. Christy married Peter B. MacNeil, Highland Hill (see **234**) and had no family. Mary Lizzie married Rory C. MacDonald, Upper Washabuck (see **382**) and had a family.

MACNEIL

Katie died unmarried.

Hugh (Malcolm, Iain "Ban") married Elizabeth (Norman) MacNeil, Piper's Cove. They lived in Barra Glen and their family: Norman, Rory, Neil H., Elizabeth, Mary Ann, and a girl who died unmarried. **237**

Norman (Hugh) and Rory married in New Glasgow. Elizabeth married John MacNeil, Piper's Cove, lived in Piper's Cove, and had a family. Mary Ann married Stephen (Neil, Donald) MacNeil, Jamesville, lived in Jamesville, and had no family.

Neil H. (Hugh) married first Mary (Donald) Nash, St. Columba (see **565**). They lived in Barra Glen and their family: Hugh Dan, Dan Rory, Mary Catherine, and Lizzie Ann. In a second marriage he married Mary Ann (Donald, Murdock) MacKenzie, Washabuck (see **437**) and their family: John Dan and Margaret. After Neil H.'s death, Joe MacNeil was brought up in the family. **238**

Hugh Dan (Neil H.) died unmarried in the United States. Dan Rory married in the United States. Mary Catherine married John N. MacKinnon, Rear Iona (see **461**) and had a large family. Lizzie Ann married John MacLean, Boisdale, lived in Boisdale, had a family, and moved to the United States. Margaret married Walter Arsenault, from P.E.I. (see **275**), lived in Barra Glen, and had a family. John Dan married Catherine (James C., Donald "Beag") MacNeil, Iona (see **50**), lived in Sydney, and had a family.

●   ●   ●

John Dan (James, Donald "Og") MacNeil, Castle Bay married Annie Catherine (Rory R.) MacNeil, Barra Glen (see **10**). They lived in Barra Glen and their family: Annie, Monica, Teresa, Roddie, Mendel, Jamie, Joseph, Marie, and Mary Louise. **239**

Annie (John Dan, James Donald "Og") married Cyril O'Toole, Sydney Mines, lives in Sydney Mines, and has a large family. Mendel married Pauline George from Western Nova Scotia and has a family. Jamie married Mary Louise, adopted daughter of Rory G. MacNeil, Iona Rear (see **202**), lives in Boisdale, and has a large family. Joseph married Alice Moore and lives in Toronto. Mary Louise married John A. (Rod F.) Gillis, Jamesville West (see **336**), lives in Antigonish, and has a large family. Marie is married in Montreal.

Roddie (John Dan, James Donald "Og") married Helen Devon from Ontario. They live in Barra Glen and their family: Marian, Lorne, Myrna, Timmie, Rosemary, and Paul. **240**

● ● ●

James "Pearson" MacNeil came to Iona through an unusual set of circumstances. Two brothers, James and Alexander, had come to the New World from a hamlet in Barra called "Pearson." On arriving in this land, they went immediately to Mabou, where a relative of theirs — also a native of Pearson in Barra — had already settled. This "Pearson" MacNeil who had settled in Mabou was married to Mary, sister of Donald (Ruairi) MacNeil, one of the first four MacNeils to come to Iona. Alexander, one of the brothers newly come from Pearson, managed to secure land near Mabou, but James had to come eastward to Skye Glen, before he found suitable land. In Skye Glen, however, James found himself surrounded by fine people, all of them belonging to the Protestant faith. It happened that, about this same time, a man by the name of MacLeod had come from North Uist in Scotland and settled in Iona. Here he, a Protestant, found himself surrounded by people who all embraced the Catholic faith. Most likely it was through the connection between the original "Pearson" MacNeil in Mabou and his sister married in Iona that a decision was reached, whereby James "Pearson" in Skye Glen and the MacLeod in Iona swapped land titles. Thus it was that James "Pearson" came to Iona. He married a Flora MacNeil and their family: Neil, James Jr., Murdock, and Catherine. **241**

Catherine (James "Pearson") married Eoin "Mor" MacNeil, Jamesville (see **58**), lived in Jamesville, and had a family. Murdock went to the United States as a young man, married an Irish girl, and had two sons. One of Murdock's sons, whose name was James, was for a time Councillor in Salem, Mass. Some of the descendants of this James in the United States changed their name from MacNeil to MacPherson, wrongly taking "Pearson" to be a corruption of MacPherson.

Neil (James "Pearson") married first a Mary MacNeil and had a daughter who died in infancy. In a second marriage he married Margaret (James, Alexander) MacDonald, St. Columba (see **365**). They lived in Iona and their family: James N.P., Hector, Dan, Mary, Elizabeth, and Flora. **242**

Mary (Neil, James "Pearson"), Dan, and Hector were unmarried. Flora married Rory (Neil, Archibald) MacLean, MacKinnon's Harbour (see **533**), lived in MacKinnon's Harbour, and had a family. Elizabeth married first Thomas "Ban" MacNeil, Iona (see **193**), had a family; and in a second marriage she married William MacKenzie, Washabuck (see **439**) and had a family.

James N.P. (Neil, James "Pearson"), known as "Fisherman," married Sarah (John), MacNeil, Grand Narrows. They lived in Iona and their family: Dan Stephen, John Neil, Eliza, Maggie, Mary, and Mary Lizzie. **243**

Dan Stephen (James N.P.) married in the Cape Breton mining area and had no family. John Neil is unmarried in the United States. Eliza married Rory S. MacNeil, Rear Christmas Island and had a family. Maggie married in the United States. Mary married a Mr. Roulan, Fall River, Mass. Mary Lizzie married Michael Morrison, Frenchvale, had a family, and moved to the United States. Stephen James, a grandson of James N.P., lives now on the family property in Iona. He married Mary (Dan S.) MacNeil, MacNeil's Vale (see **122**) and their family: Dan S., Stephen Osmond, Genevieve, and Sandra Rhodena. **244**

James Jr. (James "Pearson") married Annie (James, Eoin) MacNeil, Iona (see **77**). They lived in Iona and their family: Flora, Mary, Maggie, Sarah, Mary Ann, James F., Alex P., Frank, and John. **245**

Flora (James Jr., James "Pearson") was the first wife of Paul MacKinnon, Iona Rear (see **458**) and had a family. Mary married Rory P. MacNeil, Iona Rear (see **217**) and had a family that died young. Maggie married John A. MacKinnon, Iona Rear (see **463**) and had a family. Sarah married Angus MacMillan, MacKay's Corner in Glace Bay and had a family. Mary Ann married first a Mr. O'Handley in the United States, had a son; and in a second marriage she married Amos Curry in the United States. James F. married a daughter of Donald Chisholm, Antigonish, lives in Inverness, and had a large family. Frank married, had a family in Truro, and moved to the United States. John died young.

Alex P. (James Jr., James "Pearson") married first Mary Ann MacLeod, Benacadie. They lived in Iona and their family: Mary Ann, Alice, Cecilia, Ann, Angus, James, Norman, Dan Neil, John Peter, and Malcolm. In a second marriage he married Mary Ann MacNeil, Barra Glen, widow of Donald (Iain, Domhnull) MacNeil, Gillis Point (see **102**) and had no family. **246**

> Mary Ann (Alex P.) married first Jack Sinclair in the United States, and in a second marriage she married Art Smith, Vancouver. Alice married Donald Cox and lived in Truro. Cecilia married Gilbert Gordon, Halifax and had a family. Ann became a Sister of St. Martha. Angus died young. James married, had a family, and lives in Antigonish. Norman married Rose MacNeil, Point Tupper, had a family and lives in Halifax. Dan Neil married, lived in Antigonish, had a family, and died as a result of a fire accident. John Peter married first Kay MacNeil, Hay Cove, lived in Sydney, had a family; and in a second marriage he married Eileen MacNeil, Stellarton and lives in Sydney. Malcolm married, had a family, and lives in Oshawa, Ontario.

● ● ●

Neil "Mor" MacNeil came to Ottawa Brook from East Bay. He married a daughter of John, brother of Rory "Mor" MacNeil (see **35a**). They lived in Ottawa Brook and their family: Dan Y., Neil, John J., Christy, Katie, Maggie, and Mary Sarah. **247**

John J. (Neil "Mor") married Margaret Jane (Hector, Neil) MacLean, Ottawa Brook (see **535**), lived in Sydney and had a large family, two of whom became priests in the Diocese of Antigonish and one the Provincial Superior of the Sisters of Notre Dame. Neil died as a young man. Christy died unmarried in the United States. Maggie married Angus Jackson, Boston and had a family. Katie married Timothy Riordan, Boston and had no family. Mary Sarah married Neil S. (John G.) MacKinnon, MacKinnon's Harbour (see **468**), lived in MacKinnon's Harbour, and had a family.

Dan Y. (Neil "Mor") married Eliza, sister to John J.'s wife and widow of a Mr. MacLellan, Margaree from whom she had no family (see **535**). They lived in Ottawa Brook and their family: Neil, Bessie, Rita, Mickey, Laura, Andrew, Andrew's twin sister who died in infancy, Archie, Mary Peter, and William.   **248**

Neil (Dan Y.) is unmarried. Bessie married Neil S. MacNeil, Irish Cove, lived in Boston, and had a family. Rita married Angus MacNeil, St. Rose, lives in Sydney, and has a family. Mickey died young. Laura married James (Joseph "Doctor") MacNeil, Red Point (see **230**) and has a family. Archie married Margaret (Michael, Rory Alex) MacNeil, Iona (see **214**), lives in Sydney, and has a family. Mary Peter married Angus MacDonald, Glace Bay, lives in Saskatoon, and has a family.

Andrew (Dan Y.) married Mary Ellen MacDonald, Estmere. They lived in Ottawa Brook and their family: Jackie, Gordon, Hugh, Franklin, and Shirley.   **249**

William (Dan Y.) married Mildred (Hugh N.) Gillis, MacKinnon's Harbour (see **332**). They lived in MacKinnon's Harbour and their family: Alphonsus who died in infancy, Theresa and Lily (twins), Meliton, Leonarda and Gillis.   **250**

● ● ●

Michael "Saor" or "Carpenter" MacNeil who settled in Red Point and Alexander MacNeil who settled in Ottawa Brook were brothers.

Michael "Saor" lived in Red Point on the property later owned by George Small. Michael "Saor" married Ann (Neil, Barra) MacNeil, Red Point (see **33**) and is reported to have had a son on whom we have no information. When Michael "Saor" died, his property was taken by Malcolm D. (Donald "Mor") MacNeil (see **43**) who was married to Catherine (Ben) MacNeil (see **35**). Malcolm D. and Catherine had no family. When Malcolm D. died, his widow married George Small, continued to live on the property, and had a family. **251**

Alexander MacNeil married Jessie or Seonaid (Rory "Mor") MacDonald, MacKinnon's Harbour (see **391**) and settled on land immediately East of the present Walker property in Ottawa Brook. His family was: Alexander, a daughter who married John B. MacKinnon, Highland Hill (see **453**), Catherine who married Donald Walker, Ottawa Brook (see **575**), and probably others. **252**

Alexander (Alexander) or, as he was commonly called by his mother's name Alexander (Seonaid), married a daughter of John (Charles) MacKinnon, MacKinnon's Harbour (see **475**). They lived in Ottawa Brook and their family: Mary Ann, John Alex, Joseph, and Katie "Beag." **253**

Joseph (Alexander, Seonaid) and Mary Ann died unmarried. Katie "Beag" married Fred McCluskey, Grand Falls, N.B., lived in Ottawa Brook, and had no family. They adopted George, who was killed in World War II, and Margaret.

John Alex (Alexander, Seonaid) married Lizzie (Peter B.) MacDonald, Ottawa Brook (see **352**). They lived in Ottawa Brook, had no family, but they adopted two: Leo (Joseph) Bonaparte and Genevieve MacNeil. **254**

● ● ●

Donald (Iain Domhnull ic Iain) MacNeil, Red Point married Katie (Donald "Mor") MacKinnon, MacKinnon's Harbour (see **486**). They lived in MacKinnon's Harbour and their family: John D., Dan, and Hugh. They also adopted two: Mary, commonly called "Maisheag," and Molly. **255**

John D. (Donald Iain Domhnull ic Iain), a Captain in the Boer War, married twice, had a family from his first wife, and lived his latter years in Grand Narrows. Hugh went to the United States. Dan married Molly Redquest, Red Point (see **571**), lived in Sydney, and had a family. "Maisheag" married Hector MacEachern, a blacksmith from Arichat (see **34**), and had a son Simon who had a large family in Glace Bay. (Molly married Malcolm Morrison, St. Ann's, lived in Sydney, and had a family.)

● ● ●

Stephen (Alasdair) MacNeil, Grand Narrows, who settled in Grass Cove, was a direct descendant of Roderick MacNeil, Laird of Barra. The Laird had a son James, who had a son Hector, who came from Barra and settled in Grand Narrows about 1804. Stephen (Alasdair) was this Hector's grandson. He married Catherine (Hector, John "Ban") MacNeil, Grand Narrows, settled in Grass Cove, and their family: James S., Jim Hugh, Alex, Isabelle, and Kate. **256**

Jim Hugh (Stephen, Alasdair) married and had a family in Sydney. Alex died unmarried. Isabelle married Dan A. (James) MacDonald, St. Columba (see **360**), lived in Iona, and had a family. Katie married in the United States.

James S. (Stephen, Alasdair) married Mary Ann (John "Saor") MacInnis, Iona (see **408**). They lived in Grass Cove and their family: John Stephen, Joseph, Roddie, Sylvester, Margaret, Annie May, and Mary Belle. **257**

John Stephen (James S.), Joseph, Roddie, and Sylvester are unmarried. Margaret married Frank Vitelli, Agincourt in Ontario and has a family. Annie May married Allan Booth, Agincourt in Ontario and has a family. Mary Belle married Allan Dixon, lives in Calgary, and has a family.

● ● ●

James (John) MacNeil, known as "Lieutenant," settled in Grass Cove on the property East of that which once belonged to Stephen (Alasdair) MacNeil. He served in the Armed Forces and this explains the label "Lieutenant." He married Mary Ann (Archibald) MacDougall, Christmas Island and their family: John Archibald and Mary Ann. **258**

John Archibald (James "Lieutenant") died unmarried. Mary Ann married John D. (Donald, Norman) MacNeil, Piper's Cove, lived in Grass Cove, and had a family.

● ● ●

John D. "Blacksmith" (Donald, Norman) MacNeil, Piper's Cove married Mary Ann (James "Lieutenant") MacNeil, Grass Cove (see **258**). After residing elsewhere for a time, he settled on the property of his father-in-law in Grass Cove. Here he built a forge and continued his trade of blacksmith for many years. He was interested also in politics and was Councillor for District No. 18 for a number of terms. When the Gypsum Plant was built in Grass Cove in 1914, he built a combined home and general store at the juncture of the Gillis Point and St. Columba highways. Thus he provided a general store for the community and a boarding house for persons working in the plant. His family was: James, Daniel, Maria, Maggie, and Eliza. After the death of his wife, he married a MacNeil woman from Boisdale. **259**

Daniel (John D.) married in the United States, had a family, lived for a time in Iona, and later moved to the Nova Scotia mainland. Marie married a Mr. Deveau, Little Bras d'Or, had a family, lived for a time in Iona, and, after the death of her husband, moved away with her family. Maggie married a Mr. Bagnell, lived in Sydney, and had a family. Eliza married John Young, Little Bras d'Or, lived in Little Bras d'Or, and had a family.

James (John D.) married Lucy (Neil S.) MacNeil, Gillis Point (see **17**). They lived in Grass Cove and their family: Duncan, Joseph Neil, and Columba. **260**

● ● ●

Francis F. (Mor Ruairi) MacNeil, Barra Glen married Margaret (James, Michael) MacDonald, St. Columba (see **359**). They lived in Barra Glen and had an adopted family: John Anderson, Margaret Burke, Annie MacNeil, and Bennie MacNeil. **261**

MACNEIL

For John Anderson see **274**. For Margaret Burke see **68**. For Bennie MacNeil see **93**. Annie MacNeil married a Mr. White in Ontario and had a family.

● ● ●

Eoin MacNeil came from Scotland with the family of Lachlan MacLean and settled in Washabuck Center. He married Mary "Mhor" (Lachlan) MacLean, Washabuck (see **487**) and had a large family: Michael, Angus, Ann, Flora, "Big" Betsy, Theresa, Catherine, a daughter whose name we do not know, and quite likely others who died young. **262**

Ann (Eoin) married Donald (Rory "Miller") MacDougall, Big Beach and had a family. Flora and Catherine married MacPhee brothers, Shenacadie and had families. "Big" Betsy and Theresa were unmarried. Angus married Christena (Rory "Miller") MacDougall, Big Beach and their family: Hector, Sarah, and Alexander who was brother-in-law of Francis X.S. MacNeil, Iona and father-in-law of Joseph (Iain "Ban") MacKinnon, Highland Hill. Eoin's daughter whose name we do not know had a daughter Isabel, who was brought up by her uncle Michael (see **263**), married a Mr. MacEachern in Columbus, Ohio, and had a family, one of whom was Reverend Roderick A. MacEachern, who spoke seven languages, wrote many books, lived in Rome for several years, and became an authority on the Roman catacombs (see also **452**).

Michael (Eoin) married Lucy (Murdock "Beag") MacNeil, Upper Washabuck (see **268**). They lived in Washabuck and their family: Johnnie A., Theresa, Mary, Joseph, Alex, Michael, Ellen, Mary Ann, and Isabel (niece of Michael) whom they adopted (see **262**). **263**

Theresa (Michael) married Vincent (Peter Francis) Mac-Lean, MacKay's Point in Washabuck (see **505**) and had a large family. Mary married John Campbell, Washabuck and had no family. Joseph spent most of his life in the North West Territory, had a family of four who died young, and spent his last days in Iona. Alex, known as "Captain Alex," lived in Washabuck, and with his sister Mary, who was unmarried at the time, brought up Donald Porter and Elizabeth Ongo, both of whom married later in Western Canada, as well as Stella who later married and had a family in the United States. Michael, known as "Captain Michael," married in the United States and had a family. Ellen and Mary went to the United States and had families there.

Johnnie A. (Michael) married a daughter of John (Rory, Neil) MacNeil, Washabuck (see **266**). They lived for a time in Washabuck and moved to the United States. Their family was: Neil F., Murdock, Lucy, and a girl who died in infancy. **264**

> Neil F. (Johnnie A.), a Night Editor of the *New York Times* and author of *Highland Heart of Nova Scotia*, was honoured by his Alma Mater in Antigonish with the degree LL.D. *honoris causa*. Murdock was killed in World War I. Lucy married Jack Hayes, Montreal and had a daughter who died in infancy.

● ● ●

Neil "Geal" MacNeil, one of the "Piper's" of Piper's Cove, came from Scotland. He married Catherine (Angus "Og") MacLean in Scotland. They settled in Washabuck and their family: Ann, Catherine, Christy, Lucy, Jane, Rory and John. **265**

Ann (Neil "Geal") married Neil (Lachlan) MacLean in Scotland, came to Cape Breton in 1817, and had a family (see **488**). Catherine married Donald (Philip) MacKinnon, Lower Washabuck (see **479**) and had a family. Christy married Malcolm (Rory Donald "Og") MacNeil, Barra Glen (see **1**) and had a family. Lucy married John "Ban" (Hugh) Gillis, Jamesville West (see **334**) and had a family. Jane married John (Murdock) MacNeil, Gillis Point (see **25**) and had a family. John died young.

Rory (Neil "Geal"), a carpenter, married Mary (Hector, John "Og") MacKinnon. They lived in Lower Washabuck and their family: Hector, John, Michael, Neil, Ann, Mary, and Kate. **266**

> Hector (Rory) married Catherine (John, Neil "Ban") MacNeil, had this family: Sarah, Katie, George, and John, and went to the United States. John married Helen Murphy and had a daughter who married Johnnie A. (Michael, Eoin) MacNeil, Washabuck (see **264**). Michael married

Ann Mahoney, Antigonish, and their family: Mary and Bessie. Neil, a millionaire, lived in the United States, married Susan Jordan, had no family, and was honoured by Saint Francis Xavier University in Antigonish with the degree LL.D. *honoris causa* for his financial assistance to that institution. Ann married John (Murdock) MacNeil, Upper Washabuck (see **269**), lived in Washabuck, and had a family. Katie died young. Mary married first Michael (Murdock) MacNeil, had a son Murdock who was a builder in Boston; and in a second marriage she married Peter (Neil, Hector) MacNeil, Gillis Point (see **89**) and had a family.

● ● ●

'Red" Dan MacNeil, formerly of Piper's Cove, married Margaret Ann (Hugh, Darby) Campbell, Jamesville (see **300**). They lived in Jamesville and their family: John Pat, Mary Elizabeth, and Sadie May. **267**

John Pat ("Red" Dan) was unmarried. Mary Elizabeth and Sadie May became Sisters of Charity.

● ● ●

Murdock "Beag" (Donald "Piper") MacNeil settled in Washabuck Bridge. He married, in Barra, Nellie Robertson, daughter of Robertson of the Kirk Sessions of Barra, and their family: Hector, John, Ann, Michael, Mary, Peggy, Lucy, and Sarah. **268**

Ann (Murdock "Beag") married John "Soldier" MacDonald, Grand Narrows and had a family. Mary married Sandy MacNeil, Big Beach and had a family. Hector married and lived in Baddeck. Peggy married Paul (Neil, Lachlan) MacLean, Washabuck Center (see **500**) and had a family. Sarah married Hector (Neil) MacLean, Washabuck (see **499**) and had a family. Lucy married Michael (Eoin) MacNeil, Upper Washabuck (see **263**) and had a family.

John (Murdock "Beag") married Ann (Rory, Neil) MacNeil, Washabuck (see **266**). They lived in Upper Washabuck and their family: Hector, Murdock, Joe, Dan Murdock, Mary Ann, Katie,

Ann, Margaret, and Nellie. **269**

Nellie (John) and Margaret lived in Boston. Ann married a Mr. Cadegan and lived away. Katie married John C. MacNeil, Grand Narrows. Mary Ann married John E. Campbell, Baddeck. Joe, a builder, lived in San Francisco. Murdock died in Boston. Hector, known as "Black Hector," lived in Baddeck. We have no information on Dan Murdock.

Michael (Murdock "Beag"), a blacksmith, lived in Iona. He married Jane MacIntyre, Big Pond and had a son, a merchant at Grand Narrows, who married Josephine (Norman) MacNeil, Arichat. **270**

● ● ●

Malcolm MacNeil, known as "Calum I' Ruadh" and whose father settled in Christmas Island, settled in Washabuck Bridge. He married Katie (Allan, Donald "Ban") MacKinnon, MacKinnon's Harbour (see **465**). They had no family but they adopted Mary, known as "Mary Red," who married Jack (Peter) Murphy (see **561**). Our friend, Neil Devoe, informs us that Calum I' Ruadh had a brother James, who married Mary Ban of P.E.I., and who had two children who died young and are buried on a Washabuck hillside. **271**

● ● ●

Malcolm "Ruadh" MacNeil, of whom we know little, lived in Washabuck Center on the property later owned by Murdock (Paul) MacLean. He married a woman from Grand Narrows and their family: Michael and Nancy. **272**

Michael (Malcolm "Ruadh") did not marry. Nancy married William Munroe (see **555**) and had no family.

● ● ●

Jonathan (Seamus) MacNeil, Grand Narrows settled in Iona in 1804. He married Mary (Iain, Eachain) Campbell, sister of Malcolm Campbell, Barra Glen (see **36**). Their family was: Hector, Annie, and Elizabeth. **273**

MACNEIL

Hector (Jonathan, Seamus) was drowned in Gillis Point Harbour. Elizabeth was drowned while crossing the Barra Strait on the ice. Annie married Donald (Calum "Ban") MacDonald, Grand Narrows, lived in Boston, where her daughter Margaret married Hector "Framer" MacKenzie, Washabuck (see **434**), and became the mother of the famed missionary, Reverend Charles MacKenzie, C.M.

● ● ●

Malcolm Dan (Norman D.) MacNeil, Benacadie settled in Grass Cove after World War I. He had married Christy (Peter) MacDonald, Boisdale and their family: Norman, Mary, Peter, Dorothy, Angus, Patsy, Malcolm, Cathy, and a daughter who died in infancy. In 1950 the family moved to Halifax. 273a

● ● ●

John Anderson, adopted son of Francis F. MacNeil, Barra Glen (see **261**) married Mary Connolly from Ireland. They lived in Barra Glen and their family: Annie, Agnes, Martin, and John. **274**

● ● ●

Walter Arsenault from P.E.I. married Margaret (Neil H.) MacNeil, Barra Glen (see **238**). They lived in Barra Glen and their family: Joan, Neil, Ernie, Donnie, and twins who died young. **275**

● ● ●

Seward and Joseph Bonaparte, brothers, came from Soldier's Cove and settled in MacKinnon's Harbour, Seward in 1918 and Joseph in 1919. Both were already married and had part of their families.

Seward married Sadie (Michael, Alasdair) MacDonald, James- ville West (see **369**) and their family: Nora May, Michael Charlie, Angus Louis, Seward Joseph, Sadie Madeline, John Alex, Roddie James, Gregory, Isabel, Stephen, Donald, Tena May, along with a son and two daughters who died in in- fancy. **276**

Roddie James (Seward) married, in England during World War II, Daphne Muldoon and, after the war, settled in MacKinnon's Harbour. He had a large family. The rest of Seward's family also married and had families of their own, ten of them in Sydney, and the remaining one in Reserve Mines. Four of them married natives of the parish: Angus Louis who married Josephine (Charles) Northen, Ottawa Brook (see **568**); Sadie Madeline and Isabel who married Neil Peter and Mickey, sons of John J. MacLean, formerly of Ottawa Brook (see **537**); and John Alex who married Catherine (Angus) MacLellan, Ottawa Brook (see **543** **277**

Joseph was married twice before he came to MacKinnon's Harbour, and both times to a Miss Mombourquette. His family from the first wife was: Annie May, Bertha, and Cecilia who died in infancy. His family from the second wife was: Rita, Charlie, Cecilia, Kathleen, Nora, Abe, Felix, Annie, Leo who was adopted by John Alex (Seonaid) MacNeil, Ottawa Brook (see **254**), and a son and two daughters who died in infancy. **278**

Annie May (Joseph) married first a Mr. MacSween, lived in Sydney, had a family; and in a second marriage she married a Mr. Bailey, lived in Sydney, and had a family. Bertha married Colin MacLeod, adopted son of Ambrose (John G.) MacKinnon, MacKinnon's Harbour (see **467**) and had a family. Rita married and has a family in Sydney. Charlie lives in Sydney and has an adopted son. Cecilia married John Malcolm (Michael D.) MacNeil, Red Point (see **46**), lives in Red Point, and has a family. Kathleen married Leonard (John Archie) MacLean, Ottawa Brook (see **541**), lives in Ottawa Brook, and has a family. Nora married in Quebec and has a family.

● ● ●

John C. Boyd, a school teacher and a justice of the peace, lived and taught in Washabuck for some years. He married Catherine (Malcolm, Lachlan Malcolm) MacLean, Washabuck (see **503**) and had a family. After his death, his widow married Joseph Arsenault, Cheticamp and they are believed to have lived in Baddeck. There are no Boyds in the parish today. **279**

● ● ●

John Brown from Northern Cape Breton married Mary (Peggy, Calum William) MacDougall, Washabuck (see **402**). They lived in Washabuck and their family: Johnnie, Michael, Dan, Angus, Calum, and Maggie who died young. All died unmarried. **280**

● ● ●

Malcolm (John, Hector) Campbell came from Scotland to Cape Breton in 1817. He had a sister Mary, who was the second wife of Rory "Mor" (Donald, Rory) MacNeil, Iona (see **36**) and the widow of Jonathan (Seamus) MacNeil, Iona (see **273**). Malcolm had lived in Uist for a time as a shoemaker, and then he returned to his native Barra. By this time, so many of his friends had migrated to the New World, that he decided to follow after them. When he came to Cape Breton, he searched for his friend, Rory (Donald "Og") MacNeil who, with his brother Ben had settled in Rear Christmas Island about four years earlier. Most of the land in that area had already been taken, so Malcolm and Rory (Donald "Og") "granted" land in Barra Glen, approximately seven hundred acres of it. Malcolm and Rory settled side-by-side, and Rory's son-in-law took land to the North of them. Malcolm had married Catherine MacLeod in Uist and their family: Hugh, Archibald, John, Catherine, Elizabeth, and Peggy. **281**

John (Malcolm, John Hector) married in Sydney Mines. Catherine married Stephen (James) MacDonald, Washabuck (see **366**) and had a family. Elizabeth died unmarried. Peggy was the second wife of Hugh (Domhnull, Ruairi) MacNeil, Iona Rear (see **196**), lived in St. Columba, and had a family.

Hugh (Malcolm, John Hector) married first Mary (Malcolm "Red") MacNeil, Iona Rear (see **206**). They settled in Barra Glen and their family: Rory H., Catherine, Sarah, and Mary Ann. In a second marriage he married Sarah (Rory "Glen Mor") MacNeil, Barra Glen (see **9**) and their family: Malcolm and Rory. **282**

Rory (Hugh, Malcolm John Hector) died unmarried. Catherine married Michael S. (Stephen) MacNeil, Barra Glen (see **12**), lived in Barra Glen, and had a family. Sarah married Rory S. (Stephen) MacNeil, Barra Glen (see **15**), lived in Barra Glen, and had a family. Mary Ann married Donald (Iain, Domhnull) MacNeil, Gillis Point (see **102**), lived in Gillis Point, had a son John Hugh who was killed, as a young man, in a mining accident; and in second marriage she married Alex P. (James "Pearson"), Iona (see **246**), and had no family. Rory H. married Elizabeth (John Mac Iain "Og") MacNeil, Benacadie, lived in Newfoundland, and their family: Margaret and Catherine.

CAMPBELL

Malcolm (Hugh, Malcolm John Hector) married Eliza (Archibald "Red") MacKenzie, Washabuck (see **427**). They lived in St. Columba and their family: Archibald, Sarah Margaret, Hugh, and Angus. **283**

Archibald (Malcolm) died young. Sarah Margaret married Robert Bonvie, Tracadie, lived in Tracadie, and had no family. Angus, a medical doctor and radiologist in Halifax, married and has a family in Halifax. Hugh is unmarried.

Archibald (Malcolm, John Hector) married first Mary (Eoin, "Glas") MacNeil, Jamesville. They lived in Barra Glen and had a daughter Elizabeth who lived in the United States. In a second marriage he married Christy (Malcolm "Mor") MacNeil, Rear Iona (see **206**) and their family: Rory "Mor," Rory "Beag," Paul, Sally Ann, and Malcolm. The family moved to the United States and all married there, except Malcolm. In a third marriage, Archibald married Flora (Alexander) MacDougall, Red Point (see **393**) and their family: Alex, Hugh, Mary, and Bessie. **284**

Hugh (Archibald, Malcolm John Hector) died unmarried. Mary married a Mr. Bouzzan in the United States, had two sons — William and George — who were brought up by their uncle Alex in Red Point. Bessie married George MacNeil, Grand Narrows and died soon after her marriage.

Alex (Archibald, Malcolm John Hector) married Christy (Rory I) MacNeil, Red Point (see **41a**). They lived in Red Point and had a daughter Mary who lives unmarried in Point Edward. **285**

● ● ●

Malcolm Campbell, the first Campbell to come to Iona, married Flora (Donald "Ban") MacNeil (see **164**) and their family: Angus, Mary, and Sarah. **286**

Mary, daughter of the pioneer Campbell to Iona, married Rory

CAMPBELL

"Mor" MacNeil, one of the first four MacNeils to come to Iona (see **36**). Sarah married Malcolm (Rory, Donald "Og") MacNeil, Barra Glen (see **2**).

Angus, son of the pioneer Campbell to Iona, married Jessie MacNeil. They lived in Iona and had a son Malcolm. **287**

Malcolm (Angus) married Christy (Neil, Domhnull) MacNeil, Jamesville (see **172**). They lived in Iona and their family: Peter, Annie and John. **288**

John (Malcolm) died unmarried. Peter married in Sydney and had a family. Annie married Peter McLaughlin, lived in Sydney, had a family, two of whom became priests in the Diocese of Antigonish.

• • •

Hugh Campbell, who settled in Gillis Point East, was apparently a nephew of Malcolm, the pioneer Campbell to Iona (see **286**). The Campbells in Boisdale are apparently the same Campbells. Hugh's family was: Allan, George, Angus, and Sarah. **289**

Sarah (Hugh) married Rory (Hector "Mor") MacNeil, Iona (see **143**), lived in Gillis Point, and had a family.

Allan (Hugh) married Catherine (Hector "Mor") MacNeil, Iona (see **142**). They lived in Gillis Point East and their family: Angus, Hughie, Dan, Hector, Annie, Mary and Margaret. **290**

Angus (Allan, Hugh), Dan, and Margaret died unmarried. Hughie, still a young man, was accidentally killed. Annie married Alfred Tucker, Truro and had a family. Mary married Alex Tucker and had a family.

CAMPBELL

Hector (Allan, Hugh) married Mary (John, Alasdair "Mor") MacNeil, Gillis Point (see **130**). They lived in Gillis Point and their family: Catherine Margaret, John A., Daniel Joseph, and Angus J. **291**

Catherine Margaret (Hector) married Michael F. (John) MacInnis, Iona (see **409**), lived in Iona, and had a family. Angus J. died unmarried. Daniel Joseph is unmarried.

John A. (Hector) married Mary (Hector) MacDonald, Grass Cove (see **386**). They lived in Grass Cove and their family: Mary, Margaret, John, and Catherine. **292**

George (Hugh) had this family: Peter, Mary, and another daughter. **293**

Mary (George) married Stephen "Banker" MacNeil, Iona (see **167**), lived in Gillis Point East, and had a family.

Peter (George) married Elizabeth (Peter S.) MacLean, Washabuck (see **517**). They had a son Joseph S. **294**

Joseph S. (Peter) married Margaret Jessome and their family: Eliza, Elizabeth, and William. **295**

Angus (Hugh) married Flora MacLean, Washabuck (see **513**). They lived in Gillis Point and their family: Dan, Lauchlin, and Maggie. **296**

Lauchlin (Angus, Hugh) died young. Maggie died unmarried.

Dan (Angus, Hugh) married Sarah (Allan, Alasdair) MacNeil, Gillis Point (see **135**). They lived in Gillis Point and their family: Angus, Mary, Agnes, Michael, Alex, Lauchlin, and Florence whom they adopted. **297**

CAMPBELL

Donald (Hector) Campbell settled first in Irish Cove where his brother Colin had already settled. Later he moved to Jamesville East. His family was: Darby, Hector "Ban," Anna, Katie, and Peggy "Red." **298**

Anna (Donald, Hector) died unmarried. Katie married James "Mor" MacNeil, Jamesville (see **178**) and had a family. Peggy "Red" married Neil (Donald) MacNeil, Jamesville (see **171**) and had a family.

Darby (Donald, Hector) married Annie (Rory, Donald "Og") MacNeil, Barra Glen (see **1**). They lived in Jamesville East and their family: James, Hugh, Sarah, Jane, Donald, and two others. **299**

Jane (Darby, Donald Hector) died unmarried. Donald married in Mabou and had a family. Sarah married Donald (Allan, Donald) MacLean, Washabuck (see **522**). Another member of the family married a man from Arichat. Still another married John MacSween, Low Point.

Hugh (Darby, Donald Hector) married Sarah (John, Norman) MacNeil, Piper's Cove. They lived in Jamesville East and their family: John, Dan, Katie, Mary Ann, Darby, and Margaret Ann. **300**

Darby (Hugh) was killed in World War I. Katie married Archibald MacKenzie, Rear Christmas Island and had a family. Mary Ann married a Mr. Healy in the United States and had a family. Margaret Ann married "Red" Dan MacNeil, Piper's Cove, lived in Jamesville, and had a family (see **267**).

John (Hugh) married Margaret (Sandy) MacNeil, Benacadie. They lived in Jamesville East, had a family, and moved to New Waterford. **301**

Dan (Hugh) married first Sarah (Donald, James) MacNeil

CAMPBELL

(see **80**). They lived in Jamesville East and their family: Mary Sarah, Agnes, and Dan Joe. In a second marriage he married Bessie (Malcolm) MacLeod, Benacadie and their family: Sadie, Margaret, Jerry, Angus, and Hugh. All the family of Dan (Hugh) moved away from the parish. **302**

James (Darby, Donald Hector) married Sarah (Iain "Saighdear") MacDonald, Grand Narrows. They lived in Jamesville and their family: Darby, Colin, John Francis, Michael, Jane, Annie, Mary, and Lucy. **303**

Darby (James) and Mary died unmarried. John Francis and Michael died young. Jane married James C. (Iain, Alasdair) MacNeil, Gillis Point (see **131**), lived in Gillis Point, and had a family. Annie and Lucy both married Gillises from Rear Christmas Island and had families.

Colin (James) married Catherine Beaton, Mabou. They lived in Jamesville and their family: John James, John Francis, Michael, and a daughter who died in infancy. **304**

Hector "Ban" (Donald, Hector) settled in Jamesville. With the exception of Colin, his family all died young. **305**

Colin (Hector, "Ban," Donald Hector) married Catherine (Eoin "Mor") MacNeil, Jamesville East (see **58**). They lived in Jamesville East and had a family. A daughter Mary Sarah married Charles S. (James, Hector) MacNeil, Red Point (see **93**), lived in Red Point, and had a family. Other children died young. **306**

•   •   •

Donald Campbell was married in Barra to Mary Pheadair. His sons, Donald and Angus, settled in Grand Narrows, and his son, Neil, settled in Jamesville West. **307**

CAMPBELL

Neil (Donald) Campbell married Peggy (Hugh) Gillis, Jamesville West (see 325) and their family: Rory I, Hugh, Stephen, Donald, James I, James II, Angus, Joseph, Mary, Michael, and Rory II. They also adopted James, who was a son of Angus (Donald) in Grand Narrows. **308**

Hugh (Neil, Donald) married Lucy (Donald "Halifax") MacKenzie, lived in Arichat, and had a family. Stephen married Ann MacNeil and had a family. Donald and Angus settled in Grand Narrows. Joseph, a sea-captain, married Catherine MacNeil and had a family. Michael married Ann MacEachern and had a family. Rory II married Sarah (Eoin, Niall) MacNeil (see **116**), and had a family. James was drowned soon after his marriage. Mary married Murdock (Eoin, Plant) MacNeil, Barra Glen (see 7), lived in Barra Glen, and had a family.

Rory I (Neil, Donald) married first Theresa (Allan, Domhnull "Ban") MacKinnon, MacKinnon's Harbour (see **465**). They lived in Jamesville West and their family: Angus, Michael R., and Donald, all of whom died unmarried. In a second marriage he married Maggie (Aonghas, Eoin) MacNeil, Highland Hill (see **183**) and their family: Angus R., John R., and Theresa. **309**

Theresa (Rory I, Neil Donald) married first Rod M. (Michael, Calum "Mor") MacNeil, Iona Rear (see **207**) and had a son Michael Roddie who died unmarried. In a second marriage she married Rory MacNeil, Glace Bay, lived in Glace Bay, and had a family.

John R. (Rory I, Neil Donald), a merchant in Jamesville West, married Nellie Scott, Truro and their family: Roddie, Arthur, Frank, Victor, Ethel, Helena and Catherine. **310**

Arthur (John R.), a merchant, and Victor are unmarried. Helena became a Sister of Charity. Ethel married John F. Kennedy, Mulgrave, lived in Truro, and had no family. Catherine married and had a family in Western Canada.

CAMPBELL

Roddie (John R.) married Tena MacDonald, Ottawa Brook. They lived in Jamesville West, had no family, but adopted a son Stanley. **311**

Frank (John R.) married Patsy O'Donnell, adopted daughter of Philip O'Donnell, Jamesville West (see **570**). They lived in MacKinnon's Harbour and had a daughter Marion. **312**

Angus R. (Rory I, Neil Donald) married Jessie, sister of John R.'s wife. They lived in Shubenacadie where he was the C.N.R. Station Agent. Their family: Donald S. and John R., both of whom became priests in the Archdiocese of Halifax.

James I (Neil, Donald), commonly known as "Shapa," married Katie (Iain, Alasdair) MacNeil, Gillis Point (see **130**). They lived in Jamesville West and their family: Neil J.R., Roddie, Alexander, Margaret, Sadie, Florence and Mary Jane. **313**

Roddie (James, Neil Donald) married and had a family in Western Canada. Alexander, a famed physician and surgeon in the United States who was honoured by Saint Francis Xavier University with the degree LL.D. *honoris causa*, married Marie MacPherson, lived in Boston, and had a family. Margaret, a nurse, married Edward A. MacNeil, Iona (see **30**), lived in Iona, and had a family. Florence married a Mr. Mulane and had a family in the United States. Mary Jane married a Mr. MacDonald and had a family in the United States. Sadie married James M. "Red" (Malcolm) MacNeil, Jamesville (see **181**), lived in Jamesville, and had a family.

Neil J.R. (James, Neil Donald) married Mary Sarah (John R.) MacNeil, Piper's Cove. They lived in Jamesville West and their family: Kathleen, Theresa, Florence, James, Pius, Jackie, and Francis. **314**

Theresa (Neil J.R.) married William MacCabe and had a family in Halifax. Florence married Walter MacNeil and has a family in Sydney. Pius married Pauline Mackley and has no family. Francis is married in Ontario. James became a priest in the Diocese of Antigonish. Kathleen, unmarried,

CAMPBELL

teaches in Calgary. Jackie is unmarried.

● ● ●

James (Angus) Campbell, commonly called "Shapa Beag," lived in Jamesville West. He was a nephew of Neil (Donald) Campbell and adopted by him. He married Mary Ann (Archie "Ruadh") MacKenzie, Birch Point in Washabuck (see **427**) and their family: Josephine and Sadie who sent to the United States. **315**

● ● ●

Archie Campbell, Iona was the son of Flora (Rory "Mor") MacNeil, Iona (see **36**) and Michael Campbell, Antigonish and Margaree. Archie's father had been married before and, after the death of his wife from whom he had a son, he came to Iona, leaving the son in Margaree. After he remarried in Iona, he returned to Margaree where he set about building a new home to which to bring his second wife. Unfortunately he was drowned in the Margaree Harbour, and before his son Archie was born in Iona. Archie married Ann (John, Domhnull) MacNeil, Gillis Point (see **99**). They lived in Iona and their family: John Francis, Dan Rory, Elizabeth, Mary Ann, and Michael. **316**

Michael (Archie) married a Miss MacIsaac, Big Pond, lived in Sydney, and had a family. Dan Rory, Elizabeth, and Mary Ann were unmarried.

John Francis (Archie) married Elizabeth Ann (Donald, Donald "Beag") MacNeil, Iona (see **56**). They lived in Iona and their family: Leo, Andy, Bernard, Stanley, and Marie. **317**

● ● ●

Arthur Campbell, adopted son of the widow of Rory R. MacNeil, Barra Glen (see **10**) married Mary MacDonald, adopted daughter of Sarah MacLean, Washabuck (see **510**). They lived in Iona and their family: Eulalia, Hughie, and Rhodena. **318**

● ● ●

Donald Campbell settled in MacNeil's Vale in the early 1800's.

He married Jane or Sine MacInnis, Lower Washabuck, a relative of the wife of Lachlan MacLean. Their son was known as "Eachain Ban."

Eachain "Ban" (Donald) married Mary (Philip, Donald) MacNeil, Gillis Point (see **96**). They lived in MacNeil's Vale and their family: Stephen, Philip, Dan H., Neil H., Betsy, Jane, Margaret, and John. With the exception of Stephen who lived unmarried in Gillis Point, the family moved to Baddeck. **319**

> John (Eachain "Ban") returned from Baddeck to Iona. He married Catherine, a daughter of "Banker," and lived on the "Banker" property (see **166**). He did not have a family of his own, but adopted Annie Morrison, who married John F. (Michael) MacInnis, Iona (see **410**), lived in Iona, and had a family. **320**

● ● ●

Donald Carmichael, born in Oban, Scotland, left the Old Country to settle in Cape Breton. When he arrived on this side of the Atlantic, the boat on which he made the crossing ran into a series of such fierce and prolonged storms, that he had to land in the Ingonish area. Later he came to Washabuck, lived there for a time, and then moved to his family to Frizzleton in Inverness County. **321**

● ● ●

Peter Devoe came from Little Bras d'Or to MacKinnon's Harbour. He married Christy (Donald "Og") Murphy, MacKinnon's Harbour (see **556**) and their family: Simon, Dan, and Magdalen. **322**

Magdalen (Peter) died unmarried.

Simon (Peter) married Helen (Hector, Eoin) MacKenzie, Washabuck (see **443**). They lived in Washabuck and their family: Tena, Neil, Mary Ann, and Tony MacNaughton whom they adopted. **323**

> Tena (Simon) married John Murdock (Ruairi, Neil) MacNeil, Gillis Point (see **109**), had a family; and in a second marriage she married Allan Alex (Alasdair, Neil)

MacNeil, Gillis Point (see **112**) and had a son Dennis who was drowned. Neil is unmarried. Mary Ann married John Stephen MacKenzie, Washabuck Bridge (see **436**).

Dan (Peter) married Catherine (Rory, Iain Eoin) MacDonald, Piper's Cove and their family: John, Minnie, Tena, Christy, Mary Ann, Annie, Joe, and Margaret. He married a second time and had no family. He married a third time, his third wife being Sarah Ann (Donald S.) MacNeil, Jamesville (see **66**), and had a daughter Magdalen. **324**

Margaret (Dan) was the first wife of Dan Neil (Michael John) Nash (see **567**), lived in Iona, and had a daughter Judy.

● ● ●

Bill Deveau came with his family to Grass Cove about the year 1925. He had married Florence MacMaster, Princeville in Inverness County and their family: Lawrence who died in Grass Cove as a young man, Rita who died before the family came to Grass Cove, Wilfred, Russell, and Nan. The family moved away about the year 1950. **324a**

● ● ●

Hugh Gillis, a native of Lorn, Argyllshire moved to Barra. He married Ann MacIntyre and their family: Rory, John "Ban," Margaret, Jane, Flora, and Catherine. Hugh was killed in the army and soon thereafter his widow and family — with the exception of Rory — migrated to the New World and settled in Jamesville West. **325**

Margaret (Hugh) married Neil (Donald) Campbell, Jamesville West (see **308**) and had a large family. Jane married Alex MacPhee in Shenacadie. Flora married Donald "Mor" MacKinnon, MacKinnon's Harbour (see **486**). Catherine married John MacNeil, Shenacadie.

GILLIS

Rory (Hugh) did not come with his mother and family at the time that they came to the New World. He was already married to Mary MacKinnon in Barra before he did come and, when he came, he settled in Gillis Point. It was from him that Gillis Point took its name. In about 1819, he left Gillis Point and came to settle near his mother, but by that time the Campbells had "granted" land in Jamesville West, and the MacKinnon brothers — Allan, John, and Charles — had "granted" land in MacKinnon's Harbour. So Rory Gillis had no option but to "grant" land between the MacKinnons on the East and Donald "Og" Murphy and Donald "Mor" MacKinnon on the West. Rory's family was: Catherine, James, Hugh, and Donald. **326**

Catherine (Rory) and Hugh died unmarried. James died a few days before his marriage.

Donald (Rory) married first Ann (John) MacInnis, Red Point (see **412**). They lived in MacKinnon's Harbour and their family: Flora and James. In a second marriage he married Flora (John, Donald Rory) MacNeil, Ottawa Brook (see **35a**) and their family: John Y., Margaret, Mary, Michael A.J., Dan R., Hugh N., Catherine, Hugh, Mary Jane, and Rory Joseph. **327**

Flora (Donald) married Peter (Rory) MacLean, Rear Ottawa Brook (see **527**) and had a family. Mary married Donald (Isabella) MacNeil, Jamesville (see **70**) and had twin daughters who died in infancy. Margaret married Michael Gallant in the United States and had a family. Mary Jane married James Fitzgerald in the United States and had no family. Catherine died unmarried in the United States. Hugh died young. Rory Joseph died unmarried.

James (Donald) married Lucy MacInnis, West Lake Ainslie. They lived in MacKinnon's Harbour and their family: Joseph, Mary Ann, Dan Joe, Charles, Roddie, and Neillie. **328**

Joseph (James) was killed on the railroad as a young man. Mary Ann died young. Charles died unmarried in the United States. Dan Joe married Mary Campbell from P.E.I., lived in Sydney, and had a daughter Marie. Roddie married Mary Aucoin, Reserve Mines,

GILLIS

lived in Westville, and had no family.

Neillie (James) married first Mary Catherine (Stephen J.) MacNeil, Jamesville (see **64**). They lived in MacKinnon's Harbour and had no family. In a second marriage he married Frances Ann (Rory, John Rory) MacNeil, Upper Washabuck (see **38**) and their family: Joseph, Camillus, and Rosaire. **329**

John Y. (Donald), a postmaster, married Flora (Donald) Walker, Ottawa Brook (see **575**). They lived in MacKinnon's Harbour and their family: Dolena, Dan Hugh I, Dan Hugh II, Catherine, Flora May, Alexina, and Josephine. **330**

Dolena (John Y.) married John Dan (Michael, Alasdair) MacDonald, Jamesville West (see **369**), lived in Sydney, and had a family. Catherine married Jimmy Sheilds in the United States and had no family. Dan Hugh I died in infancy. Dan Hugh II and Josephine were unmarried. Alexina married Douglas Fraser, Baddeck, lived away from the parish, and had a family. Flora May married Peter F. (Vincent) MacLean, Washabuck (see **506**), lived in Iona, and had a family.

Dan R. (Donald) married Helena MacDonald, Gillis Lake, lived in Red Point, and had no family. **331**

Hugh N. (Donald), a merchant, married Mary Lucy (Michael S.) MacNeil, Barra Glen (see **12**). They lived in MacKinnon's Harbour and their family: Wilfred, John Hugh, Mary, Marcy, Lex, Rose, Mildred, John Y., and Mary Catherine who died in infancy. **332**

Wilfred (Hugh N.), Rose, and John Y. were unmarried. John Hugh became a priest in the Diocese of Antigonish. Mary became a Sister of Charity. Marcy and Lex became priests in the Oblates of Mary Immaculate. Mildred married William (Dan Y.) MacNeil, Ottawa Brook (see **250**), lived in MacKinnon's Harbour, and had a family.

Michael A.J. (Donald) married first Maggie Belle (Allan, Michael "Mor") MacDonald, Iona (see **361**). They lived in Alba Station and their family: Marion, Florence, Rannie,

GILLIS

Lawrence and Mary Sarah or "Chippy." In a second marriage he married Annie (Malcolm, Michael) MacInnis, Iona (see **407**) and their family: Margaret, Rodriguez, and Charlie. **333**

> Marion (Michael A.J.) married Alex Livingstone in the United States and had a family. Florence married Bill Owens in the United States and had a family. Lawrence, as a young man, was drowned. Rannie married May (Joseph "Doctor") MacNeil, Red Point (see **229**), lived in Sydney, and their family: Ronald, Joseph, Lawrence, and Rochelle. Mary Sarah or "Chippy" was brought up by her aunt Mary (Hector, Neil) MacNeil, Gillis Point (see **90**), married Chesley Fraser, Eureka, and had a family.

John "Ban" (Hugh) married Lucy (Neil "Geal") MacNeil, Washabuck (see **265**). They lived in Jamesville West and their family: Neil, John, Lauchlin, Rory, Hugh, Ann, Flora, Mary and Annie. **334**

John (John "Ban") and Mary were unmarried. Ann and Annie died young. Lauchlin married a Miss O'Leary, Springhill and had two sons, John and Neil, who died young. Flora married Hugh (Hector "Mor") MacNeil, Iona (see **145**) and had a family. Hugh married Mary MacDonald, West Bay Road, lived first in Jamesville and later in Glace Bay, and their family: Neil J., John, Dan, Ranald, John R., Joseph J., Alex F., and Annie. Rory married Mary MacIntyre, Sydney Mines and had no family.

Neil (John "Ban") married in the United States Mary II (Alasdair, Barra) MacNeil, Ottawa Brook (see **31**) and their family: John, Annie, Margaret, Mary Jane, Peter, Michael, Lucy, Rory F., Catherine, and Mary Elizabeth. **335**

> John (Neil) was killed in a mine explosion in Springhill. Annie married Roderick (Archibald) Campbell in Boston. Margaret married Charles Franks in Boston and had no family. Michael died young. Lucy married James (Iain, Pheadair) MacNeil, Castle Bay and died a year after her marriage. Catherine married Dan Cameron, Castle Bay and had a large family. Mary Elizabeth married Joseph

MacInnis, Glace Bay and had a family. Mary Jane was unmarried in the United States. Peter married Catherine (John) Cameron, Shenacadie, lived in Boston, and had a family.

Rory F. (Neil) married Catherine (Hector, John Donald) MacNeil, Big Beach. They lived in Jamesville West and their family: Lucy, Mary Jane, Neil John, Agnes, Hector, Margaret, James, John Anthony, May, Annie, Teresa, three boys who died in infancy, and Faye whom they adopted. **336**

Agnes (Rory F.) married Francis (Michael D.) MacNeil, Iona (see **53**), lived in Iona, and had a family. Lucy married John L. MacDonald, Antigonish, lived in Antigonish, and had a family. Mary Jane married Leo MacDonald, Sydney and had an adopted family. Hector, as a young man, was killed on the railroad. James was killed in World War II. Margaret married Robert Douglas, a R.C.M.P. officer, lived in Dartmouth, and has a family. May married James Moore, Sydney and has a large family. Annie married Frank Blois in the United States and has a family. Teresa married Albert Gerber in the United States and has a family. Faye married Gerry LeFort in Ontario and has a family. John Anthony married Louise (John Dan) MacNeil, Barra Glen (see **239**), lives in Antigonish, and their family: David, Frankie, Jocelyn, Ian, Tommie, Peter, Mary Lou, Edward, Annie Catherine and twins who died in infancy.

Neil John (Rory F.) married Marge Sharkey, Saint John. They live in Jamesville West and their family: Kevin, Roddie, Jimmie, Maria, Barbara, Janet, Cathy, John, and Carmel. **337**

● ● ●

Victor Jankowski, a Displaced Person during World War II, married Catherine (Rory John) MacNeil, Iona (see **74**). They lived in Iona and their family: Vincent and Richard. **338**

● ● ●

MACAULAY - MACCORMACK

MacAulay is a name that occurs in the earliest history of Washabuck. As there are none by that name in the area today, we cannot be too certain of how the persons we mention here are related. Donald "Piper" MacAulay would appear to be the pioneer. Isabel, who was unmarried, was his sister. Donald's family was: Angus, Jane, Allan, and Margaret.

Jane (Donald "Piper") married Malcolm MacInnis (see **414**) and had a family. Angus married, lived in West Bay, and had a family. Margaret married Allie Donn MacAulay, Washabuck (see **339a**).

Allan (Donald "Piper") married a Miss MacDonald, Whycocomagh. They lived in Washabuck and their family: Dan, Margaret, Catherine, Belle, John Rudolphe, Tena, Mary, and Sarah. **339**

> Dan (Allan) and Belle were unmarried. Mary died young. Margaret married John Dan MacRitchie (see **549**). Catherine married a Mr. Stewart in the United States, and had at least one son, Allan, who lived in Washabuck, as a young man. John Rudolphe married a woman from Scotland, lived in the United States, and had no family. Tena married in the United States. Sarah married at Mr. Patterson in the United States.

● ● ●

Alexander MacAulay, familiarly known as "Allie Donn," married Margaret (Donald "Piper") MacAulay and their family: Liza who married a Mr. Langille, lived in Baddeck, and had a son Bill who married Collena (John) MacIver (see **423a**); and Allan, an accomplished step-dancer, who was accidentally killed in St. Peter's. **339a**

● ● ●

William L. MacCormack, Lower River Inhabitants, a C.N.R. Station Agent married Irene (John P.) MacNeil, Iona (see **163**). They lived in Iona and their family: Patricia, Brian, and Martin. **340**

● ● ●

MACDONALD

Donald (Malcolm) MacDonald came from the Isle of Wish early in 1800 and settled in Ottawa Brook. His family, born in Scotland, was: Philip, Donald, Jessie, and Katie Ann. All but Philip were unmarried. **341**

Philip (Donald, Malcolm) married Sarah, sister of Donald "Doctor" MacNeil, Ottawa Brook (see **225**). They lived in Ottawa Brook and their family: John, Donald, Annie, Sarah, and Jonathan. **342**

Annie (Philip, Donald Malcolm) married Joseph MacNeil, Shenacadie, had a family, and moved to Bridgeport. Sarah married Neil MacKenzie and had a family (see **432**).

John (Philip, Donald Malcolm) married Katie (Iain, Domhnull) MacNeil, Gillis Point (see **99**). They lived in Ottawa Brook and their family: Mary, Annie, and Katie. **343**

Mary (John) was unmarried. Annie married Rod Steele and had a family. Sadie married a Mr. Ferguson.

Donald (Philip, Donald Malcolm) married Sarah (Michael, John "Lewis") MacDonald, Ottawa Brook (see **351**). They lived in Ottawa Brook and their family: Philip, Angus, Mary, Margaret, Kate, and Dan Angus. **344**

Philip (Donald) was unmarried. Mary married a Mr. Gillis, Inverness, and had a family. Kate married Rod J. (Peter, Rory) MacLean, Ottawa Brook (see **528**), lived in Ottawa Brook, and had a family. Margaret married Joseph MacNeil, lived in Ottawa Brook and, after the death of her husband, lived with her brother Philip.

Angus (Donald) married Veronica MacNeil, Benacadie. They lived in Ottawa Brook and their family: Donald, Joseph, Wilfred, Sadie, and Kathleen. **345**

Dan Angus (Donald) married a daughter of James (Seamus, Eoin) MacNeil, Rear Christmas Island. They lived in Ottawa Brook and had nine daughters and three sons. With the exception of John and Dan James, the family went to the United States. **346**

Jonathan (Philip, Donald Malcolm) married Kate (Donald "Og") Murphy, MacKinnon's Harbour (see **556**). They lived in Ottawa Brook and their family: Philip, Dan D., James, Mary, Katie, Bessie, Annie, Sadie, Catherine, and Margaret. **347**

Philip (Jonathan) married Mary MacCormack, lived in Sydney, and their family: John, Donald, Tom, Michael, Mary, Margaret, Josie, and Dan. Dan D. married Mary MacNeil, Sydney, lived in Sydney, and their family: John, Hugh, Wilfred, Catherine, Francis, Josie, and Margaret. Mary married John White and had a family. Katie married Martin Joyce and had a family. Annie married Dan Campbell, Sydney and had a family. Sadie married Hector MacNeil, Glace Bay and had a family. Margaret married Bill O'Toole and had no family. Bessie married Bill Wells and had a family. We have no information on Catherine.

James (Jonathan) married Elizabeth Effie (John, John Charles) MacKinnon, MacKinnon's Harbour (see **476**). They lived in Ottawa Brook and their family: John Dan and Hugh. **348**

Hugh (James) married Irene Belliveau, lives in Halifax, and has a family.

John Dan (James) married Sarah (MacNeil) MacInnis, daughter of Neil D. MacNeil, Jamesville (see **175**). They lived in Ottawa Brook and had no family. **349**

● ● ●

John "Lewis" MacDonald came to Christmas Island and settled in Benacadie. He married Sarah (James "Big") MacNeil, Big Beach, sister of Iain (Seamus) MacNeil, Goose Pond. Their sons, Michael and James, settled in Big Beach on the property now owned by John Neil MacKinnon, but later they moved to Ottawa Brook. They still carried the label "Lewis," and it is said that it was they who gave the name Cape Lewis to the point of land, off Red Point, where first they settled. **350**

James (John "Lewis") married Ann (Donald "Halifax") Mac-Kenzie. They both died soon after their marriage.

Michael (John "Lewis") married Elizabeth (Donald, Donald) MacNeil, Big Beach. They lived in Ottawa Brook, Michael annexing to his own the property left by his deceased brother James. Michael's family was: Peter, Kate, John, Dan and Sarah. **351**

Sarah (Michael, John "Lewis") married Donald (Philip) MacDonald, Ottawa Brook (see **344**), lived in Ottawa Brook, and had a family. Kate married Dan (Donald, Donald "Ban") MacNeil and had no family (see **165**).

Peter (Michael, John "Lewis") married Catherine II (Michael, Murdock Donald "Og") MacNeil, sister of Piper Stephen B. MacNeil, Port Hawkesbury (see **27**). They lived in Ottawa Brook and their family: James, Katie Margaret, Lizzie and Mamie. In a second marriage he married Bessie (Donald) Nash (see **565**) and had no family. **352**

Katie Margaret (Peter) became a Sister of Mercy. Lizzie married John Alex (Alasdair, Seonaid) MacNeil, Ottawa Brook (see **254**), lived in Ottawa Brook, had no family, but adopted Genevieve MacNeil and Leo Bonaparte. Mamie, a nurse, married James MacNeil, Little Bras d'Or and had a family.

James (Peter) married Margaret (Joseph "Doctor") MacNeil, Red Point (see **229**). They lived in Ottawa Brook and their family: Cyril, Freddie, Anthony, Theresa, and Hilda. **353**

John (Michael, John "Lewis") married Sarah, sister to Peter's wife (see **27**). They lived in Ottawa Brook and had a daughter Tena. **354**

Tena (John) married John J. (Eoin) MacLean, Ottawa Brook (see **536**), lived in Sydney, and had a large family.

Dan (Michael, John "Lewis") married Margaret (Iain, Domhnull)

MacNeil, Gillis Point (see **99**). They lived in Ottawa Brook and had a son James, a carpenter and boat-builder, who died unmarried. **355**

•   •   •

At the time that Lord MacDonald abandoned the Catholic religion in favour of Protestantism, Alasdair MacDonald left South Uist and went to live in Barra. He married Margaret, sister of Hugh Gillis whose wife and family settled in Jamesville West at the time of the clearances (see **325**). One of his sons, Michael "Mor," married Catherine MacIntyre in Barra, and at least one of his children was born there. He came to the New World and settled in Mabou. His brothers, James, Donald, and Rory followed him to the New World and settled in Washabuck, that part of it today called St. Columba. A sister of theirs, Flora, had already come to the New World and was by this time settled in Washabuck (likely in Lower Washabuck) and the wife of Allan "Leathaineach" MacLean. After his brother had settled in St. Columba, Michael "Mor" decided to leave Mabou and join them. He settled on the property in St. Columba later owned by Michael E. MacDonald, and his brothers — James, Donald, and Rory — settled close by.

Michael "Mor" (Alasdair) had seven sons and two daughters, the last of whom was born in St. Columba. His sons were: Alexander, Allan I, Archibald, Michael, James, Allan II, and John; and the daughters were: Christy and Mary. **356**

Allan I (Michael "Mor," Alasdair) died in infancy. Christy married first Hector (Murdock) MacKenzie who died soon after their marriage, leaving a son who died young; in a second marriage she married Stephen "Roger" MacNeil, Highland Hill (see **233**) and had a family. Mary was the second wife of Angus MacDougall, Christmas Island, lived in North Sydney, and had a family. Archibald, a shoemaker by trade, died as a young man in North Sydney. We have no information on Michael.

Alexander (Michael "Mor," Alasdair) married Catherine (Neil "Soldier") MacDonald, Grand Narrows. They lived in St. Columba and their family: Michael B., Neil, Peter D., Stephen

A., Mary C., Betsy, and Archibald. **357**

Michael B. (Alexander), a famous school teacher, who taught for nearly fifty years, died unmarried. Neil drowned on his way from Baddeck. Peter D. married first Maggie Bell MacLean who died shortly after her marriage, and, after the death of his wife, he left St. Columba, married Matilda MacInnis, Inverness, settled in South Bar, and their family: Alex J., Angus, Maggie, Mary Ann, Catherine, and Clare. Mary C. married Donald R. MacLean, Whycocomagh and had a family. Betsy was the first wife of Rory (Neil) MacNeil, St. Columba (see **107**) and had a family. Archibald married Margaret O'Handley, Long Island who died, leaving a son Michael; in a second marriage he married Christy Fraser from Richmond County and their family: James, Joseph, Marie, and John Archibald; and in a third marriage he married Eliza Musgrave and had a son who died young.

Michael, son of Archibald (Alexander) from his first marriage, was a deep-sea captain. It was he who brought the S.S. Cape Breton to this country on her maiden voyage. He married a woman from Pictou, had three children, and died in Havana, Cuba. James and Joseph, his children from his second marriage, died at sea. Marie, his daughter from his second marriage, married a Mr. Smith, Pictou, and had no family.

Stephen A. (Alexander) married Mary Ann (Neil, James Charles) MacNeil, Shenacadie. They lived in St. Columba and their family: Neil, Alex, John Archibald, James Joseph, Michael John, and Peter Francis. Of these only Peter Francis married and he lived in Halifax. Michael died in Truro on his way overseas in World War I. **358**

James (Michael "Mor," Alasdair) married Elizabeth (Allan) MacKinnon, MacKinnon's Harbour (see **465**). They lived in St. Columba and their family: Michael, Mary, Maggie, Stephen Francis, Neil S., John Michael, Stephen B. and Dan A. (Twins), Catherine, Elizabeth, and Allan. **359**

Michael (James) married Ann MacKinnon, Frenchvale, lived in Copper Mines, and their family: Murdock, John,

Neil, Hector, Mary Ann, Catherine, and James. Mary married Rory R. MacNeil, Barra Glen (see **10**), lived in Barra Glen, and had a family. Maggie married Francis F. MacNeil, Barra Glen (see **261**), lived in Barra Glen and had an adopted family. Stephen Francis died unmarried in the United States. Neil S., unmarried, was drowned on his way from Baddeck. John Michael died unmarried. Stephen B. married Georgie MacInnis, lived in Bangor, and their family: Anne, Francis, James, Mary, Helen, and Lucille. Allan died young. We have no information on Catherine and Elizabeth.

Dan A. (James) married Isabella (Stephen, Alasdair) MacNeil, Grass Cove (see **256**). They lived in Iona and their family: Mary E., James, Stephen, Margaret, Mary Catherine, Dan A. Jr., Francis, Annie, and Michael. **360**

James (Dan A.) died as a young man. Margaret married in Halifax and has no family. Mary Catherine married a Mr. Nicholson, Florance, lives in North Sydney, and has a family.

Allan II (Michael "Mor," Alasdair) married Sarah (Eoin, Ruairi) MacNeil, Hector's Point in Iona (see **152**). They lived in St. Columba and later in Iona. Their family was: Michael A.J., Rory, Mary, Katie, Katie Ann, John A., Eliza, Archie, Maggie Bell, and Alex Joseph. **361**

Katie (Allan II) married Francis (Philip) MacKenzie, Benacadie, lived in Benacadie and Iona, and adopted Margaret Devoe and Eugene MacKenzie, the latter drowning early in life. Katie Ann married Dan S. (Murdock) MacNeil, Gillis Point (see **122**), lived in Gillis Point, and had a large family. Rory died unmarried. Mary married Hector (Neil, Hector) MacNeil, Gillis Point (see **90**), lived in Gillis Point East, had a family of her own, and adopted Mary Sarah or "Chippy," daughter of her sister Maggie Bell. Maggie Bell married Michael A.J. (Donald) Gillis, MacKinnon's Harbour (see **333**), lived in Alba Station, and had a family. Eliza became a Sister of Charity. Archie married Margaret Gillis, Soldier's Cove, and had no family. Alex Joseph married first Mary A. MacKinnon, had a son, and in a second marriage he married Edna MacNeil, lived in North Sydney, and had a family.

Michael A.J. (Allan II) married Mary MacDonald, Soldier's Cove. They lived in Iona and their family: Minnie, Agnes, Hanna, Eliza, Catherine, Rita, Rose, Hugh, and two boys who died in infancy. **362**

Minnie (Michael A.J.) married Stephen N. MacKinnon, Big Beach, lived in Sydney, and had a family, one of whom became a priest in the Diocese of Antigonish. Agnes married Malcolm J. MacLean, Boisdale, lived in Boisdale, and had a family. Hanna married Victor L. MacDonald, Windsor in Nova Scotia, lived in Boston, and had a family. Eliza married James Murphy, Margaree, lived in Detroit, and had a family, one of whom became a priest and another a Sister. Catherine married Peter Smith, Arisaig, lived in Detroit, and had a family. Rita married Joseph MacLean, West River in Antigonish County, lived in Detroit, and had no family. Rose married Malcolm (Neil M.) MacNeil in the United States, lived in Detroit, and had no family. Hugh became a priest in the Archdiocese of Halifax and later transferred to the Archdiocese of Detroit.

John A. (Allan II), a merchant in Iona, married Mary Agnes MacKinnon, Shenacadie. They lived in Iona and their family: Leonard, Mary, Joseph Allan, Sylvester, Mildred, Hector, Cecilia, Collette, Martin, Leo, and Christena. **363**

Leonard (John A.), a medical doctor, married and settled in Colorado. Joseph Allan, a medical doctor, settled in Glace Bay and had a family. Martin, a medical doctor, settled in Halifax and had a family. With the exception of Hector who died young, the rest of the family live in Halifax where they went from Iona in the thirties.

John (Michael "Mor," Alasdair) married Mary (Neil, Barra) MacNeil, Red Point (see 33). They lived in St. Columba and their family: Maggie, Mary, Michael E., Mary Catherine, Katie, Michael John, and Christy. **364**

Maggie (John) married Michael MacNeil, lived in Bangor, and had no family. Mary married Malcolm MacDonald,

MACDONALD

brother of R.C. MacDonald, Washabuck (see **381**), and had a son Murdock who did not marry. Michael E. was unmarried. Mary Catherine was the second wife of John P. MacNeil, Iona (see **163**), lived in Iona, and had a large family. Katie married Hector "Lighthouse" MacLean, Gillis Point (see **491**), lived in Gillis Point, and had a large family. Michael John died while attending Saint Francis Xavier University. Christy married a Mr. Shannon, Bangor, lived in Bangor, and had a family.

James (Alasdair) MacDonald married Catherine (Hector) MacNeil, Grand Narrows. They lived in St. Columba and their family: Stephen, John, James, Peggy, Mary, and Elizabeth. **365**

Elizabeth (James, Alasdair) died unmarried. John and James married in the United States and had families. Peggy married Neil (James "Pearson") MacNeil, Iona (see **242**), and had a family. Mary married Murdock B. MacNeil, Highland Hill (see **189**) and had a family.

Stephen (James, Alasdair) married Catherine (Malcolm) Campbell, Barra Glen (see **281**). They lived in Upper Washabuck and their family: James, John Rory, Hugh J., Hector, Malcolm, and Annie. **366**

James (Stephen), a deep-sea captain, and Hector died unmarried. Annie married in the United States. Malcolm lived in Detroit. Hugh J. married a Miss MacNeil, Big Beach and had a family in Glace Bay.

Donald (Alasdair) married Catherine (Archibald) MacKenzie, Birch Point in Washabuck (see **425**). They lived in St. Columba and their family: Alexander, James, Archibald, Jane, Bessie, Ann, and Catherine. **367**

Archibald (Donald, Alasdair) married and had a large family. Jane married in the Cape Breton mining area. Bessie married

MACDONALD

Michael MacDougall, Washabuck (see **396**) and had a large family. Annie married Hector MacLean, Ottawa Brook (see **535**) and had a large family. Catherine married Hector MacLean, Ingonish and had a family. We have no information on James.

Alexander (Donald, Alasdair) married Elizabeth (Charles, Donald "Ban") MacKinnon, MacKinnon's Harbour (see **474**). They lived in St. Columba and, after the death of Alexander, his widow moved the family to MacKinnon's Harbour: Michael, Stephen, Hector, Maggie, and Mary. **368**

Maggie (Alexander) married John MacKenzie, a blacksmith in Shenacadie, and had a family. Stephen married Annie (Dan, Archibald) MacLean, Ottawa Brook (see **532**), lived near St. Peter's, and had a family of three, one of whom married John Alex MacKinnon, Big Beach and lived in Sydney. We have no information on Mary.

Michael (Alexander) married Sarah (John "Cooper") MacNeil, Grand Narrows. They lived in Jamesville West and their family: Dan, Angus, Maggie, John Dan, Alexander, Roddie, Sarah, and Mamie. **369**

Dan (Michael) married a Miss MacInnis, Shenacadie and had a large family in Western Canada. Angus died unmarried in the United States. Maggie married a Mr. MacIntosh and lived in Western Canada. John Dan married Dolena (John Y.) Gillis, MacKinnon's Harbour (see **330**), lived in Sydney, and their family: Lyla and two others who died in infancy. Alexander married in Western Canada. Roddie, a C.N.R. Conductor, married Mary Ann (Rory S.) MacNeil, Barra Glen (See **15**), lived in Sydney, and had a large family. Sadie married Seward Bonaparte, MacKinnon's Harbour (see **276**) and had a large family. Mamie married Philip O'Donnell, MacKinnon's Harbour (see **570**), lived in Jamesville West, and had a family.

Hector (Alexander) married Margaret (Colin, Seamus "Mor") MacNeil, Jamesville (see **179**). They lived in Jamesville and their family: Alex, Joseph, Frank, and Mary Catherine. **370**

MACDONALD

Alex (Hector) married in Western Canada. Joseph and Frank died young. Mary Catherine, adopted by Donald (Isabella) MacNeil, Jamesville (see **70**), married Joseph MacNeil, Baddeck (see **114**), had a child, and died about a year after her marriage.

Rory (Alasdair) married Catherine, sister of James "Lieutenant" MacNeil, Grass Cove (see **258**). They lived in Upper Washabuck (where John A. MacDougall now lives). Their family was: Alexander, Donald, John, Angus, Annie, Mary I, Sarah, Margaret, and Mary II. **371**

Donald (Rory, Alasdair) lived away and had a family. John married in the United States. Angus married Eliza MacLean, South Side Whycocomagh and, after a second marriage, went to Western Canada. Annie married Peter (Neil, Lachlan) MacLean, Washabuck (see **496**) and had a family. Mary I married Donald (Neil, Lachlan) MacLean, Washabuck (see **494**) and had a family. Sarah married Archibald MacKenzie, Birch Point in Washabuck (see **427**) and had a family.

Alexander (Rory, Alasdair) married Annie (John) MacNeil, Shenacadie. They lived in Gillis Point (where later Dan D. MacNeil lived) and their family: Mary, Katie, Mary E., Rory Stephen, and two others who died young. **372**

Mary (Alexander) was the first wife of John P. MacNeil, Iona (see **163**), lived in Iona, and had a family. Annie died in the United States. Mary E. married a Captain Allen in P.E.I. Rory Stephen married a Miss MacLean and lived in Whitney Pier.

● ● ●

Ronald "Mor" MacDonald came from Boularderie to Washabuck, settling on land there once owned by a Mr. Sutherland. He married Catherine (Donald, Philip) MacKinnon, Washabuck (see **479**) and their family: Angus, Rory R., Dan and Annie. **373**

Annie (Ronald "Mor") died unmarried. Dan married an Irish girl, settled in Lynn, Mass. and their family: Katie, Ellise, Mary Ann, Theresa, and Richard.

Rory R. (Ronald "Mor") married Agnes (Stephen, Calum) MacLean, Lower Washabuck (see **509**). They lived in Lower Washabuck and their family: Joseph, Rory R. Jr., Francis B., Quentin, Donald, Stephen, George, and Margaret Creighton whom they adopted. **374**

Joseph (Rory R.) married a Miss Brophy from Antigonish County, lives in Baddeck, and has a family. Rory R. Jr. married and has a family in Halifax. Quentin married Sadie E. (Dan) MacKinnon, Cain's Mountain (see **483**), lived out West, had a family, and died as the result of a fire.

Francis B. (Rory R.) married Margaret (Dan S.) MacNeil, Gillis Point (see **122**). They lived in Lower Washabuck and their family: Clara, Geraldine and Roddie. **375**

Angus (Ronald "Mor") married Eliza (Rory J., Iain Ruairi) MacNeil, Washabuck (see **38**). They lived in Upper Washabuck and their family: Katie Ann, Theresa, Ranald, Angus, Alex, Rose, Lexena, Betty, Mary C., Margaret, Roddie, Johnnie, Dan F., and Mary Agnes. They also adopted Josie, Andy, and Raymond. **376**

Katie Ann (Angus) married Neil S. MacLean, Washabuck Center (see **498**) and had a family. Theresa married in the United States. Alex was killed as a young man. Rose married Michael Anthony (Vincent) MacLean, Lower Washabuck (see **507**) and had a family. Lexena married a Mr. Fraser in the United States. Betty married a Mr. Fownes and has a family in Nyanza.

Ranald (Angus) married Joan (John Stephen) MacKenzie, Washabuck (see **436**). They live in Upper Washabuck and their family: Stephen, Ann, Sarah, Helen, Quentin, and a girl who died in infancy. **377**

Angus (Angus) married Annie (James Allan) MacNeil, Gillis Point (see **136**). They live in Upper Washabuck and their family: Elizabeth, Margaret Ann, and Johnnie. **378**

Dan F. (Angus) married Kathleen (Dan P.) Murphy, Washabuck (see **564**). They live in Upper Washabuck and their family: Gertrude, Marie, Charlotte, Patsy, Gregory, Mary Louise, Brenda, Blair, and Donna. **379**

● ● ●

Alasdair "Glas" MacDonald came to Washabuck with his wife. He came from Red Head, the district about Beinn Breagh, the favourite haunt of Dr. Alexander Graham Bell. He married a Mrs. Johnston from Mabou and their family: at least a son Murdock; a daughter Margaret, who was the first wife of Michael (James "Miller") MacDougall, Washabuck (see **396**); and Kate, who married Michael MacDougall, Washabuck (see **403**). **380**

Murdock (Alasdair) married Elizabeth (Jonathan) MacKenzie, Washabuck (see **442**). They lived in Washabuck and their family: Rory C., Malcolm, Neil, John, Sandy, Jim, Mary, and Ann. **381**

Neil (Murdock), John, Sandy, and Jim moved away early in life. Malcolm married Mary (John, Michael "Mor") MacDonald, St. Columba (see **364**) and, after the father died, their only child Murdock was brought up by the grandfather, John MacDonald, in St. Columba. Mary married Rod MacIsaac, Upper Washabuck (see **417**), lived in Upper Washabuck, and had a family. Ann married Rory J. (Iain, Ruairi) MacNeil, Upper Washabuck (see **38**) and had a family.

Rory C. (Murdock) married Lizzie (John, Calum) MacNeil, Barra Glen (see **236**). They lived in Upper Washabuck and their family: Mary Ann who married in the United States, and Malcolm. They also adopted Angus Gardiner who died unmarried. **382**

Malcolm (Rory C.) married Agnes Rankin, Creignish. They lived in Upper Washabuck and their family: Buddy, Roddie, Duncan, Elizabeth, Joseph, and Mary Margaret. **383**

● ● ●

MACDONALD

Angus MacDonald, called "Tuathach" and also "Lord," was a native of North Uist who settled in Washabuck. The label "Tuathach" means "Northern." He married a sister of Peggy (Calum William) MacDougall, Washabuck (see **402**) and their family: Catherine, Sarah, Ann, Mary, Dannie, and Rachel. **384**

Catherine (Angus) married Rory "Tailor" MacKinnon, Upper Washabuck (see **481**) and had a family. Sarah married Rory D. (Donald "Mor") MacNeil, Red Point (see **41a**) and had a family. Ann and Dannie were drowned. Mary married a Mr. Morrison, Blues Mills and had a family. Rachel was unmarried.

● ● ●

Donald "Soldier" MacDonald, Grand Narrows married in Ottawa Brook and his family: Hector and Flora "Beag." **384a**

Flora "Beag" (Donald "Soldier") was the wife of Angus "Beag" MacNeil, Ottawa Brook (see **218**).

Hector (Donald "Soldier") married Ann "Mhor" (Philip, Donald) MacNeil, Gillis Point (see **96**). They lived in Ottawa Brook and their family: Eliza, Lizzie Ann, Katie, Christy, Ann, and Dan Neil who died young. **385**

Eliza (Hector) married Alex "Red" MacNeil, Mabou, lived in Sydney, had a family, and later moved away. Lizzie Ann married first Ronald MacDonald, Hay Cove, had a family; and in a second marriage she married Angus D. MacDonald, MacLeod's Hill, Sydney, and had a son Vincent. Katie married James MacDonald, Grand Narrows. Christy married John M. MacNeil, Barra Glen (see **208**), lived in Barra Glen, and had a family. Ann married a Mr. Griffin in the United States and had a son, Dan Neil, on whom we have no information.

● ● ●

Hector (Ronald) MacDonald, Hay Cove in Richmond County settled in Gillis Point. His mother was Lizzie Ann (Hector "Soldier") MacDonald (see **385**). He enlisted in World War I, married Mary Dixon from Scotland, and, after his return from overseas, he purchased the property of Hector (Iain, Domhnull) MacNeil, Gillis Point, and settled on it. His family was: Hector, Dannie, John, Joseph, Ronald I, Ronald II, Adam, Mary, Agnes, Jean, Margaret, Betty and Famie. **386**

Hector (Hector, Ronald) is unmarried. Dannie married and had a family in Sydney. Joseph married and has a family in Toronto. Ronald I died in a drowning accident in Gillis Point. Adam was killed in World War II.

Ronald II (Hector, Ronald) married Rose (John Stephen) MacKenzie, Washabuck (see **436**). They live in Washabuck and have a family. **387**

●　　●　　●

James (Donald "Ban") MacDonald settled early in Gillis Point and had a family. He and his descendants moved away. It is therefore quite difficult to get information on him and his family, but we give what we were able to piece together. His family was: Mary, Bessie, Jane, Ann, Nicholas, and another daughter. **388**

Mary (James, Donald) married Donald "Beag" MacNeil, Iona (see **50**) and had a large family. Bessie married Eoin "Dunn" MacNeil, Jamesville (see **65**), lived in Jamesville, had a large family, and moved to Glace Bay. Jane died unmarried. Nicholas is believed to have gone to the United States. Ann, known as "Annie Mhor Fiddler," was unmarried but she adopted a nephew, Donald Morrison, known as "Donald Ann James," who married a woman from Richmond County, lived in Gillis Point, had a large family, and moved to Glace Bay. James' daughter whose name we do not know was the wife of Rory (John) Morrison, Gillis Point (see **553**) and the mother of "Donald Ann James," referred to above.

●　　●　　●

A Mr. MacDonald from River Deny's married Annie (James, Eachain) MacNeil, a sister of Charles S. MacNeil, Red Point (see **92**). They lived in Ottawa Brook and had a son James. **389**

James, known as "James Section Man," married Margaret (Michael "Doctor") MacNeil, Ottawa Brook (see **226**). They lived in Ottawa Brook and their family: Theresa, Katie, Clemy, Catherine, Annie May, Cassie, Angus, Alex and Stanley. **390**

●   ●   ●

Rory "Mor" MacDonald came from West Scotland and settled in Ottawa Brook. He married a Miss Walker whose relations live in Mira and Point Aconi. They lived in MacKinnon's Harbour and their family: John, Donald, Alex, Jessie, and Angus "Red." **391**

Alex (Rory "Mor") married in the United States and had two daughters. Jessie married Alexander MacNeil, Ottawa Brook (see **252**). We have no information on John and Donald.

Angus "Red" (Rory "Mor") married first Sarah (Rory, Donald "Ban") MacKinnon, McKinnon's Harbour (see **471**). They lived in MacKinnon's Harbour and their family: Donald, Rory, and Kate. In a second marriage he married Annie MacLean and their family: Annie, and another daughter who married in the United States. **392**

Annie (Angus "Red") married a Hugh MacDonald and had a family. Donald, Rory, and Kate were unmarried.

●   ●   ●

John "Miller" MacDougall settled in Christmas Island about 1821. His son Alexander moved to Red Point. We cannot say for certain who Alexander's wife was (see **35a**), but their family was: James, Joseph, Flora, and Mary. **393**

Flora (Alexander) married Archibald Campbell, Red Point (see **284**), lived in Red Point, and had a family. Mary married Donald "Doctor" MacNeil, Ottawa Brook (see **225**), lived in Ottawa Brook, and had a family. We have no information on Joseph.

James (Alexander) married Ann (Alasdair, Barra) MacNeil, Ottawa Brook (see **31**). They lived in Red Point, had no family, but they adopted Michael MacInnis and Christy MacNeil, respectively nephew and niece of Ann. **394**

Michael MacInnis married Sarah (Rory D., Donald "Mor") MacNeil, Red Point (see **41a**) and had no family. Christy

MACDOUGALL

MacNeil married a Mr. Wilford in the United States.

● ● ●

MacDougalls also settled in Washabuck. Owing to the fact that the older folk have moved away, it is rather difficult to get accurate information on these families.

James "Miller" MacDougall and his sister Mary came to Washabuck along with the MacLeans in 1817. Mary married Alexander (Lachlan) MacLean, Washabuck (see **501**). There appears to have been another sister, Jane, but we have no information on her. We do not know whom James "Miller" married, but it is reported that she was connected with the family of Lachlan MacLean. All we can say is that he married an Ann who was the daughter of a Hugh, and that they had a son Michael. **395**

Michael (James "Miller") MacDougall married first Margaret (Alexander "Glas") MacDonald, Washabuck (see **380**). They lived in Upper Washabuck and their family: James, Mary, and Kate. In a second marriage he married Bessie (Donald, Alexander) MacDonald, St. Columba (see **367**) and their family: Jim Alex, Dan, Hugh Archie, John Peter, Annie Jane, and Hector. **396**

James (Michael, James "Miller") is not known to have married. Mary was unmarried. Kate married John J. MacKinnon, Ohio in Antigonish County, lived in Eureka in Pictou County, and her daughter Mary married there Arthur Frasier, whose son Chesley married Mary Sarah or "Chippy" Gillis, who was brought up by her aunt, Mary (Allan) MacDonald, Gillis Point and Iona (see **361**). Annie Jane married Angus MacDonald, Mira, lived in Mira, and had a large family. Hector married Mary MacKinnon, sister of Hugh Archie's wife (see **485**), lived in Paschendale, had a family, and married a second time without family. We have no information on John Peter.

MACDOUGALL

Jim Alex (Michael, James "Miller") married Sarah (Peter) Murphy, Washabuck Bridge (see **561**). They lived in Upper Washabuck and their family: Muriel, Martha, Walter, John A., Joe, Frances, and Mary. They also adopted John Campbell who married Mary (Michael, Eoin) MacNeil, Washabuck (see **263**). **397**

Muriel (Jim Alex) married a Mr. Moore and had a family in the United States. Martha married Dan Alex (Rory) MacKinnon, Upper Washabuck (see **482**) and had a family.

Walter (Jim Alex) married Helen (Dan) MacKinnon, Washabuck and Cain's Mountain (see **483**). They lived in Jamesville West and their family: Leo, Angela, Mary Jane, Duncan F., Dan E., and Joanne. **398**

Dan (Michael, James "Miller") married Flora MacCormack, River Inhabitants. They lived in Washabuck Bridge and their family: Anna May, Cassie, Theresa, Mary Ann, Sarah, Michael, Dan Hugh, George, and James. **399**

Sarah (Dan), Michael, Dan Hugh, and James were unmarried. Anna May married away. Cassie married Tom MacKenzie, Lower Washabuck (see **440**) and had a family. Theresa and Mary Ann married in the United States. George married in Baddeck.

Hugh Archie (Michael, James "Miller") married Theresa (Michael) MacKinnon, Lower Washabuck (see **485**). They lived in Lower Washabuck and their family: Michael Rory, Catherine, Elizabeth, and Lucy who died in infancy. **400**

Catherine (Hugh Archie) married John Ferguson and had a family.

Michael Rory (Hugh Archie) married Rita LaRusic, Bay St. Lawrence. They lived in Lower Washabuck and their family: Patrice, Mary, Theresa, Leo, Catherine, Louise, Ernest, Michelle, Peggy, Dan E., Lucy, Ernest A. who died young, and Francis whom they adopted. **401**

● ● ●

A family of MacDougalls, known as "the Williams," lived in

Washabuck. Not much is known about them, except that Malcolm MacDougall, known as "Calum William," had this family in Washabuck: "Captain" Michael, Peggy, and another daughter. **402**

Peggy (Calum William) married Jack MacDougall, Christmas Island, apparently a son of John MacDougall. This Jack MacDougall was drowned near Shenacadie and, after the drowning, his widow Peggy came back to Washabuck with her daughter Mary, who married John Brown (see **280**). Peggy's other children, Neil and John, did not come to Washabuck. (Neil married in Sydney Mines. John died young.) The other daughters of "Calum William" married Angus "Tuathach" MacDonald, Washabuck and had a family (see **384**).

"Captain" Michael (Calum William) married Kate (Alexander "Glas") MacDonald, Washabuck (see **380**). They lived on the North side of the Washabuck River and their family: Mary Ann, Sandy, Neil, Jim, Angus, and Mary. **403**

Mary Ann (Michael), Sandy, Neil, and Angus died unmarried. Jim married away and had two sons. Mary married first Johnnie Morrison, South Cove, had a daughter Cassie; and in a second marriage she married John MacNeil, Washabuck Center (see **39**) and had no family.

● ● ●

Rory (Donald, Hector) MacDougall, Ingonish lived for a short time in Upper Washabuck. He married Mary (Thomas, Johnnie) MacKinnon, Iona Rear (see **456**) and had a son Daniel. **404**

Daniel (Rory, Donald Hector) married Christena (Donald, Roderick Lachlan) MacLean, Washabuck (see **514**), had a family, and moved to Ingonish.

● ● ●

Rory MacInnis came from Barra in about 1817. He married Annie "Ban" (Rory, Malcolm) MacNeil, Christmas Island. They lived in Iona and their family: Michael, Donald, Rory, and Catherine. **405**

MACINNIS

Donald (Rory) lived in the United States. Rory married and had a family in North Sydney. Catherine married Neil (Barra) MacNeil, Red Point (see **33**), lived in Red Point, and had a large family.

Michael (Rory) married Christy Ann MacNeil, Shenacadie. They lived in Iona and their family: Malcolm, John, Michael D., Peter, Charles, Mary I, Christy I, Mary II, Christy II, Bessie, and Annie. **406**

Michael D. (Michael, Rory) married in Bangor and had two daughters. Peter and Charles were drowned at sea. Mary I died unmarried. Christy I married Donald (Neil) MacNeil, Gillis Point (see **106**), lived in Iona, and had a family. Mary II married Neil MacPhee, Sydney Mines, and had a family. Bessie married Malcolm (Eoin) MacNeil, Iona (see **154**), lived in Iona, and had a family. Christy II married Michael (Iain, Edward) MacNeil, Christmas Island and had a family. Annie married Colin (James "Mor") MacNeil, Jamesville (see **179**) and had a family.

Malcolm (Michael, Rory) married Mary (Donald "Mor") MacNeil, Red Point (see **41**). They lived in Iona and their family: Annie, Katie, Joseph, Dan and Michael. **407**

> Joseph (Malcolm) and Michael died unmarried. Annie was the second wife of Michael A.J. (Donald) Gillis, MacKinnon's Harbour (see **333**), lived in Alba, and had a family. Katie married William McGovern, lived in Saint John, and had a family. Dan married Mary Ann (Archie) MacKenzie, Christmas Island, lived in Grand Narrows, and had a family.

John (Michael, Rory) married first Ann MacNeil, Boularderie. They lived in Iona and had a son, Michael Joseph, who died in infancy. In a second marriage he married Annie (John "Mason") MacNeil, Gillis Point (see **78**) and their family: Michael F., John F., and Mary Ann. **408**

> Mary Ann (John) married James S. (Stephen, Alasdair) MacNeil, Grass Cove (see **257**), lived in Grass Cove, and had a family.

MACINNIS

Michael F. (John) married Margaret (Hector) Campbell, Gillis Point (see **291**). They lived in Iona and their family: Joan, and a son Joseph who died in infancy. **409**

John F. (John) married Annie Morrison, adopted daughter of John (Hector) Campbell, Gillis Point (see **320**). They lived in Iona and their family: Jean, Catherine, Donald, and Francis. **410**

● ● ●

Michael MacInnis, son of Peter MacInnis, Castle Bay, settled in Red Point. His mother was Katie I (Alasdair' Barra) MacNeil, Ottawa Brook (see **31**) and his wife was Sarah (Rory D., Donald "Mor") MacNeil, Red Point (see **41a**). He had no family. **411**

● ● ●

A Mr. MacInnis, commonly called "MacIain Mhinistir," married Catherine (Rory, Donald "Ban") MacKinnon, MacKinnon's Harbour (see **471**). They lived in Red Point and their family: Annie, Sarah, and Lucy. **412**

Annie (Mac Iain "Mhinistir") was the first wife of Donald (Rory) Gillis, MacKinnon's Harbour (see **327**), lived in MacKinnon's Harbour, and had a family. Sarah was the grandmother of the wife of Judd Halliday, who had a summer residence in MacKinnon's Harbour in her latter years. Lucy married a Mr. MacNutt in Truro.

● ● ●

John MacInnis came to Washabuck Bridge from Hume's River in Victoria County. He was married to Ann (Dan) MacDonald and their family: Danny, Annie, Mary, Rachael, Tena, Murdock, and Ella. **413**

Danny (John), Mary, Rachael, and Murdock are unmarried. Annie married Tom Roberts, Baddeck and has a family. Tena married. Ella married Gordon Beers and has a family in Dartmouth.

● ● ●

MACINNIS - MACISAAC

Malcolm MacInnis, who had a brother Donald in South Cove, married Jane (Donald "Piper") MacAulay and had three daughters — Margaret, Christie, and Annie — and a son Murdock. All four were unmarried. An adopted son, Duncan, lived on the Northside of Washabuck River, married Almena ("Little" Norman) MacIver, and had no family. **414**

• • •

A Mr. MacIntosh settled in Lower Washabuck from the earliest days. We have no information on this family. None of his descendants live in the area today. **415**

• • •

Roderick "Ur" MacIntyre, brother of the wife of Michael "Mor" MacDonald, St. Columba, left Scotland to come to Cape Breton. He was an excellent seaman. Before he left the Old Country, he promised his mother that, as soon as he was able to put her passage money together, he would send for her. It turned out that on the way coming across the Atlantic, they ran into exceptionally severe storms. The Captain was convinced that, were it not for Roderick's skill as a seaman, he could never have kept the ship afloat. The Captain feared to make the return trip without Roderick. So he made this agreement: If Roderick would accompany the boat back, the Captain would refund him his passage money and, more than that, on the next voyage to America, he would take both Roderick and his mother at no cost to them. Roderick and his mother settled in St. Columba. He married Sarah (Archibald) MacKenzie, Washabuck (see **425**) and their family: Allan, Archie, Hector, Sarah, Christy, and Mary. The family later moved to Sydney Mines. **416**

• • •

Rod MacIsaac who settled in Washabuck married Mary (Murdock) MacDonald, sister of R.C. MacDonald, Washabuck (see **381**). Their family was: Malcolm, Donald, Catherine, Annie, and Agnes. All moved away from Washabuck about the beginning of World War II. **417**

• • •

A Mr. MacIsaac from Northern Cape Breton settled in Red

Point. He married a daughter of Donald (Iain, Donald) MacNeil, Red Point and had no family. **418**

● ● ●

George MacIver from Scotland is believed to be the first MacIver to settle in Washabuck. And "Big" Colin MacIver is believed to have been a son of his.

"Big" Colin MacIver had this family: Betsy, Esther, "Little" Colin, George, Henry, and John. **419**

Betsy ("Big" Colin) was unmarried. Esther married Robert Clarke, Miramichi, and both are buried in Washabuck. "Little" Colin married a sister of Alex Murphy, had a family, and lived in Baddeck. George, who was married to a Murphy girl (see **562**), was killed in a lumber camp.

Henry ("Big" Colin) had this family: Dan or "Dolly," Angus, Jim, Mary Ann, Betty Jane, and Joe. **420**

Betty Jane (Henry) was unmarried. Joe moved away. Angus married and had a family in Inlet. Jim married and had a family in Big Baddeck. Mary Ann married Kenny MacRitchie, Northside St. Patrick's Channel (see **547**).

Dan or "Dolly" (Henry) whose wife was a Miss Matheson from the South Side had this family: Christena, Mary, Katie Margaret, Jamie, Dan Henry, and Joe. **421**

Mary ("Dolly"), Katie Margaret, and Jamie were unmarried. Christena married in Inlet. Dan Henry married and had a family in Bras d'Or.

Joe ("Dolly") married Mary MacInnis, South Cove. They lived in Washabuck and their family: Joe, Harold, Betty, and Mary. The family later moved to the United States. **422**

John ("Big" Colin) had a son John.

John (John) married Nancy (Angus, Allan) MacAulay, then of West Bay and their family: Agnes, Collena, Dolena, Anna Belle, Kate, and two other daughters. **423**

Agnes (John, John) married Oram Waite of the United States, adopted Jackie Whitehouse and Beatrice Bragg, both of England, and brought them up in her father's house in Washabuck. (Jackie is unmarried in Little Narrows; Beatrice married and has a family in the United States.) Collena married Bill Langille, lives in North Sydney, and has an adopted family. Dolena married in the United States. Anna Belle married a Mr. Durlette in the United States. Kate is married in the United States.

John Charles MacIver lived in Upper Washabuck and had a family. **423a**

"Buddy" (John Charles) married Elizabeth (Neil P.S.) MacLean, Lower Washabuck (see **518**), lives in Sydney, and has a family. For Collena see **339a**.

● ● ●

George MacKay, who gave his name to MacKay's Point in Washabuck, was among Washabuck's earliest settlers. He died in MacKay's Point and was buried in Baddeck. The family moved to Baddeck after 1850. **424**

● ● ●

Archibald (Eachain) MacKenzie came from Barra in 1821 and settled in Washabuck. He had already married Catherine (John) MacKinnon, a shoemaker, and their family: Donald, John, Rory, Neil, Sarah, Catherine, Mary, Mary "Og," and Christy. **425**

Neil (Archibald) was drowned. Sarah married Rory MacIntyre (see **416**) and had a family. Catherine married Donald (Alasdair)

MACKENZIE

MacDonald, St. Columba (see **367**), lived in Upper Washabuck, and had a large family. Mary married Alexander "Framer" MacKenzie, Lake Ainslie, lived in Washabuck (see **434**) and had a family, one of whom, Hector, went to the United States, married Margaret (Donald, Calum "Ban") MacDonald, Grand Narrows, and was the father of the famous Vincentian missionary, Reverend Charles MacKenzie. Ann and Christy lived in Sydney Mines. We have no information on Mary "Og."

Donald (Archibald) married Ann MacLean. They lived in Birch Point in Washabuck and their family: Neil W., Archibald, Angus, Hector, Mary, and Elizabeth. **426**

Hector (Donald, Archibald) died young. Neil W. married Mary Crowdis, Baddeck and had no family. Angus married Alice Rocket. Mary married Alex (Peter) Murphy, Washabuck (see **563**) and had a family. Elizabeth married Malcolm (Angus, Eoin) MacNeil, Highland Hill (see **183**), lived in Sydney and had no family.

Archibald (Donald, Archibald) married Sarah (Rory, Alasdair) MacDonald, Upper Washabuck (see **371**). They lived in Birch Point and their family: Mary Ann, Catherine, Eliza Ann, Mary Elizabeth, Mary Jane, Daniel J., and Roderick H. **427**

> Roderick H. (Archibald) died umarried. Mary Ann married James Campbell, Jamesville West (see **315**) and had a family. Catherine married John E. Ross in the United States. Eliza Ann married Malcolm (Hugh) Campbell, Barra Glen (see **283**), lived in St. Columba, and had a family. Mary Jane married Malcolm B. MacLean, Lower Washabuck (see **511**) and had a family. Mary Elizabeth married Roderick V. MacKenzie, Christmas Island and had a family.

> Dan J. (Archibald) married Cassie (Donald) Walker, Ottawa Brook (see **575**). They lived in Ottawa Brook and their family: Archie, Catherine, Jessie, J.D., and Ada. **428**

> Archie (Daniel J.) married Catherine Ann (John H.)

MacNeil, Jamesville (see **182**), lives in Sydney, and has no family. Catherine married Angus (John J.) MacLean, Ottawa Brook (see **537**), lives in Sydney, and has no family. Ada, brought up by her Aunt Flora, married Alex (John J.) MacLean, Ottawa Brook (see **538**), lives in MacKinnon's Harbour, and has a family. Jessie and J.D. are unmarried.

John (Archibald), called "Iain Mor," married Jessie MacDonald, niece of Father Angus MacDonald in Barra. They lived in Washabuck and their family: Neil, Archibald, and five daughters. **429**

Neil (John, Archibald) was drowned in the United States. Archibald married Elizabeth MacNeil, Big Beach and had no family. We have no information on the daughters.

Rory (Archibald) married Jane MacDougall, Washabuck. They lived in Washabuck Bridge and their family: Archie, Neil, Hector, James, Mary, Katie, Sarah, and Ann. **430**

James (Rory, Archibald) lived in New York. Mary, Sarah, and Ann died unmarried. Katie married Harry McGowan and had no family.

Archie (Rory, Archibald) married a Miss MacKenzie, Margaree. They lived in Washabuck Bridge and their family: William, James, Jessie, and Archie. **431**

Neil (Rory, Archibald) married Sarah (Philip) MacDonald, Ottawa Brook (see **342**). They lived in St. Columba and their family: Rory, Hector, Sarah, Mary, and Annie. **432**

Hector (Rory, Archibald) married Christy (Peter) Murphy, Washabuck (see **562**). They lived in Washabuck and their family: Rory, James, Alex, and Katie Ann. **433**

MACKENZIE

Alexander "Framer" MacKenzie, Lake Ainslie married Mary (Archibald, Hector) MacKenzie, Washabuck (see **425**). They lived in Washabuck and their family: Charles, Hector, Archie, Mary, Katie, and Flora. **434**

We have no information on Archie (Alexander "Framer"), Mary, Katie, and Flora. For Hector see **273**.

Charles (Alexander "Framer") married Ann (Stephen "Roger") MacNeil, Highland Hill. They lived in Washabuck Bridge and their family: John Stephen, Joe, Mary Ann, Hector, Catherine, and Christy. **435**

Joe (Charles), Hector, and Christy died unmarried. Mary Ann married Dan P. (Alex, Peter) Murphy, Washabuck (see **564**), lived in Washabuck, and had a large family. Catherine is unmarried.

John Stephen (Charles) married Mary Ann (Simon) Devoe, Washabuck (see **323**). They lived in Washabuck Bridge and their family: Murdock, Hector, Charles, Carleton, Simon, Helen, Mary, Annie, Joan, Jean, Rose, and Charlotte. **436**

Helen (John Stephen) married Andrew (Hector) MacLean, Gillis Point East (see **492**), lives in Iona, and has a family. Mary married Stanley Campbell, Hunter's Mountain and had a family. Annie married Benny (Neil P.S.) MacLean, Washabuck (see **518**), lives in Sydney Mines, and has a family of sixteen. Joan married Ranald (Angus, Ronald) MacDonald, Upper Washabuck (see **176**) and has a family. Rose married Ronald (Hector, Ronald) MacDonald, Washabuck (see **387**) and has a family.

● ● ●

Murdock (Hector) MacKenzie came from Barra in 1817 and settled in Washabuck. He had already married Lucy (Donald "Piper") MacNeil and their family: Donald I, Donald II, James, Rory, John, Hector, Archie, Mary I, Mary II, Katie, and Sarah. **437**

Donald I (Murdock), Rory, Archie, Mary I, Mary II, and Katie were unmarried. Donald II married Ann (Jonathan) MacNeil, Christmas Island and had a daughter Mary Ann, who married Neil H. (Hugh, Malcolm) MacNeil, Barra Glen and had a family (see **238**). John lives in Newfoundland. Sarah married Neil (Johnnie) MacKinnon, Iona Rear (see **460**), lived in Iona Rear, and had a family.

James (Murdock) married Katie Ross, Margaree (see **572**). They had a family of which only William remained in Washabuck. **438**

William (James) married Bessie (Neil, James "Pearson") MacNeil, Iona (see **242**). They lived in Washabuck and their family: Tom, James, Michael Hector, and Catherine. They also adopted Leonard MacKenzie who now lives in Montreal. **439**

Tom (William) married Cassie (Dan) MacDougall, Washabuck (see **399**). They live in Lower Washabuck and their family: James, Donnie, Florence, Patsy, Shirley, and Lawrence whom they adopted. **440**

James (William) married Annie Smith, Portage. They lived in Lower Washabuck and their family: Elizabeth, Ann, Betty, James Carleton, Gregory, Michael, John, Mary, and Gary. **441**

Jonathan (Hector) MacKenzie came from Barra in 1821 and settled in Washabuck. He had already married Sarah "Gobha" MacLean and their family: Hector I, Hector II, Donald, Murdock, Neil, James, Mary I, Mary II, Elizabeth, and Catherine. **442**

Hector I (Jonathan), Neil, and James lived in the United States. Mary II was unmarried. Murdock married and lived in Big Beach. Mary I married Rory (James) MacNeil, Big Beach. Elizabeth married Murdock (Alasdair) MacDonald, Washabuck (see **381**), lived in Upper Washabuck, and had a family. Catherine married Allan (Donald) MacLean, Washabuck (see **522**), lived in Washabuck, and had a large family, one of whom, Donald, appears to have married Sarah, daughter of Darby, the first Campbell to come to Jamesville.

Hector II (Jonathan) married Katie Ann MacDonald, Washabuck. They lived in Washabuck and had a family of eight. One daughter, Ellen, married Simon Devoe, Washabuck (see **323**). Another daughter, Catherine, married Dan MacKinnon, Cain's Mountain and Washabuck (see **483**) and had a family. **443**

Donald (Jonathan) married Elizabeth (Donald, Donald Rory) MacNeil, Big Beach. They lived in Washabuck and their family: Peter, Jim, Mary, John and another son. **444**

Mary (Donald), Jim, and the other son died unmarried. John married Flora (Eoin, James) MacNeil, MacNeil's Vale and had a family (see **78**).

Peter (Donald) married Flora (Michael) MacLean, Washabuck (see **512**). They lived in Upper Washabuck and their family: John Michael, and Elizabeth (who married in Inverness). They also adopted Agatha Moore. **445**

● ● ●

John Dan (Alex) MacKenzie, Benacadie came to the parish after World War II. He married Lucille (Allan Austin) MacNeil, Gillis Point (see **108**). They live in Gillis Point and their family: Austin Alexander, John Stanislaus, and Robert Daniel. **446**

● ● ●

John "Big" MacKinnon was quite likely among the immigrants who came to Pictou in 1802. He had married a woman from the Isle of Mull. They settled in Highland Hill and their family: Neil, Rachel, Catherine, Hector, Rory, Donald and John. **447**

Rachel (John "Big") married Malcolm (Hector) MacNeil, Piper's Cove and had a family. Donald and James were drowned, going to Baddeck with a load of shingles. We have no information on Catherine.

MACKINNON

Neil (John "Big") married Catherine (Norman) MacNeil, Piper's Cove. They lived in Highland Hill and their family: Michael, Norman, Catherine, Rory, Stephen and one other. **448**

Rory (Neil, John "Big") was drowned. Stephen married in the United States and had a family of six. Catherine was unmarried.

Norman (Neil, John "Big") married Catherine (Stephen, Neil "Roger") MacNeil, Highland Hill (see **233**). They lived in Highland Hill and their family: Stephen A., Mary Ann, Elizabeth, James, and Neil. Neil was killed in an accident. No one in the family was married. **449**

Michael (Neil, John "Big") married Annie (Eoin, Iain "Mor") MacNeil, Big Beach, and their family: Rory, Neil, Jonathan, John Neil, John Nicholas, Sarah Catherine, and Sarah who died young. **450**

> Rory (Michael) and John Nicholas died unmarried. Neil and Jonathan were unmarried. John Neil married Catherine MacKenzie, Christmas Island, lived in Big Beach, and had a family. Sarah Catherine married Rod MacDonald, Big Beach and had no family.

Hector (John "Big") married Catherine (Alex, Rory) MacNeil, Piper's Cove. They lived in Highland Hill and their family: Alex, Donald, Rory, and Rachel. The father was drowned, and the mother moved the family to Rear Castle Bay. **451**

Rory (John "Big"), whose wife's name we do not know, settled in Highland Hill. He met a tragic death from perishing in the snow. He had a son, John Bernard "Ban," and a daughter, Isabel. **452**

Isabel (Rory, John "Big") married first Thomas MacNeil, who was drowned off Jamesville on May 22, 1863 (see **192**). In a second marriage she married Neil MacEachern, Inverness and went to the United States, where she had a family. (Rory, one of

Isabel's sons, became a priest and a daughter became a Sister. See also **262**).

John Bernard (Rory, John "Big") married a Miss MacNeil, sister of Alex (Seonaid) MacNeil, Ottawa Brook (see **252**). They lived in Highland Hill and their family: Sandy, Joe, Roderick, Florence, Jessie, and John Ambrose. **453**

Sandy (John Bernard) married a daughter of Hector Brackie, lived in Sydney, and had a family. Florence married Rory (Donald, Eoin "Plant") MacNeil, Barra Glen (see **4**), lived in Sydney, and had no family. Jessie married John MacLean, Boisdale and had a family. Joe married a daughter of Alexander (Aonghas, Eoin) MacNeil, Washabuck (see **262**), lived in the Cape Breton mining area, and had a family. John Ambrose married a Miss Curry and had a family in Sydney, one of whom became a priest in the Diocese of Antigonish.

Roderick (John Bernard) married Betsy Ann (Murdock B.) MacNeil, Highland Hill (see **189**). They lived in Highland Hill, had a family, and moved to Sydney. **454**

● ● ●

We do not know precisely when Johnnie MacKinnon (of whom we know little) and his wife Effie (of whom we also know little) came to Iona Rear. Their family was: Thomas, Neil, Malcolm, and Annie. **455**

Annie (Johnnie) married John (Charles) MacKinnon, MacKinnon's Harbour (see **475**), lived in MacKinnon's Harbour, and had a family.

Thomas (Johnnie) married Elizabeth (Donald, Rory "Red") MacNeil, Iona Rear (see **195**). They lived in Iona Rear and their family: Eoin, Paul, John, Annie, Effie, Mary, and Sarah. **456**

John (Thomas, Johnnie) went to Ontario as a young man, married, and had a son Charles who became a priest. Annie married a Mr. MacNeil, Bay St. Lawrence and had a family. Effie married a Mr. Brown, Bay St. Lawrence and had a family. Mary married Rory MacDougall, Ingonish (see **404**) and had a family, one of whom, Daniel, married a sister of "Red" Rory MacLean, Washabuck (see **514**). Sarah married Donald MacLean, Baddeck (see **521**) and had a family.

Eoin (Thomas, Johnnie) married Mary (Murdock, Donald Eoin) MacNeil, MacNeil's Vale (see **121**). They lived in Iona Rear and had no family. Eoin was drowned off Baddeck. **457**

Paul (Thomas, Johnnie) married first Flora (James Jr., James "Pearson") MacNeil, Iona (see **245**). They lived in Iona Rear and their family: Annie and Mary. In a second marriage he married Catherine (Stephen, Rory Donald "Og") MacNeil, Barra Glen (see **11**) and their family: Flora and John P. **458**

Annie (Paul) married Jack MacPherson, Mira and had a family in Sydney. Mary married a Mr. Cole, lived in Sydney, and had a family. Flora married Michael K. (Kenneth, James) MacNeil, Iona (see **82**), lived in Iona, and had a family.

John P. (Paul) married Veronica (Hector "Lighthouse") MacLean, Gillis Point (see **491**). They lived in Iona Rear and their family: Theresa, Pauline, Rosemary, Eleanor, Priscilla, Vera, Barbara, Sarah, Rosamund, and Aloysius. **459**

Neil (Johnnie) married first Sarah (Murdock, Hector) MacKenzie, Washabuck (see **437**). They lived in Iona Rear and their family: Jonathan, Lucy, Effie, and Murdock. They adopted James, brother of Hector MacDonald, Gillis Point who died young. In a second marriage Neil married Katie (Philip) MacNeil, Gillis Point (see **96**) and had no family. **460**

Lucy (Neil, Johnnie) married Neil D. MacNeil, Sydney (see **80**) and had no family. Effie married and had a family in the United States. Murdock was killed in a mining accident, while still a young man.

Jonathan (Neil, Johnnie) married Mary Catherine (Neil H.) MacNeil, Barra Glen (see **238**). They lived in Iona Rear and their family: Sarah, Joseph, Lizzie, Rita, Annie, Charles, Roderick, Duncan, Effie, Ronald, Clara, and Bernadette. The family moved away from the parish. Clara became a Sister of Notre Dame. **461**

Malcolm (Johnnie) married Effie (Aonghas, Eoin) MacNeil, Highland Hill (see **183**). They lived in Iona Rear and their family: John A., Neil A., Thomas, Angus, Effie, Sarah, Margaret, and Annie. **462**

Sarah (Malcolm, Johnnie), Effie, and Angus were unmarried. Thomas married and had no family. Margaret was the second wife of Rory Paul MacNeil, Iona Rear (see **217**) and had a family. Annie married Neil S. (Stephen) MacNeil, Gillis Point (see **17**) and had a family.

John A. (Malcolm, Johnnie) married Peggy (James Jr., James "Pearson") MacNeil, Iona (see **245**). They lived in Iona Rear and their family: Malcolm Joseph, Murdock, James, Thomas, and Mary Ann. **463**

Malcolm Joseph (John A.) was killed in World War I. Murdock was unmarried. James married in Western Canada. Thomas died young. Mary Ann married in the United States.

Neil A. (Malcolm, Johnnie) married Sarah Bell (Donald, Seamus) MacNeil, Iona (see **80**). They lived in Iona Rear and their family: Dan Malcolm, Mary, Peter, Joseph, Jerome, Columba, and Teresa. **464**

Mary (Neil A.) died young. Columba, as a boy, was killed by a runaway horse. Dan Malcolm and Jerome died unmarried. Peter and Joseph are unmarried. Teresa became a Sister of St. Martha.

● ● ●

MACKINNON

Donald "Ban" (Malcolm) MacKinnon came to Pictou in 1802 with his family. He settled in Cooper's Pond on the property now owned by Rod MacKinnon. He had already married Ann MacInnis and their family: Neil, Flora, Ann, Mary, Allan, Rory, and Charles. Land was scarce in the area, so Allan, Rory, and Charles left to settle in MacKinnon's Harbour. Their sister Mary had married John (Rory "Red") MacNeil, Iona Rear and had a family (see **199**).

Allan (Donald "Ban") married Christy, whose father, Donald (Ruairi) MacNeil, was one of the first four MacNeils to come to Iona. They lived in MacKinnon's Harbour and their family: John G., Donald, James, Michael, Anna "Mhor," Mary, Anna "Beag," Katie, Catherine, Sarah, Elizabeth, Theresa, and Margaret who died young. **465**

James (Allan, Donald "Ban"), Michael, Anna "Mhor," and Mary died unmarried. Anna "Beag" married Hugh Murphy, MacKinnon's Harbour (see **558**) and had a son Joseph Francis, who was adopted by his uncles and aunts in MacKinnon's Harbour. Catherine married Hector MacNeil, Gillis Point (see **126**). Sarah married Michael MacLean, Washabuck (see **489**). Elizabeth married James MacDonald, St. Columba (see **359**). Katie married Malcolm MacNeil, Washabuck Bridge (see **271**) and had no family. Theresa married Rory "Mor" Campbell, Jamesville West and had a family (see **309**).

John G. (Allan, Donald "Ban") married Mary (Calum, Lachlan) MacLean, Washabuck (see **503**). They lived in MacKinnon's Harbour and their family: Mary, Annie, Monica, Michael, Francis, Ambrose, Neil S., and Hugh. They also adopted James MacLean and Christy MacNeil, both of whom died unmarried. **466**

Mary (John G.), Monica, and Francis died unmarried. Hugh was lost at sea. Annie married Hector (Philip) MacNeil, Gillis Point (see **96**), lived in the United States, and had a family. Michael went away from the parish.

Ambrose (John G.) married Mary MacEachern, Mira. They

lived in MacKinnon's Harbour and their family: Dan Francis, and a daughter who died in infancy. They also adopted several children, among them: Philip O'Donnell (see **570**), Colin MacLeod (see **545**), Minnie Devoe (see **324**), and Sadie and Elizabeth (sisters). **467**

Dan Francis (Ambrose) married Lizzie Curry, Boisdale, lived in Sydney, and had a family.

Neil S. (John G.) married Mary Sarah (Neil "Mor") MacNeil, Ottawa Brook (see **247**). They lived in MacKinnon's Harbour and their family: Cassie Ann, Mary, Catherine, Neil Roddie, John Vincent, Michael, and Mary Margaret. **468**

Cassie Ann (Neil S.) married John (Donald) Campbell, Grand Narrows, lived in Grand Narrows, and had a family. Mary Catherine married Angus (Eoin) MacLean, Ottawa Brook (see **536**), lived in Sydney, and had a family. Neil Roddie who lived in Ontario, John Vincent, Michael, and Mary Margaret were unmarried.

Donald (Allan, Donald "Ban") married Margaret MacNeil, Grand Narrows. They lived in MacKinnon's Harbour and their family: Michael, Allan D., Isabella, Theresa, and Margaret. **469**

Michael (Donald) and Isabella died unmarried. Margaret lived unmarried in the United States. Theresa married a Captain Hall in the United States and had no family.

Allan D. (Donald) married Katie MacNeil, Piper's Cove. They lived in MacKinnon's Harbour and had no family. Allan D. and his sister Isabella adopted Mary Agnes MacNeil; he and his wife adopted William and Lucy Hart. **470**

Mary Agnes MacNeil (Allan D.) married Anthony (Dan S.) MacNeil, Gillis Point (see **124**), lived in Iona, and had a family. Lucy Hart married a Mr. Doiron, Pomquet and had a family. William Hart was unmarried.

MACKINNON

Rory (Donald "Ban") had this family: John, Annie, Catherine, Mary, and Sarah. They lived in MacKinnon's Harbour. **471**

Annie (Rory, Donald "Ban") died unmarried. Catherine married a Mr. MacInnis, commonly called "Mac Iain Mhinistir," Red Point (see **412**) and had a family. Mary married Donald (Eoin) MacDonald, Grand Narrows and had a son, Stephen "Ban," who was brought up in MacKinnon's Harbour. Sarah married Angus "Mor" MacDonald, MacKinnon's Harbour (see **392**) and had a family.

John (Rory, Donald "Ban") married Lucy (John "Red") MacNeil, Grand Narrows. They lived in MacKinnon's Harbour and their family: Rory S., Neil, Lucy, Mary Ann, and Rory John. **472**

Rory John (John) died in the United States. Mary Ann married a Mr. Barry in the United States. Neil and Lucy died unmarried.

Rory S. (John) married Margaret Monica (Donald "Plant") MacNeil, Barra Glen (see **4**). They lived in MacKinnon's Harbour and their family: Roddie, Donald, and Stephen who died in infancy. **473**

Roddie (Rory S.) died unmarried. Donald was killed in World War II.

Charles (Donald "Ban") had this family: John, Elizabeth, Mary, Catherine, and Annie. **474**

Annie (Charles, Donald "Ban") married James (Hector) MacNeil, Red Point (see **92**) and had a family. Elizabeth married Alexander (Donald, Alasdair) MacDonald, St. Columba (see **368**) and had a family. Mary died unmarried. Catherine married John (Angus, Eoin) MacNeil, Highland Hill (see **184**) and had a family.

John (Charles, Donald "Ban") married Annie (Johnnie) MacKinnon, Iona Rear (see **455**). They lived in MacKinnon's Harbour and their family: John J., Stephen J., Neil, Donald, and Mary. **475**

Neil (John) died unmarried. Mary married Neil (Philip) MacNeil, Barra Glen (see **98**) and had a family. Donald, a tailor, lived in Sydney. A daughter of John (Charles) married Alasdair (Seonaid) MacNeil, Ottawa Brook (see **253**), lived in Ottawa Brook, and had a family.

John J. (John) married Mary (Angus, Eoin) MacNeil, Highland Hill (see **183**). They lived in MacKinnon's Harbour and their family: Margaret, Mary Ann, and Lizzie Effie. **476**

Margaret (John J.) married first Ignatius MacKenzie, Christmas Island, lived in MacKinnon's Harbour, had no family; and in a second marriage she married Joe MacDonald, Boisdale and had no family. Mary Ann was the first wife of Donald (Donald) Walker (see **577**), lived in Ottawa Brook, and had a child who died in infancy. Lizzie Effie married James (Jonathan) MacDonald, Ottawa Brook (see **348**), lived in Ottawa Brook, and had a family.

Stephen J. (John) married Catherine (Donald "Plant") MacNeil, Barra Glen (see **4**). They lived in MacKinnon's Harbour and their family: John Murdock, Charles, Mary Ann, Marion, Annie May, Florence, and Josephine. **477**

Charles (Stephen J.) married and had a family in Sydney. Annie May married in the United States. Mary Ann married in the United States and had no family. Josephine married in the United States and had a family. Marion became a Sister of Notre Dame. Florence died young.

Johh Murdock (Stephen J.) married Angela MacIntyre, Big Pond. They lived in MacKinnon's Harbour and had no family. **478**

● ● ●

Donald (Philip) MacKinnon settled in Washabuck around 1817. He married Catherine (Neil "Geal") MacNeil, Lower Washabuck (see **265**) and their family: Murdock, John, Philip, Neil I, Neil II, and Catherine. **479**

MACKINNON

John (Donald, Philip), Philip, and Neil I moved away. Neil II lived in Baddeck. Catherine married Ronald "Mor" MacDonald, Upper Washabuck (see **373**) and had a family.

Murdock (Donald, Philip), a tailor, married Catherine (Donald, Donald) MacNeil, Big Beach. They lived in Upper Washabuck and their family: Rory, Dan, Philip, and Neil. We have no information on Philip and Neil. **480**

Rory (Murdock, Donald Philip) married Catherine (Angus) MacDonald, Washabuck Bridge (see **384**). They lived in Upper Washabuck and their family: Angus, Murdock, Dan Alex, Annie, Katie Ann, and Marie whom they adopted. **481**

Angus (Rory) married a girl from Inverness and lived in Sydney. Murdock married in Ontario. Annie married a Mr. MacMillan from Richmond County, lived in Sydney, and had a family. Katie Ann married in the United States. We have no information on Marie.

Dan Alex (Rory) married Martha (Jim Alex) MacDougall, Upper Washabuck (see **397**). They lived in Upper Washabuck and their family: Roddie, Jane, Donnie, Jim, and Muriel. **482**

Dan (Murdock, Donald Philip) married Catherine (Hector) MacKenzie, Washabuck (see **443**). They lived in Upper Washabuck and Cain's Mountain, and their family: Hector, Murdock, Neil, Jimmie, Philip, Dan Joe, Leo, John Neil, Columba, Helen, Cecilia, Ann, Katie, Walter, Sadie E., Roddie, and a set of twins. **483**

Hector (Dan) was unmarried. Murdock married twice and had a family in each marriage. Neil was drowned. Philip married in Ontario. Dan Joe married in British Columbia, had a family, and was accidentally killed. Leo drowned in Washabuck River. John Neil married in Ontario. Columba drowned in British Columbia. Helen married Walter MacDougall, Washabuck (see **398**), lives in Jamesville West, and has a family. Cecilia married Alex (George) Small, Red Point (see **573**), lives in Sydney, and has a family Ann married and has no family. Katie married in the United States. Walter died young. One of the twins and Katie died young. Sadie E. married Quentin MacDonald, Washabuck (see **374**) and had a family in Western Canada. Roddie married a daughter of Dan X. MacNeil, Benacadie Pond and has a family in Sydney.

Jimmie (Dan) married Anna May (Rory J.) MacNeil, Washabuck (see **38**). They live in MacKinnon's Harbour and their family: Andre, Ann, Rory S., Anthony, Francis, and Dan. **484**

● ● ●

Michael "Dubh" MacKinnon, Lower Washabuck was generally believed to have been a son of Donald (Philip) MacKinnon (see **479**). As we cannot verify this, we assign him here a section of his own. He married first Mary (Neil, Eachain) MacNeil, Gillis Point East (see **87**). In a second marriage he married Peggy (Hector) MacNeil, MacNeil's Vale (see **126**) and their family: Theresa, Mary, Katie, Margaret, and John. **485**

Theresa (Michael "Dubh") married Hugh Archie MacDougall, Washabuck (see **400**) and had a family. Mary married Hector (Michael) MacDougall, Washabuck (see **396**) and lives in the Cape Breton mining area. John moved away when young. We have no information on Katie and Margaret.

● ● ●

Donald "Mor" MacKinnon came from Barra in the early 1800's with his half-brother Donald "Og" Murphy (see **556**). He married Flora (Hugh) Gillis, Jamesville West (see **325**). They lived in MacKinnon's Harbour and their family: Angus, Katie, Mary I, Mary II, Ann, and Sarah. **486**

Angus (Donald "Mor") married Mary (Donald, Hector James) MacNeil, Grand Narrows, lived in MacKinnon's Harbour, later moved to the Glace Bay area, and had a family. Katie married Donald (John, Donald John) MacNeil, Red Point (see **255**), lived in MacKinnon's Harbour, and had a family. Mary I married Donald MacNeil, Grand Narrows and had a family. Mary II adopted Agnes who married a Mr. Vivorus in the United States. Ann married John (John) MacNeil, Barra Glen (see **21**), lived in Barra Glen, and had a family. Sarah married Neil (John

"Soldier") MacDonald, Grand Narrows and lived in the United States.

●   ●   ●

Lachlan MacLean was only seventeen when in 1745 he took part in the Battle of Culloden. He lived the latter part of his life in Lower Washabuck and was known, far and wide, for the great clarity with which he could describe events that occurred during the Uprising that ended disastrously at Culloden. He died in the summer of 1842, having attained the patriarchal age of 114. He married Annie MacPhee and their family: Michael, Neil, Alexander, Mary "Mhor," Peter, Malcolm, Roderick, Jan, and Mary "Og." **487**

Michael (Lachlan) remained in the Old Country and enlisted in the Royal Navy. Mary "Mhor" married Eoin MacNeil, Lower Washabuck (see **262**), lived in Washabuck Center, and had a family. Mary "Og" married John Ross, Margaree (see **572**). Jan married a Mr. Almon, George River and their descendants live in George River and Little Bras d'Or. Peter lost his life in St. Andrew's Channel, along with a man named Cann and despite the valiant effort of Peter's brother Alexander.

Neil (Lachlan) married Ann (Neil "Geal") MacNeil (see **265**) in Scotland. They came to Cape Breton in 1819 and their family: Michael and Ann who were born in Scotland, Donald who was the first MacLean to be born in Washabuck, Peter, Hector, Paul, Ann "Bheag," Stephen, another daughter, and an infant who died on the way to the New World and was buried on the Cape Breton Coast before the Ship "Ann" entered Sydney Harbour. **488**

FOOTNOTE:
*For helping us to record the MacLeans of Washabuck — and indeed the people of Washabuck in general — we are indebted to the late Alex D. MacLean and his widow Marjory (see **497**), Neil Devoe (see **323**), and Vincent (Michael Anthony) MacLean (see **507**).

MACLEAN

Ann (Neil, Lachlan) married Philip MacNeil, Gillis Point (see **96**) and had a family. Ann "Bheag" married Michael MacNeil and had a family. Stephen, a teacher, died in his twenties.

Michael (Neil, Lachlan) married Sarah (Allan, Donald "Ban") MacKinnon, MacKinnon's Harbour (see **465**). They lived in Washabuck Center and their family: Mary, John, Elizabeth, Catherine and Margaret (twins), Christena, Hector, Allan, Theresa, and Annie. **489**

Mary (Michael) married Murdock (Neil, Hector) MacNeil, Gillis Point (see **88**). Margaret married Roderick (Alexander) MacNeil, Iona Rear (see **214**) and had a family. Christena married Neil MacMullin and moved to California. Annie married Charles Munroe in Boston. Theresa was unmarried. We do not know whether Elizabeth and Catherine married.

John (Michael) married Elizabeth (Neil, Hector) MacNeil, Gillis Point East (see **87**). They lived in Washabuck Center and had a family. **490**

Hector (Michael) married Catherine (John) MacDonald, St. Columba (see **364**). They lived in Gillis Point East and their family: Mary Elizabeth, Sadie, Michael John, Kathryn, Andrew, John, Malcolm, Veronica, Joseph, Stephen, Hector, and Mary Ann. **491**

Sadie (Hector), Michael John, Kathryn who was a nurse, John, and Malcolm were unmarried. Mary Elizabeth married Malcolm MacNeil; Iona Rear (see **211**), had no family, but adopted James MacNeil, now living in St. Columba. Veronica married John P. (Paul) MacKinnon, Iona Rear (see **459**) and had a family. Joseph married Isabella MacLean, Grand Narrows, lived in Grand Narrows, and had a family. Stephen married Peggy (Rod) MacKinnon, Grand Narrows, lived in Baddeck, and had a family. Mary Ann married John Graves, lived in the United States, and had a family. Hector married Johanna (Archie) MacDougall, Christmas Island, lived in Liverpool, and had a family.

Andrew (Hector) married Helen (John Stephen)

MacKenzie, Washabuck Bridge (see **436**). They live in Iona and their family: Gordon, Roslyn, Charlene, Grace, Hector, Jacinta, Mary, and Kenzie who died young. **492**

Allan (Michael) married Mary Ann (Donald, James) MacNeil, Iona (see **80**). They live in Washabuck Center and their family: Michael, Donald Malcolm, Mary Elizabeth, Peter, Neil Stephen, Rod James, Catherine, Sarah, Michael Joseph, John, James Andrew, and Sarah Veronica. **493**

Sarah (Allan) and James Andrew died young. Peter lost his life in a flood in Florida. Mary Elizabeth, Neil Stephen, and Catherine were unmarried. Donald Malcolm married and had a family in Paschendaele. Michael married a Miss MacDonald, lived in Glace Bay, had a family; and in a second marriage he married Theresa MacIsaac and had a family. Rod James married Maude Boutilier, Sydney and had a family. Michael Joseph married Cecilia (Dan P.) Murphy, Washabuck (see **564**). Sarah Veronica married.

Donald (Neil, Lachlan), the first MacLean to be born in Washabuck, married Mary (Rory) MacDonald, Upper Washabuck (see **371**). They lived in Washabuck Center and their family: Alexander D., Annie, Catherine D., Neil Stephen, Roderick D., Elizabeth Ann, and a daughter who died in infancy. **494**

Alexander D. (Donald), Annie, Catherine D., and Elizabeth Ann who died in the United States, were unmarried. Roderick D. married Mary Ann MacNeil, St. Peter's and had a daughter who died young.

Neil Stephen (Donald) married Christena Campbell, Baddeck. They lived in Washabuck and Baddeck and their family: Alex D. and Michael Donald. **495**

Michael Donald (Neil Stephen), unmarried, was killed in World War I. Alex D. married Marjory Ann (Neil P.) MacLean, Washabuck Center (see **497**) and lived in Baddeck.

MACLEAN

Peter (Neil, Lachlan) married Annie (Rory) MacDonald, Upper Washabuck (see **371**). They lived in Washabuck Center and their family: Mary, Neil P., Elizabeth, Stephen P., Catherine, and two daughters who died in infancy. **496**

Mary (Peter) married Neil MacDonald, Sydney Mines and had a family. Elizabeth married Peter D. MacNeil, Sydney Mines and had a family. Stephen P. married a Miss Heary in Boston and had a family. Catherine married Roderick J. MacNeil, Upper Washabuck (see **38**) and had a family.

Neil P. (Peter) married Marjory Druhan from Antigonish County. They lived in Washabuck Center and their family: Peter D., Catherine Ann, John D., Marjory Ann, Neil Stephen, Roderick Angus, Mary Christena, Annie May, and Mary Theresa. **497**

Peter D. (Neil P.) and Roderick Angus were unmarried. Catherine Ann married James P. Gillis, North Sydney and had no family. John D. married Eve Pearl, Kentville and had no family. Marjory Ann married Alex D. MacLean, Baddeck (see **495**) and had a daughter Marjory MacLean. Mary Christena married Edward Hartigan, Whitney Pier and had a son who died in infancy. Annie May married Chester Hallett in the United States and had a family. Mary Theresa married Hexon Vail in the United States and had no family.

Neil Stephen (Neil P.) married Katie Ann (Angus, Ranald) MacDonald, Upper Washabuck (see **376**). They lived in Washabuck Center and their family: Roderick, Carmie, Bernard, Cyril, and Joseph. **498**

Hector (Neil, Lachlan) married Sarah (Murdock "Beag") MacNeil, Upper Washabuck (see **268**). They lived in Washabuck and their family: Hector, Mary, Neil, Murdock, Michael, Stephen, Ellen, Roderick, and John. **499**

Mary (Hector), Neil who was drowned, Stephen, Ellen, and Roderick were unmarried. Michael was killed in Boston. John died in Washabuck as the result of an accident. Hector, a builder, married a Miss MacPhee from P.E.I. Murdock married Janet MacPhee from P.E.I.

MACLEAN

Paul (Neil, Lachlan) married Margaret (Murdock "Beag") MacNeil, Upper Washabuck (see **268**). They lived in Washabuck Center and their family: Mary, Stephen, John, Neil, Murdock, Michael, Malcolm, Catherine, and Ellen Ann. **500**

Neil (Paul), Murdock, Michael, Malcolm, Catherine, and Ellen Ann were unmarried. Stephen married Mary Ann (Eoin) MacNeil, Iona (see **73**), lived in Baddeck, and had a son John M. Mary married Donald J. MacNeil, lived in Sydney, and had a family. John married first Catherine Fraser, Morristown in Antigonish County, had a family; and in a second marriage he married Mary (Eoin) MacNeil, Iona (see **73**) and their family: Tena and John J.

Alexander (Lachlan) married Mary MacDougall who came with her brother James to Upper Washabuck in 1817. They lived in Lower Washabuck and their family: James, Catherine, Sarah, Paul, Stephen, Peter, Michael, and Nicholas. **501**

Michael (Alexander, Lachlan), James, and Nicholas lost their lives in the sinking of the Ship "Alexander." Michael and Nicholas were unmarried. James married Catherine MacNeil, Washabuck and had no family. Catherine married Roderick MacNeil, Baddeck Bay and had a family. Sarah married Allan ("I' Ruadh") MacNeil, Christmas Island, lived in St. Peter's, and had a family. Stephen was twice married and had a son, Reverend Neil MacLean, Sydney. Peter married Flora Gillis, Glasgow in Cape Breton, lived in the old homestead in Lower Washabuck, and had no family.

Paul (Alexander, Lachlan) married Ann Carmichael, Whycocomagh. They lived in Washabuck and their family: Catherine, Mary, Anastasia, Alexander, and a daughter who died young. **502**

Anastasia (Paul) was unmarried. Catherine married Henry MacKinnon, Sydney Mines and had no family. Mary married Alex MacIntyre, Sydney Mines and had a family. Alexander married Elizabeth Oram, Little Bras d'Or, lives in George's River, and has this family: Alex, Mary Ann, Catherine, John, Paul James, Mary, Anastasia, and Alexander.

MACLEAN

Malcolm (Lachlan) married Catherine (Eoin) MacDonald, Grand Narrows. They lived in Washabuck and their family: Peter Francis, Jonathan, Stephen, Michael, Donald, Elizabeth, Flora, Mary, Anna, Christena, Catherine, and Martin who died in infancy. **503**

Donald (Malcolm, Lachlan) married Catherine Beaton, Boularderie, lived in Boston, and had a family. Elizabeth married Angus MacNeil, Big Bank in Boularderie and had a family. Flora married Hector MacLean, Boisdale and had a family, one of whom was the father of Right Reverend Ronald MacLean. Mary married John G. (Allan) MacKinnon, MacKinnon's Harbour (see **466**) and had a family. Christena married Charles MacNeil, Shenacadie and had a family. Anna married Donald MacSween, Glasgow in Cape Breton and had a family. Catherine married first John C. Boyd, South River in Antigonish County who spent his last days in Washabuck, had a family; and in a second marriage she married Joseph Arsenault, Cheticamp, lived in Baddeck, and had a family.

Peter Francis (Malcolm, Lachlan) married Ellen Denison, Baddeck River. They lived in Washabuck and their family: Annie, Esther, Joseph, Elizabeth, Mary Ellen, Christena, Vincent, Alexander, and Martin who died young. **504**

Elizabeth (Peter Francis) and Alexander were unmarried. Annie married Daniel H. Campbell, Baddeck and had a family. Esther married Joseph Tinkham in the United States and had a family. Joseph married Harriet Brown in the United States and had a family. Mary Ellen married Richard Broderick, lived in Florence, and had a family. Christena married Napoleon Charon in the United States.

Vincent (Peter Francis) married Theresa (Michael, Eoin) MacNeil, Washabuck Center (see **263**). They lived in MacKay's Point in Washabuck and their family: Peter F., Helen, Lucy, Alexander, Murdock, John, Leo, Annie Helen, Mary, Joseph, Theresa, and Michael Anthony. **505**

Helen (Vincent) married Stephen L. (Francis) MacNeil, Iona (see **40**), lived in Sydney, and had a family. Lucy married George Bush, Swan Lake in Manitoba and lives in Windsor in Ontario. Alexander, a student at Saint Francis Xavier University, died young. Murdock is unmarried. John married Betty (Jim Hugh) MacNeil, Sydney, lives in the United States, and has a family. Leo married Loretta Gauthier, Sudbury and has a family. Annie Helen married Bill Gallagher, Montreal, lives in Florida, and has a family. Mary married Alfred MacDonald, Middle River, lives in Baddeck, and has no family. Joseph married Marguerite (Jim Hugh) MacNeil, Sydney, lives in Sydney, and has a family. Theresa married Peter Morrison, lives in Sydney, and has a family.

Peter F. (Vincent) married Flora May (John Y.) Gillis, MacKinnon's Harbour (see **330**). They live in Iona and their family: Alexander, Ann, Florence, Theresa, and Helen. **506**

Michael Anthony (Vincent) married Rose Rhodena (Angus, Ranald) MacDonald, Upper Washabuck (see **376**). They live in the old homestead in MacKay's Point and their family: Vincent, Angus, Martin, Judy, and Robert. **507**

Jonathan (Malcolm, Lachlan) married Mary MacNeil, Boularderie. They live in Washabuck and their family: Catherine, Lachlan, Donald, Ian, Vincent, Anna Belle, Stephen, and Angus. **508**

Stephen (Jonathan), Angus, and Catherine were unmarried. Vincent married Josephine Beaton, lives in Ontario, and his family: Edna and Michael. Donald married Mary Reiden, Sydney Mines and has a family. Lachlan married Jane MacLean and their family: Josephine, Hector, Elizabeth, Ann, Catherine, and Mary Ann. Ian married Margaret Fitzgerald, lives in Sydney Mines and his family: Peter, Charles, Ambrose, Anthony, Bernard, Mary Ellen, Elizabeth, Ruth, Gertrude Patricia, and Ann. Anna Belle married Joseph MacNeil and has a family in Ontario.

Stephen (Malcolm, Lachlan) married Mary Gillis, Whycocomagh. They lived in Lower Washabuck and their family: Charles, Margaret, Mary Ann, Agnes, Roderick Joseph, Malcolm B., Christena, and Elizabeth. **509**

MACLEAN

Charles (Stephen), Margaret, and Christena were unmarried. Mary Ann became a Franciscan Sister. Agnes married Roderick R. MacDonald, Upper Washabuck (see **374**), lived in Lower Washabuck, and had a family. Elizabeth married Neil MacKenzie, Upper Washabuck, had a family, and lived away.

Roderick Joseph (Stephen) married Sarah (Murdock B.) MacNeil, Highland Hill (see **189**). They lived in Lower Washabuck, had no family, but they adopted Mary MacDonald, Mina MacNeil, and Teddy Porter. **510**

> Mary MacDonald (Roderick Joseph) married Arthur Campbell, Iona (see **318**), lived in Iona, and had a family. Mina MacNeil married John Rory (Michael John) Nash, St. Columba (see **566**), lives in Sydney, and has a family. Teddy Porter married and has a family in Sydney Mines.

Malcolm B. (Stephen) married Mary Jane (Archie "Red") MacKenzie, Birch Point in Washabuck (see **427**). They lived in Lower Washabuck and their family: Mary Margaret, Archibald A., Eulalia, and Stephen. **511**

Michael (Malcolm, Lachlan) married Mary MacRitchie, Little Narrows. They lived in Washabuck and their family: Euphemia Ann, Ellen, Christena, Flora, Ellen Ann, Mary Jane, and Elizabeth. **512**

> Euphemia Ann (Michael) married Neil MacKinnon, Grand Narrows and had no family, but they adopted Catherine Devoe who married a Mr. Anderson. Ellen married William C. Bonnyman and we have no record as to whether she had a family. Christena married Michael H. Burns in the United States and had a family. Flora married Peter D. (Donald, Jonathan) MacKenzie, Upper Washabuck (see **445**). Ellen Ann married "Red" Rory MacLean, Washabuck (see **515**), lived in Lower Washabuck, and had a family. Mary Jane married Michael O'Handley, Sydney Mines and had a family. Elizabeth married John D. MacKinnon, Sydney and had no family.

MACLEAN

Roderick (Lachlan) married Ann MacIntyre, Big Bank in Boularderie. They lived in Washabuck and their family: Donald, Flora, Peter S., Mary, Catherine, Lachlan, Angus, Mary "Og," Alexander, Michael, and Elizabeth. **513**

Flora (Roderick, Lachlan) married Angus (Hugh "Red") Campbell, Gillis Point East (see **296**) and had a family. Angus married three times, away from the parish, and had a family from each marriage. Alexander was unmarried. Mary married John (Alasdair "Mor") MacNeil, Gillis Point (see **130**) and had a family. Catherine married Roderick Morrison, Baddeck and had a family. Mary "Og" married Jonathan (Neil, Eoin) MacNeil, Iona (see **73**). Michael married first a Miss MacLeod, North Shore; and in a second marriage he married a woman from Upper Canada, and we have no record whether he had any family. Elizabeth married first Michael (Neil, Eoin) MacNeil (see **73**), had a family; and in a second marriage she married Michael MacNeil, Glace Bay and had no family.

Donald (Roderick, Lachlan) married Ann MacNeil, Shenacadie. They lived in Washabuck and their family: John I, Christena, Sarah Elizabeth, "Red" Rory, Mary Jane, John II, Michael, and three daughters who died in infancy. **514**

John I (Donald) was unmarried. Sarah Elizabeth married Allan MacDonald, Glace Bay and had a family. Mary Jane married William Lehman in the United States and had no family. Christena married Daniel (Rory, Donald Hector) MacDougall, Washabuck (see **403**) and moved to Ingonish with her family. John II and Michael died in infancy.

"Red" Rory (Donald) married Ellen Ann (Michael, Calum) MacLean, Washabuck (see **512**). They lived in Washabuck and their family: Michael Dan, Mary Ann, Joseph A., Elizabeth, Florence, Euphemia, Agnes, John Charles, and Nancy whom they adopted. **515**

Michael Dan ("Red" Rory) married Mary Ann (James A.) MacNeil, Gillis Point (see **136**), lives in Baddeck, and has a family. Mary Ann married Charles Doherty, lives in Baddeck, and has a family. Elizabeth married John R. (Michael S.) MacNeil, Barra Glen (see **14**) and has a family. Florence married Angus MacDonald, Sydney and has a family. Euphemia married

MACLEAN

Jackie (John "Ban") MacNeil, Barra Glen (see **22**) and has a family. Agnes married Neil Francis MacLennan, Benacadie and has a family. John Charles married Jean Curry and has a family in Toronto.

Joseph A. ("Red" Rory) married Josephine LaRusic, Bay St. Lawrence. They live in Washabuck and their family: Ann, Sandra, Alice, Martina, Joanne, Jim, Theresa, and Maureen. **516**

Peter S. (Roderick, Lachlan) married Jessie MacDonald, Highlands in Christmas Island. They lived in Washabuck and their family: Mary Ann, Elizabeth, Annie, Neil P.S., Francis Alexander, Michael, and Theresa. **517**

Michael (Peter S.) and Theresa died in infancy. Francis Alexander died young. Mary Ann and Annie became Sisters of Sacred Heart. Elizabeth married first Peter Campbell, Gillis Point East (see **294**), had a family; and in a second marriage she married Daniel MacKenzie, Glace Bay and had a family.

Neil P.S. (Peter S.) married first Elizabeth (Eoin, Seamus) MacNeil, MacNeil's Vale (see **78**). They lived in Washabuck and their family: Francis Alexander, Peter, John Joseph, Michael Ambrose, James A., Matthias, Neil Stephen, and Jessie who died in infancy. In a second marriage he married Christena (John, Michael) MacLean, Washabuck Center (see **490**) and their family: John Benedict, Madeline, and Elizabeth. Mary and Joseph died in infancy. **518**

Francis Alexander (Neil P.S.) and Peter, both war veterans, were unmarried. John Joseph married away and had a family. Michael Ambrose married away and had a family. Matthias married Sadie MacNeil, Piper's Cove and had a family in Sydney. Neil Stephen married a daughter of John MacLennan, Benacadie and has a family in Sydney. John Benedict married Annie (John Stephen) MacKenzie, Washabuck Bridge (see **436**), lives in Sydney Mines, and has a family of sixteen. Madeline married Peter (Charles) Northen, Ottawa Brook (see **568**), lives in Little Narrows, and had a family. Elizabeth married

"Buddy" (John Charles) MacIver, Washabuck (see **423a**) and has a family in Sydney.

James A. (Neil P.S.) married Irene Deon, Pomquet. They live in Washabuck and their family: James, Yvonne, Annette, Joey, Tony, Louise, Loretta, and Louis. **519**

Lachlan (Roderick, Lachlan) married Mary MacNeil, Shenacadie. They lived in Washabuck and their family: Elizabeth, 'Red" Lachlan, Alexander, Sarah Ann, and John. **520**

John (Lachlan) was unmarried. Elizabeth married first Hugh Ronnayne, had a family; and in a second marriage she married John Hicks and had a family. "Red" Lachlan married first Beatrice Peck and their family: Blanche, Pearl, Violet, Russell, Seward Hilary, and Claude; and in a second marriage he married Agnes Love Selfridge and their family: Lachlan and Francis Sampson. Alexander married Margaret Peck, a sister of "Red" Lachlan's wife, and their family: Alexander, George A., Thomas P., Joseph L., and Francis C., Sarah Ann married Jacob Johnstone in the United States and had no family.

● ● ●

Neil "Dubh" (Donald) MacLean settled in Washabuck, and later moved to Baddeck. His son Donald married Sarah (Thomas, Johnnie) MacKinnon, Iona Rear (see **456**) and had a daughter. **521**

Allan, a brother of Neil "Dubh," married Catherine (Eoin, Hector) MacKenzie, Washabuck (see **442**), settled in Washabuck, and had five sons and six daughters. The family did not remain in the parish, but one of the sons, Donald, married Sarah (Darby) Campbell, Jamesville (see **299**) and later moved to the Cape Breton mining area. **522**

● ● ●

Allan MacLean, known as "Leathaineach," a native of the mainland of Scotland, came to Washabuck in 1817. He married Flora (Alasdair) MacDonald, a sister of Michael "Mor"

MACLEAN

MacDonald (see **356**), and their family: Michael, Alexander, and Catherine. **523**

Alexander (Allan) was drowned when the vessel "Alexander" foundered on its way to Newfoundland in 1859. Catherine married Angus MacIntyre, Boisdale. Michael, a blacksmith, married Margaret (Malcolm "Ban") MacDonald, Grand Narrows, lived in Boisdale, and their family: Alex, Allan, and Stephen who was brought up on his grandfather's farm at Lighthouse Point in Grand Narrows.

● ● ●

Charles "Gobha" (Hector) MacLean from Barra, a nephew of Lachlan MacLean, came to Washabuck via Mabou in about 1817. An unmarried sister Kate accompanied him. He settled in Washabuck Bridge and his family: Kate, John, Rory, Michael Charlie, and Hector. He later moved to Baddeck with his son Michael Charles. **525**

Kate (Charles "Gobha"), John, and Rory were unmarried. Michael Charles married Euphemia Nicholson, Gairloch Mountain, had a family, and lived in Baddeck. Hector married a Lucy MacDonald and had no family.

● ● ●

Archibald MacLean came from Barra with six sons. He was twice married in Barra and both his wives died, before he came to the New World. His sons were: Rory, Neil, Dan, Michael, Peter, and Jonathan.

Michael (Archibald) married in the United States and had a family. Peter and Jonathan were unmarried.

Rory (Archibald) married a Miss Dingwall. They lived in Rear Ottawa Brook and their family: Peter, John, and Mary. We have no information on Mary. **526**

MACLEAN

Peter (Rory, Archibald) married Flora (Donald) Gillis, MacKinnon's Harbour (see **327**). They lived in Rear Ottawa Brook and their family: Rod, Ronald, Dan, Norman, Hugh, Margaret, and Marcella whom they adopted and who went to the United States. **527**

Ronald (Peter) married Flora McMullin, Reserve Mines, lived in Reserve Mines, and their family: Philip, Margaret, Mildred, Dolena, John, Jimmie, Alex, Flora, and Wilma. Dan married a sister of Ronald's wife, lived in Reserve Mines, and had no family. Margaret married Charles Northen (see **568**), lived in Ottawa Brook, and had a family.

Rod (Peter) married Katie (Philip) MacDonald, Ottawa Brook (see **344**). They lived in Ottawa Brook and their family: Florence, Margaret, John, and Lawrence. **528**

Margaret (Rod) married Murdock (Michael D.) MacNeil, Iona (see **54**), lives in Iona, and has a family.

Hugh (Peter) married a Miss Carrington. They lived in Ottawa Brook and their family: Leo, Flora, Hugh, Franklin, and Annie. **529**

Norman (Peter) married Margaret Marsh who was adopted by Tom and Katie Ann MacLean, MacKinnon's Harbour (see **533**). They lived in Rear Ottawa Brook and later moved to MacKinnon's Harbour, and their family: Marcella, Florence, Catherine, Theresa, Margaret, Dannie, Bernard, Duncan, John Thomas, Peter, Lex, Norma, and a son who died in infancy. **530**

John (Rory, Archibald) married Mary (Iain "Ban") MacNeil, Benacadie. They lived in Rear Ottawa Brook and their family: Charles, John, Mary Ann, and Jonathan. **531**

Charles (John) married Mary MacLean and lived in Estmere. John was unmarried. We have no information on Mary Ann and Jonathan.

MACLEAN

Dan (Archibald) married Christy MacLean (see **534**). They lived in MacKinnon's Harbour and their family: John, Ann, and Tilly whom they adopted. **532**

John (Dan, Archibald) died unmarried in the United States. Ann married Stephen (Alasdair, Donald) MacDonald, Jamesville West (see **368**) and later moved to Richmond County. Tilly was unmarried.

Neil (Archibald) married. We have no information on who his wife was and we have information on only a son Rory.

Rory (Neil, Archibald) married Flora (James "Pearson") MacNeil, Iona (see **242**). They lived in MacKinnon's Harbour and their family: Michael, Neil, Tom, and Katie Ann, all of whom were unmarried. In this home Margaret Marsh and Rhodena MacLean were adopted. **533**

> Margaret Marsh married Norman (Peter) MacLean, Ottawa Brook (see **530**), lived in Rear Ottawa Brook and in MacKinnon's Harbour, and had a family. Rhodena married Cosmas Northen, Ottawa Brook (see **569**), lived in MacKinnon's Harbour, and had a family.

● ● ●

Neil (Eachain) MacLean came from Scotland and settled in Ottawa Brook. He married Katie (Eoin) MacNeil, aunt of Murdock B. MacNeil (see **189**), and their family: Hector, Donald, Eoin, Christy, and Angus. **534**

Christy (Neil, Eachain) married Dan (Archibald) MacLean, Ottawa Brook (see **532**), lived in MacKinnon's Harbour, and had a family.

Hector (Neil, Eachain) married first a daughter of John (Donald, Rory) MacNeil, Iona (see **35a**). They lived towards the south shore of Ottawa Brook. His wife died shortly after their marriage. In a second marriage he married Ann (Donald, Alasdair) MacDonald, St. Columba (see **367**) and their family: Ann, Cassie, Katie Mary, Margaret Jane, Eliza, Archie, Dan, Michel, and Neil. **535**

MACLEAN

Ann (Hector) married Edward Moody in the United States and had a family, one of whom became a Sister. Katie Mary married Archie MacLean, Highlands in Christmas Island and had a family. Michael was unmarried. Archie married Tena MacNeil, Benacadie, lived in Sydney, and had a large family, one of whom became a priest in the Diocese of Antigonish and another a Sister of St. Martha. Eliza married Dan Y. (Neil) MacNeil, Ottawa Brook (see **248**) and had a family. Neil married Nellie Boutilier, Sydney and had a large family. Margaret Jane married John J. (Neil) MacNeil, Ottawa Brook (see **247**), lived in Sydney, and had a large family, two of whom became priests in the Diocese of Antigonish and another the Provincial Superior of the Sisters of Notre Dame. Dan married Cora White and had a large family in Sydney. Cassie married Hector MacKinnon, Christmas Island, lived in the United States, and had a family.

Eoin (Neil, Eachain) married Christy (Neil, Barra) MacNeil, Red Point (see **33**). They lived in Ottawa Brook and their family: Neil, Michael, John J., Cassie, Katie, and Angus.   **536**

Neil (Eoin) married in the United States, but his children — Eddie and Tena — were brought up in Ottawa Brook, Tena later marrying a John MacLean in Sydney. Michael married in the United States and had a family. Cassie married Angus MacLellan, Margaree, lived in Ottawa Brook (see **543**), and had a family. Katie married Archie MacLellan, Margaree, lived in Margaree, and had an adopted family. Angus married Mary Catherine (Neil S.) MacKinnon, MacKinnon's Harbour (see **468**), lived in Sydney, and had a family.

John J. (Eoin) married Christena (John) MacDonald, Ottawa Brook (see **354**). They lived in Ottawa Brook and their family: Joe, Tena, Neil, Angus, Catherine, Mickey, Alex, Freddie, and a twin boy who died in infancy. They also adopted Eddie and Tena, children of Neil (Eoin) MacLean (see **536**).   **537**

Tena (John J.) and Freddie are unmarried. Joe married Evangeline MacNeil, Sydney, and has a family in Sydney. Neil married Sadie Madeline (Seward) Bonaparte, MacKinnon's Harbour (see **277**), lives in Sydney, and has a family. Angus married Catherine (Daniel J.) MacKenzie, Ottawa Brook (see **428**), lives in Sydney, and has a family. Catherine married John (D.R.) MacNeil, Christmas Island, lives in Sydney, and has a family. Mickey married Isabel (Seward) Bonaparte, MacKinnon's Harbour (see **277**), lives in Sydney, and has a family.

Alex (John J.) married Ada (Daniel J.) MacKenzie, Ottawa Brook (see **428**). They live in MacKinnon's Harbour and their family: Lyla, Marina, Aileen, Mark, and Paul. **538**

Donald (Neil, Eachain) married first Sarah (James "Mor") MacNeil, Shenacadie. They lived in Ottawa Brook and their family: John Archie, Rory, and Mary Ann. In a second marriage he married Ann (Eoin "Mor") MacNeil, Benacadie and had no family. **539**

Rory (Donald) moved away. Mary Ann married John H. (Donald) Walker, Ottawa Brook (see **576**), lived in Sydney, and had a family, one of whom became a Sister of Notre Dame.

John Archie (Donald) married Sarah Gillis, MacAdam's Lake. They lived in Ottawa Brook and their family: Dan Angus, Leonard, Janie, and Sadie. **540**

Dan Angus (John Archie) married in Montreal and had a son and a daughter. Sadie married Tony MacNaughton (see **323**), lives in Ottawa Brook, and has no family.

Leonard (John Archie) married Kathleen (Joseph) Bonaparte, MacKinnon's Harbour (see **278**). They lived in Ottawa Brook and their family: Leonard Jr., May, Margaret, Ann, and Sadie. **541**

Angus (Neil, Eachain) married Mary (John, Ruairi) MacNeil, Iona (see **37**). They lived in Washabuck and their family: Alex Hector, Rory Hector, John, Neil, Pat, Florence, Mary Josephine, and Katie Ann. There could well have been two other daughters, Sarah and Mary Jane, but we cannot confirm this. **542**

MACLEAN - MACLEOD

Alex Hector (Angus) married in the United States and had a family. Rory Hector married and had a family in New Waterford. John and Neil are reported to have gone to the United States. Pat died young. Florence is reported to have married a De Rusha in the United States. Mary Josephine married Rod (Angus, Neil) MacKinnon, Cooper's Pond and had a family. Katie Ann married Jim "Cooper" MacNeil, Grand Narrows and had a family.

●   ●   ●

Angus MacLellan came to Ottawa Brook from Margaree. He married Cassie (Eoin, Neil) MacLean, Ottawa Brook (see **536**). They lived in Ottawa Brook and their family: Charlie, Tena I, Malcolm, John Angus, John Neil, Mickey, Catherine, Annie, Jackie, Peter Allan, and Tena II whom they adopted.   **543**

John Angus (Angus) and Jackie are unmarried. John Neil was killed in World War II. Malcolm became a Franciscan Priest and Tena I became a Franciscan Sister. Charlie married in Ontario and had no family. Mickey married in Toronto and had no family. Catherine married John Alex (Seward) Bonaparte, MacKinnon's Harbour (see **276**), lives in Reserve, and had a family. Annie married a Mr. Hunley in Little Bras d'Or, lives there, and has a family.

Peter Allan (Angus) married Rhodena (Dan J.J.) MacNeil, Ottawa Brook (see **228**). They lived in Ottawa Brook and their family: Charlotte, Donald, Judy, Rosaire, Neila, Stanley, David, and Harriet.   **544**

●   ●   ●

Colin MacLeod, adopted son of Ambrose MacKinnon, MacKinnon's Harbour, married Bertha (Joseph) Bonaparte, MacKinnon's Harbour (see **278**). They lived in MacKinnon's Harbour and their family: Bernard, Joe, and John Neillie.   **545**

Bernard (Colin) married a Miss Musgrave, Frenchvale, lives in Frenchvale, and has a family.

●   ●   ●

MACPHEE - MATHESON

A Mr. MacPhee lived in Lower Washabuck for a time. He married Marcella MacInnis, Lower Washabuck, a close relative of Lachlan MacLean. This Marcella MacInnis was a sister of Jane, who married Donald Campbell, MacNeil's Vale (see **319**). Mr. MacPhee was drowned, and is believed to have been the first to be buried in the new Washabuck cemetery. He had a son and a daughter. After his death, his widow moved the family to P.E.I. **546**

Kenneth MacRitchie settled in Washabuck. His family was: Norman, Murdock, Kenneth, Christy, Florence, and Ann. **547**

Chirsty (Kenneth) was unmarried. Ann was about to marry a son of Alexander (Lachlan) MacLean who drowned in the disaster of the Ship "Alexander." Murdock married and had a family in Little Narrows. Kenneth married Mary Ann (Henry) MacIver (see **420**). Florence married a Mr. MacRitchie in Alba.

Norman (Kenneth) married Mary (Donald) Matheson and their family: Kathy Bell, Annie Sarah, Cassie, John Dan, Danny, Kenny, and a brother who died young. **548**

Danny (Norman), unmarried, was killed in World War I. Kathy Bell married Angus MacAulay and had a family. Annie Sarah married a Mr. MacDonald, lived in Sydney, and had a family. Cassie married Murray Steeves and had a family. Kenny married and had a family in Sydney.

John Dan (Norman) married Margaret (Dan) MacAulay (see **339**). They lived in Washabuck Bridge where he operated a general store. **549**

● ● ●

William Matheson settled in Washabuck. He had a son Angus, who had a son Hugh, and Hugh moved to Hunter's Mountain. We have no further information on this family. There are no Mathesons in the area today. **550**

● ● ●

MORRISON - MURPHY

John Morrison, likely from the same family as the Morrisons of Baddeck, settled in Gillis Point. Very little is known of him or his family. There were at least four children: Donald "Mor," Donald "Beag," Rory, and Annie. **551**

Donald "Mor" (John) was unmarried, lived with his sister Annie who apparently was also unmarried. They adopted at least one boy and one girl. These children moved to the Cape Breton mining area.

Donald "Beag" (John) married Katie (Eoin) MacNeil, Hector's Point in Iona (see **152**) and their family: John Rory and Mary Ann, who both died unmarried. **552**

Rory (John) married a daughter of James (Donald "Ban") MacDonald, Gillis Point (see **388**) who was a sister of the wife of Donald "Beag" (Rory "Mor") MacNeil, Iona (see **338**). They had a son, known as "Domhnull Anna Sheamus," from the fact that, after his mother's death, he was brought up by his aunt, Anna (Sheamus). **553**

Donald (Rory, John) or Donald (Anna, Sheamus) married a girl from Richmond County. He lived most of his life in Gillis Point, had a large family, and moved to the Cape Breton mining area. **554**

• • •

Allan Munroe settled in Murphy's Point, Washabuck. He had at least a son, William. **555**

William (Allan) married Nancy (Calum "Ruadh") MacNeil, Washabuck (see **272**) and had no family.

• • •

Donald "Og" (Joseph) Murphy came from Barra as a young man. His mother was married first to Donald (Duncan) MacKinnon, from whom she had a son, Donald "Mor" MacKinnon. The half-brothers, Donald "Mor" MacKinnon and Donald "Og" Murphy, settled in MacKinnon's Harbour. Donald "Mor" settled on the properties later owned by Colin MacLeod and Abraham Bonaparte, and Donald "Og" settled on the property later owned by Hugh N. Gillis. Donald "Og" married Mary (Iain,

MURPHY

Eoin) MacNeil, Jamesville (see **57**) and their family: Joseph, Hugh, Mary, Annie, Margaret, Christy, Katie, Michael, James, and John. **556**

Margaret (Donald "Og") and Michael died unmarried. James, unmarried, died in a mining accident. John married in the United States and, with the exception of his son John, the family died young. Mary married Neil MacKinnon, Shenacadie and had a family. Annie married Donald (Neil, Eachain) MacNeil (see **87**), lived in the United States, and had a family. Christy married Peter Devoe (see **322**) and had a family. Katie married Jonathan MacDonald, Ottawa Brook (see **346**) and had a family.

Joseph (Donald "Og") married Susan Murphy from Ireland and their family: Hugh, Joseph, James, Minnie and Della. **557**

Hugh (Joseph), Joseph, and James were unmarried. Minnie was married. Della married in the United States.

Hugh (Donald "Og") married Annie (Allan) MacKinnon, MacKinnon's Harbour (see **465**). They lived in the United States and had a son, Joseph F., who was adopted by his aunts and uncles in MacKinnon's Harbour (see **465**). **558**

Joseph F. (Hugh) married Mary (Michael S.) MacNeil, Barra Glen (see **12**). They lived in MacKinnon's Harbour and their family: Hugh, Michael, Peter, Donald, Roddie, Margaret Teresa, and their two eldest — Annie May and Catherine Josephine — who died in infancy. **559**

Hugh (Joseph F.), Peter, Donald, and Roddie served in World War II and were fortunate enough to come out from that conflict unharmed. Donald and Roddie continued on in the Armed Forces. Roddie married Mary (Michael Dan) MacNeil, Jamesville (see **61**), serves in the Armed Forces in Saint John, and has this family: Ronnie, Carol, Shelly, and Blair.

Peter (Joseph F.) married Margaret Teresa (Roddie, Frank) MacNeil, Iona (see **160**). They live in Iona and their family: Gertrude, Roddie, Gerard, Donna, and David. **560**

●   ●   ●

MURPHY

Peter Murphy came to Washabuck Bridge from P.E.I. He had already married a Franch lady and they had this family: Kate, Sarah, Georgie, Margaret, and John. In a second marriage he married Liza MacKenzie and had no family. **561**

John (Peter) married Mary, adopted daughter of Calum I' "Ruadh" MacNeil (see **271**), had no family, but they adopted Catherine Murphy, who married Neil Hunter, Hunter's Mountain and had a daughter Violet. Katie and Margaret married in P.E.I. Georgie married a Mr. Dunn in P.E.I. Sadie married Jim Alex MacDougall, Upper Washabuck (see **397**) and had a family.

●　　●　　●

Peter Murphy came to Washabuck via Mabou. His family was: Alex, Thomas, Henry, Christy, and two other daughters. **562**

One of Peter's daughters married George MacIver, Washabuck (see **419**). Another married a Mr. Hutchinson, Inlet Baddeck. Christy married Hector (Rory) MacKenzie, Washabuck (see **433**). We have no information on Henry.

Thomas (Peter) had this family: Pat, Tom, Nick, John, Kate, Abbie, and Mary. Tom and John died young. Pat married and had a family. Nick married and had a family in Baddeck. Kate and Mary married sea-captains in the United States. Abbie married a Mr. Brown on the Nova Scotia mainland and had a family.

Alex (Peter) married Mary, sister of Archie MacKenzie, Birch Point in Washabuck (see **426**). They lived in Washabuck and their family: Neil Henry, Katie Ellen, Peter, Donald P., John Archie, Angus J., Lizzie, Sarah, and Malcolm. All moved away from the area, but Dan P. returned to Washabuck. **563**

Dan P. (Alex, Peter) married Mary Ann (Charles) MacKenzie, Washabuck (see **435**) and settled on what was the former MacIver property. They had this family in which there were three sets of twins: Charles, Alex, Peter, Kathleen, Ann, Rita, Helen, Margaret, May, Cecilia, and Gussie. **564**

Alex (Dan P.), Gussie, and Peter live in Sydney. Cecilia married Michael Joseph (Allan) MacLean, Washabuck Center (see **483**) and lived in Sydney. Kathleen married Dan Francis (Angus, Ranald) MacDonald (see **379**), lives in Washabuck, and has a family. Charles, unmarried, lives in Washabuck.

●　　●　　●

Donald Nash settled in St. Columba in the early 1800's. He married Peggy (Eoin "Beag") MacNeil, Benacadie West (see **222**) and their family: Michael John, Mary, Bessie, and another son who left home and on whom we have no information. **565**

Mary (Donald) married Neil H. MacNeil, Barra Glen (see **238**), lived in Barra Glen, and had a family. Bessie was the second wife of John (Alasdair, Barra) MacNeil, Ottawa Brook (see **32**), had no family but adopted Margaret MacDonald; and in a second marriage she married Peter B. MacDonald, Ottawa Brook (see **352**), lived in Ottawa Brook, and had no family. Margaret MacDonald married first Thomas (Murdock B.) MacNeil, Highland Hill, lived in Highland Hill, had no family; and in a second marriage she married Michael (Michael "Doctor") MacNeil, Ottawa Brook, lived in Ottawa Brook, and had no family.

Michael John (Donald) married Rachel (Neil, Malcolm) MacNeil, Benacadie. They lived in St. Columba and their family: Dan Neil, John Rory, Margaret, Peter Francis, and Agnes whom they adopted. **566**

John Rory (Michael John) married Jemina (J.T., Iain Eachain) MacNeil, Iona and St. Peter's (see **147**), lived in Sydney, and had a family. Margaret died young. Agnes became a Sister of Notre Dame.

Dan Neil (Michael John) married first Margaret (Dan) Devoe, Iona (see **324**). They lived in Iona and had a daughter Judy. He married a second time, lives in Sydney, and has no family. **567**

Judy (Dan Neil) was adopted by Francis (Michael D.) MacNeil, Iona (see **53**).

●　　●　　●

NORTHEN - REDQUEST

Charles Northen married Margaret (Peter, Rory) MacLean, Rear Ottawa Brook (see **527**). They lived in Ottawa Brook and their family: Mary Flora, Josephine, Liza, Cosmas, and Peter. **568**

Mary Flora (Charles) married John Ellis, Little Narrows and had a family. Josephine married Angus Louis (Seward) Bonaparte, MacKinnon's Harbour (see **276**), lives in Sydney, and has a family. Liza married a Mr. Fennell, lives in Sydney, and has a family. Peter married Madeline (Neil P.S.) MacLean, Washabuck (see **518**), lives in Little Narrows, and has a family.

Cosmos (Charles) married first Rhodena, who was adopted by Tom and Katie Ann MacLean, MacKinnon's Harbour (see **533**). They lived in MacKinnon's Harbour and their family: Joan and Ann. In a second marriage he married Daphne, widow of Roddie James (Seward) Bonaparte, MacKinnon's Harbour (see **277**) and has a family. **569**

● ● ●

Philip O'Donnell, adopted son of Ambrose (John G.) MacKinnon, MacKinnon's Harbour (see **467**) and a C.N.R. fireman, married Mamie (Michael, Alasdair) MacDonald, Jamesville West (see **369**). They lived in Jamesville West and their family: Betty, Raymond, Florence, James, Phyllis, and Patsy whom they adopted. **570**

Betty (Philip) married Ignatius O'Neill, Mulgrave, lived in Mulgrave, and had a large family. Phyllis became a Sister of St. Martha. Patsy married Frank (John R.) Campbell, Jamesville West (see **312**), lived in MacKinnon's Harbour, and had a daughter Marion.

● ● ●

John Redquest married Christy (James, Hector) MacNeil, Red Point (see **92**). They lived in Red Point and their family: Molly, Dan, Jim Rory, and another son who was drowned. **571**

Molly (John) married Dan (Donald) MacNeil, MacKinnon's Harbour (see **255**), lived in Sydney, and had a family. Dan married Mary Lizzie (Rory, Alasdair "Mor") MacNeil, Iona Rear (see **214**), lived in Sydney, and had a large family. Jim Rory lived in the Sydney Mines area.

● ● ●

William Ross came to Washabuck from North East Margaree. His son John married Mary "Og" (Lachlan) MacLean, Washabuck (see **487**). They lived in Washabuck for only a short time and moved back to Margaree. Their family was three sons and three daughters. One daughter, Kate, married James (Murdock) MacKenzie (see **438**), had a family of ten, only one of whom, William, settled in Lower Washabuck (see **439**).

● ● ● **572**

George Small, Glace Bay married Catherine (Ben, Neil Barra) MacNeil, Red Point (see **35**). They lived in Red Point. From a previous marriage, he had two daughters: Eunice and Mary Theresa, and, when he re-married, he took them to his home in Red Point. The family of his second marriage was: John William, James Malcolm, Tena, Alex, Mickey, and Joe. **573**

Eunice (George) and Mary Theresa both married in Glace Bay and had families. John William married Peggy MacNeil, Mabou, lives in Westmount, and has a family. James Malcolm became a Brother in the Oblates of Mary Immaculate. Tena married Mike MacInnis, Whitney Pier and has a family. Alex married Cecilia (Dan) MacKinnon, Cain's Mountain (see **483**), lives in Sydney, and has a family. Mickey married first a Miss MacKenzie, Christmas Island, had a family; and in a second marriage he married Josie (John H.) MacNeil, Jamesville (see **182**) and has a family. Joe died unmarried.

● ● ●

A Mr. Sutherland, who was a surveyor by profession, settled in Upper Washabuck. He moved back to the North Shore, and probably followed the Migration to New Zealand in 1851. **574**

● ● ●

WALKER

Donald Walker came to Ottawa Brook from the Lake Ainslie district. He was school teacher, justice of the peace, and warden of the parish. He married Catherine (Alex "Saor") MacNeil, Ottawa Brook (see **252**) and their family: John H., Alex, Dan, Flora, Jessie, Margaret, Cassie, and Dan Alex who died young. **575**

Alex (Donald) and Margaret were unmarried. Flora married John Y. (Donald) Gillis, MacKinnon's Harbour (see **330**) and had a family. Jessie married Thomas (Murdock B.) MacNeil, Highland Hill (see **190**) and had no family. Cassie married Daniel J (Archie "Red") MacKenzie, Washabuck (see **428**), lived in Ottawa Brook, and had a family.

John H. (Donald) married Mary Ann (Donald) MacLean, Ottawa Brook (see **539**). They lived in Ottawa Brook and their family: Dan R., Dolena, John Joseph, Katie Sarah who became a Sister of Notre Dame, Anna, Marion, and Bernadette. The family later moved to Sydney. **576**

Dan (Donald) married first Mary Ann (John J.) MacKinnon, MacKinnon's Harbour (see **476**). They lived in Ottawa Brook and had a child who died in infancy. In a second marriage he married Catherine MacDonald, Lake Ainslie and their family: Mary, Donald, Leonard, John Joseph, and John Alex. **577**

● ● ●